Malthus

Malthus

William Petersen

Harvard University Press · Cambridge, Massachusetts
1979

Library of Congress Cataloging in Publication Data

Petersen, William.
  Malthus.

  Bibliography: p.
  Includes index.
  1. Malthus, Thomas Robert, 1766–1834. 2. Demogra-
phers—Great Britain—Biography. 3. Economists—Great
Britain—Biography.
HB863.P47   301.32′092′4 [B]   78–31479
ISBN 0–674–54425–0

Acknowledgments

A GRANT FROM THE Guggenheim Foundation enabled me to spend a portion of a year in England, and I am grateful both for that opportunity to complete my research on Malthus and for the unbureaucratic efficiency with which the assistance was administered. In London, I did most of my work at the Goldsmiths' Library of Economic Literature of the University of London, which might have been instituted for this special purpose. The bulk of the library had been assembled by H. S. Foxwell, who continued to act as consultant after the Worshipful Company of Goldsmiths purchased it and presented it to the University College. Of the roughly 60,000 volumes on economic and social matters, about four-tenths were printed before 1851. Miss A. M. Whitelegge, the chief librarian, made its services available to me expeditiously and graciously.

Even before I went to England, I was aware that Mrs. Patricia James, the editor of an excellent edition of Malthus's travel diaries, was at work on a full biography. I was a bit fearful of a possible simultaneous publication of two similar books, but the books are far less similar than I feared. Mrs. James knows more than I ever shall both about the details of Malthus's life and about English history, and she was kind enough to read my manuscript chapter by chapter and point out my gaffes. Our books are complementary, and mine is better than it would have been without her kind cooperation.

v

Acknowledgments

Several other colleagues read a draft of the book: D. V. Glass of the London School of Economics, Philip P. Poirier and Lars G. Sandberg of the Ohio State University. Two economists, Thomas Sowell of the University of California and Julian Simon of the University of Illinois, criticized the chapter on Malthus's economic theory. James Reed of Rutgers University gave me his comments on the fertility chapter, and Peter Buck of M.I.T. on that on the Malthusian heritage. Camille Smith, my editor at Harvard University Press, showed an exceptional intelligence, conscientiousness, and tact in working on the manuscript. Particularly since I have not always accepted the advice of these experts, I absolve all from any responsibility for the final product. I hope they agree with me that my book has been much improved by their detailed critiques, and I thank them for the time they devoted to it.

Contents

Malthus

1

His Times

THOMAS ROBERT MALTHUS was born in 1766 and died in 1834. That he lived during a period of momentous and often tumultuous change is hardly a novel observation. The French Revolution and "the industrial revolution" are, after all, the dominant themes of that era's history. Most obviously, it became the age of steam power and rail transportation. After more than a decade of experimentation, Watt perfected the steam engine in 1775. From England's first rolling mill (1754) to the first one powered by steam (1790) was a full generation of steady material progress. The building of a canal in order to carry coal from Worsley to Manchester (1759–61) started a new epoch in transportation; but the first effective steam locomotive, constructed in 1814, ushered in a "railway age" that reduced all canals to second place. Such inventions as the spinning jenny (1764) were consolidated into the first of the spinning mills (1771) that radically improved the manufacture of clothing. It was typical of the period that Josiah Wedgwood, founder of the famous pottery works (1761), also invented the pyrometer (1782) used in them. Nor was the effervescence limited to Britain. In the United States, Whitney invented the cotton gin (1793) and Morse the telegraph (1832); Fulton constructed the first steamboat (1803). In France, the first telegraph linked Paris and Lille (1794), and the same year saw the establishment of the École Polytechnique, the world's first technical college.

Overlapping the development of new technology was the rise of modern sciences, in some instances from almost their first beginnings. Linnaeus's classification of species was the start of botany and zoology as we know them. The modern chemistry that grew out of the treatises of Cavendish, Rutherford, Priestley, and others soon included natural compounds; and after the inception of organic chemistry the distinction between animate and inanimate was never again so facile. There was an international upswell of mathematical genius. The work of Herschel and others marked the first significant progress in astronomy since Newton. Volta produced electricity from a cell, Ampère published his *Laws of Electrodynamic Action,* and Ohm propounded the law that would be named after him.

Some of these advances in science, both pure and applied, constituted new modes of agriculture, medicine, and sanitation, which together started the remarkable reduction in mortality associated with modern times. The invention of the threshing machine (1784) led to McCormick's reaper, perfected in 1834. In 1798 Jenner introduced vaccination against smallpox. A man named Joseph Bramah made the first flush toilet, and a sand filter was used to purify London's water supply. Dogmatic speculation about whether the population was growing or decreasing gave way to census enumerations, which eventually facilitated the start of epidemiology. Each voyage of Captain Cook brought back not only news of strange plants and animals but also the suspicion that Europeans' notions about the nature of man or of human society were perhaps provincial.

The typical view—that "the industrial revolution" was not only the key to that era's massive transformation but almost its entire content—is false. One need not depreciate the importance of new machines, of a new industrial system, to recognize that such a materialist perception omits too much. Nor is it sufficient to add the Napoleonic wars, the most obvious element of international relations, in setting the parameter of social change. After the wars were brought to a decisive end at Waterloo, after the Congress of Vienna started what Karl Polanyi called "the hundred years' peace," the ebullience of the prior decades continued unabated. The portion of the transformation that is omitted from a narrowly economic or political-economic view is the essence of what sociologists sometimes denote as the shift from gemeinschaft to gesellschaft or, more succinctly, as modernization; and to say that Britain became a "modern" society connotes much more than that it developed a rail system. The attack on mercantilism that Adam Smith had initiated gathered force, and the spread of a free market began to effect also a greater democratization of the political process. The secularization of social life, started several centuries earlier, was all but completed during Malthus's lifetime. "Moral philosophy," essentially the direct application of Christian values to current issues, gradually gave way to "political economy," whose practitioners demanded or defended "natural rights" in a "natural order" with less and less reference to a personal deity. In this process no idea inherited from the past retained its legitimacy from tradition alone; each was tested in the new context and had to prove itself anew.

From Moral Philosophy to Political Economy

Still today the central moral issues pertain to man's relation either to nature or to the state. The long process of secularization, recurrently interrupted by revivals of faith, has altered profoundly not merely the beliefs and behavior of individual adherents but the church's place in government, education, and other this-worldly institutions. And the question of how the subject/citizen relates to the state remains at the core of current disputes about the welfare state or socialism. Both of these redefinitions of man's place were well under way when Malthus was born, and the pace of change quickened during his lifetime.

The political theory of the prior era, which we know by the name "mercantilism," was of course less a unit than this single designation would imply, differing from period to period and from one country to another. Underlying this diversity, however, were several general features. The purpose of the economy, and thus of those engaged in it, was to enhance the power of the state. Since any state could prosper only at the cost of other states, power—and specifically military as well as economic power—was developed in order to be used against antagonists. In order to succeed in this permanent contest, each state endeavored to increase its supply of gold, taxes, people, colonies. With no sentimental ambiguity, the function of the mass of the population was to contribute their work,

paid for optimally at the level of subsistence, and their procreation, as large as feasible, to the greater glory of France or
England or whatever.

Specific institutions persisted long after any change in theory. The East India Company, in whose college Malthus
taught for most of his life, typified the curious public-private
enterprises of the period. The prime function of colonies, as
George III made clear to the American colonists, was to provide at cheap prices commodities not available at home. In
the ordinary view, migration was still seen as the shipment
under state auspices of persons from where they were redundant to where they would be useful. The message of *The
Wealth of Nations* that the state is not needed to run the
economy, that the right of men to move about freely brings
benefits also to society, was so widely acclaimed just because it
contradicted much current practice. And Malthus's assertion
that population tends to grow faster than the rate that social
well-being demands also contradicted the mercantilist dogma
that population is a fragile entity, which the state must nurture if it is not to wither. Much of the opposition to the
Essay was less to it directly than to Malthus's position on the
Speenhamland welfare system, which for him epitomized
the evils of mercantilist paternalism.

Though eighteenth-century concepts implicitly challenged
some mercantilist doctrines, many who voiced the new ideas
were ambivalent about the legitimacy of the state's control
of society and economy. We tend to think of the Enlightenment as a French phenomenon, brought about by a school of
thought known as the "philosophes." The French writers,
however, differed among themselves on every significant point.
Cutting across such divergencies and therefore oversimplifying
to some degree, one can define the Enlightenment as the
West's fundamental break with the methods of inquiry, the
factual conclusions, and the ethical doctrines of medieval
Europe. The attempt to substitute empirical laws of nature
for faith in the supernatural, a move toward the canons of
modern science, greatly improved the understanding of the
physical universe. But on ethical and political matters the
philosophes varied greatly, especially in their attempts to derive policy suggestions from what was common in their point
of view.

Underlying the moral thought of the Enlightenment, as of

Christianity, was "natural law." For Aquinas, writing the summa of medieval thought, the concept derived from the premise of a deity controlling the universe in a regular manner, thus enabling man to deduce the laws of nature from consistent observations. Without this premise, natural law could hardly generate a moral code as clean-cut as Newtonian science, whose comfortable certainty spread during Malthus's lifetime from mechanics to biology. In response to successful attacks on the Bible's cosmology, a French school of Christian apologists—Malebranche, Bossuet, Fénélon—used the methods of Descartes to reach Aquinas's conclusions. By precise deductions from established facts, they argued, we can demonstrate God's existence. Pascal, a convert to Jansenism, took this attempt to underpin Christianity rationally several steps further. We cannot know whether God exists or not, he held, but is it not reasonable to bet on the affirmative? If He exists, we win all; and if he does not, we lose nothing. Among the philosophes, similarly, religious belief ranged from the vehement atheism of Holbach to the neo-Calvinism of Rousseau. And if the typical philosophe was a "deist," this was a designation vague enough to permit almost any characteristic to be ascribed to the First Cause.

Britain, too, was undergoing a kind of secularization. One type of English clergyman of the period can be exemplified by William Paley (1743–1805), archdeacon of Carlisle. In his overall view, he might be called an ecclesiastic Bentham, who added to the utilitarian doctrine an almost incidental supernatural sanction, and who in most religious disputes followed the Unitarian interpretation. The social benefits of marriage, in his view, consist in "the production of the greatest number of healthy children, their better education, and the making of due provision for their settlement in life." "Promiscuous concubinage" is evil mainly because most men "will not undertake the incumbrance, expense, and restraint of married life if they can gratify their passions at a cheaper price."[1]

In secularist thought the exposition of natural law has often been more a psychological than a social theory, based not on suppositions about the functional prerequisites of human society but rather on axioms defining natural rights plus postulates concerning human nature. If man is inherently as good as Condorcet and Godwin held, then no state is needed to maintain order; the anarchism they professed, the most consistent of political theories, lacks only plausibility in the postulates on which it is based. But if men are sometimes "grasping hucksters, quarrelsome tyrants, rebels," in Hobbes's description, then government must hold them in check if there is to be a society at all. Differences on this basic point, which proliferated in the works of the Enlightenment, reached a kind of apex in Rousseau, whose self-contradictions transcended the minimum consistency one ordinarily demands of professed guides to human conduct. The well known opening sentence of *The Social Contract*—"Man is born free, and everywhere he is in chains"—suggests the philosophical anarchism to which its author was attracted; but some modern interpreters see Rousseau also, and not unreasonably, as one precursor of twentieth-century totalitarianism.

The French Enlightenment was part of an international movement. Germany had its own Aufklärung; such earlier English thinkers as Locke had started parallel developments in Britain and the American colonies. Many in France, notably Voltaire, admired England for its liberality, so different from the autocracy that under the Bourbons often verged on the tyrannical. Though among Europe's intellectual elite language barriers seemed hardly to exist, the international circulation of new ideas was encouraged by translation. For example, Voltaire's entire corpus became available in English during the decade and a half following 1760. Adam Smith deemed him "the most universal genius perhaps which France has ever produced, acknowledged to be in almost every species of writing nearly upon a level with the greatest authors of the last age who applied themselves chiefly to one."[2] Over the third quarter of the eighteenth century there appeared the successive volumes of the *Encyclopédie,* the philosophes' own summa; and this helped stimulate such other holistic surveys as Johnson's *Dictionary,* Voltaire's *Philosophical Dictionary,* and the *Encyclopaedia Brittanica.* Rousseau's rising fame in Britain is suggested by his place in the last work; in the second edition (1781) he is still not mentioned, but in the third (1797) the article on him runs to nine columns. Scotland's particular interest in Rousseau was aroused also by his protracted and notoriously petty quarrel with Hume, which scholars today are still discussing.

As contrasted with the range between Montesquieu and Diderot, or between Rousseau and Voltaire, the political doctrine of America's founding fathers was more consistent, because except in aberrant types like Tom Paine there was less appeal to extreme positions. It is more pertinent in this context that this was also true of the group of writers designated "the Scottish moralists."[3] The founder of this school was Francis Hutchinson (1694–1746), whose chair at the University of Glasgow was eventually inherited by Adam Smith (1723–90). Among the dozen other names one could list, at least David Hume (1711–76) and Adam Ferguson (1723–1816) also far transcended a merely provincial influence.

Like the philosophes, the Scottish moralists saw "human nature," the psychological foundation of their social theory, as essentially one. The discussion of this point in Hume, as in Voltaire, has been criticized for slighting even great differences between historical ages or diverse cultures.[4] According to the Scots, man is neither sinful by his fall from grace nor able through his reason to fashion the perfect world that utopians of "the age of reason" saw as the inevitable culmination of human progress. Rather, human nature comprises an interaction between passions and reason. In Hume's words, reason can never of itself produce any action; its function is to guide acts toward the realization of wants and to adjudicate between two or more partly contradictory "impulses of passion."[5] If this sounds like an early version of either utilitarian or behaviorist psychology, it may well be because the formulation was incorporated into these later constructs. The interaction in Malthus's thought between the two biological drives of hunger and sex, with reason able to lessen the tension between them, was a closer and more obvious parallel.

Since any society comprises fallible beings, it can never—according to the Scottish moralists—become merely the product of perfect reason; there are more things in the social bond than were dreamt of by the philosophes. We have retained from the eighteenth century the bizarre notion that rational planning per se has an inherent propensity to a successful fulfillment; in the 1950s the American sociologist Robert Merton achieved a modest fame for a paper proclaiming that there can be "unanticipated consequences of purposive social action." Not only was this a central theme of the Scots but they carried its analysis further than any modern theorist who does not derive directly from Adam Smith. The clarity of

Smith's point of view has been largely dissipated, however, by the present tendency to seek a cure for the inherent ineptitude of "bureaucracy" with more and better "planning."

That Adam Smith founded modern economic theory has led some commentators to trace the progress from this auspicious but rough beginning ever upward to some such pinnacle as Paul Samuelson, marking as major improvements the development of marginal utility after 1870 and Keynes's theory of capitalist development. It is important to remember, however, that this elaboration constituted also a narrowing; only a very small portion of *The Wealth of Nations* became the raw material for modern economics. The keynote of Smith's concept of "system" is that by seeking his own ends each person can contribute to the common good, and one of the book's most famous passages exemplifies this typical conjunction of private and public goals: "It is not from the benevolence of the butcher, the brewer, or the baker that we expect our dinner, but from their regard to their own interest. We address ourselves, not to their humanity but to their self-love, and never talk to them of our own necessities but of their advantages."[6] The operation of self-interest is socially beneficial, however, only within the limits set by "sympathy" or "justice," often referred to in *The Wealth of Nations* and expounded in Smith's earlier *Theory of Moral Sentiments*. In the two books together, Smith taught that man is motivated by both self-interest and what we would call social conscience.

> When I endeavor to examine my own conduct, . . . either to approve or condemn it, . . . I divide myself, as it were, into two persons . . . The first is the spectator; . . . the second is the agent . . . The first is the judge; the second the person judged of . . . To be amiable and to be meritorious, that is, to deserve love and to deserve reward, are the great characters of virtue; and to be odious and punishable, of vice. But all these characters have an immediate reference to the sentiments of others.[7]

That is to say, social integration derives not merely from the interplay of individuals' self-interest in the economic market but also, and more fundamentally, from the desire to be accepted by one's fellows. As Reisman pointed out in his analysis of Smith's "sociological economics," Smith's theory of morality is strikingly similar to the one developed more than a century later by Émile Durkheim. "Man is a moral being," Durkheim wrote, "only because he lives in society, since morality consists in being solidary with a group."[8] Thus, Smith analyzed consumer behavior (as we would term it) not only in an economic but also in a sociological framework. Not only is "consumption the sole end and purpose of all production," but the consumer judges whether a commodity is satisfactory by what his class and his nation expect of him.[9]

If within the limits of morality and law men working in their own interest generally also serve the common good, then the state's restrictions on private enterprise harm not only their direct victims but society as a whole. Smith made the point trenchantly and often. In a fascinating account of "Smith's travels on the ship of state," George Stigler noted the many contexts in which *The Wealth of Nations* exemplified one of its central doctrines: since political behavior, no less than the economic behavior, is typically motivated by self-interest, policies that are ostensibly adopted for the common good in fact generally benefit one sector of the population at the cost of all others. The obsessive intrusion of the mercantilist state into every private or quasiprivate enterprise was in Smith's opinion antisocial. He recommended that the state should limit itself to three relatively modest functions: defense, the enforcement of justice, and the provision of certain clearly defined public works.[10]

Most appropriately, since it was a clarion call to freedom, *The Wealth of Nations* was published in 1776, the year that the American republic was founded on the same moral and political principles. This means, incidentally, that the book also had its bicentennial in 1976, when many commemorative papers were published. The Keynesian revolution is receding into history, and no economist of the recent past remains as prominent, as "relevant," as Keynes still is. But the importance of Smith for judging contemporary policy is growing, partly because of his amazing prescience but partly also because government intervention is again a major problem in virtually every social or economic field. If one compares the first edition (1948) with the ninth edition (1973) of Paul Samuelson's *Economics,* the best known and most widely used American textbook, two differences are striking—the shift from a pure Keynesianism to what Samuelson terms "pragmatic Keynesianism" and the wider range of social and political factors included in the broader definition of economics, particularly in such subdisciplines as economic development.[11] Both changes reflect a renewed emphasis on the classics, and thus on Smith first of all.

During his lifetime Smith attained great honor and influence. Within a few years of its publication, members of Parliament started citing *The Wealth of Nations* to settle their debates. Outside Britain the concept of laissez-faire spread slowly, not necessarily to the centers of power but to subordinate places where the benefits of liberty were more likely to be appreciated. The first full translation of *The Wealth of Nations,* remarkably, was into Danish. In Spain the Inquisition banned it for a number of years because of "the lowness of its style and the looseness of its morals"![12] Wherever it became available, it was read as an optimistic harbinger of economic progress and political liberty. Economics as the "dismal science" came only later, partly from half-understood Malthus, mainly from Ricardo.

Of all the influences on Malthus's thought, Adam Smith was undoubtedly the strongest and most persistent. When he visited Scandinavia as a young man, Malthus jotted down the topics he wanted to investigate under the heading "Smith's Questions." As a mature and fully established scholar, he wrote a pamphlet on the Corn Laws that contradicted Smith's teaching and noted the deviation with continued deference. Smith's relatively scattered and incidental comments on population constituted a shorter and less formal statement of some of the main themes of Malthus's theory. Most generally, Malthus's *Political Economy*, like virtually all economic theory during the century following 1776, built on the principles that Smith had enunciated.

INSTITUTIONS UNDER CHANGE

With the underlying moral tenets of society changing radically, the institutions that acquired their legitimacy from them were under constant strain. This was so across the board, but I shall restrict this discussion to those most closely related to Malthus's career, which were also some of the most important institutions of British society.

The intellectual challenges to religious doctrine obviously affected the churches, whose demise was confidently predicted for over two centuries. Particularly in the cities, considerable numbers of the lower classes moved from nonconformism to indifference—and then, some decades later, to Methodism. The position of the established Anglican church, of which Malthus was an ordained member, was also complex. Several thousand churches and chapels were built, repaired, or improved during the eighteenth century; and the average annual income from a curacy rose from about £25 or £30 in the middle of the century to about £85 around 1835 (of this increase, however, a considerable portion was absorbed into the rising cost of living). Against such indications of growth and prosperity, one must put details of how the church operated and how its clergy lived. For both economic and ecclesiastical reasons, positions in the church, or "livings," were declining in number, in contrast to a probable increase in those competing for them. Livings were held through political influence, and at the upper levels of the hierarchy they provided a sometimes opulent way of life; many impropriators performed no duties themselves but hired curates to act in their stead. In theory, a curacy could be one step to a higher place in the church's ranks, but most curates either held their positions all their lives or abandoned them for secular careers. No matter what his ecclesiastical status, a curate generally had to supplement his income from such other sources as, for example, gifts from friendly parishioners, fishing and shooting, or cultivating a plot of vegetables for his own table or even for sale. Since in rural areas they were among the very few educated men, some village curates could acquire secular employment of greater dignity. By the early nineteenth century nearly one justice of the peace in four was a cleric, and it was common to combine one or more curacies with teaching in a school or university. Many of the learned Englishmen of the eighteenth century—naturalists, antiquarians, historians, classicists, lawyers—were clergymen, but few of them were deeply versed in theology.[13]

The defensive posture of organized religion was reflected in a spate of works by men whose personal views reflected the social changes under way. Thomas Chalmers (1780–1847), to take one prominent example, as a student was attracted to mathematics and almost became an atheist. As a preacher in Glasgow, he combined his very successful vocation with reform efforts, establishing day schools and Sunday schools for the poor, trying to institute the principle that a congregation's members should have a voice in choosing their own clergy. Eventually he became the first minister of the "free" disestablished Church of Scotland. Among the twenty-five volumes of his works (plus nine published posthumously) were, at the two poles, an exposition of political economy and *On the Power, Wisdom, and Goodness of God as Manifested in the Adaptation of External Nature to the Moral and Intellectual Constitution of Man,* in two volumes.[14] Many of these books by theologians put the principle of population in a religious context. A typical defense of traditional orthodoxy linked Malthus with John Leslie, who had written on the nature of heat, accusing both of mixing axioms with speculations. "Every true Christian knows that the increase of mankind can proceed from no other cause than the will of God Himself, the Supreme Governor of the world. This being unquestionably true, it is obvious that this pretended *principle of population* is nothing else but a mere name which these speculative fellows have invented for the purpose of deceiving the rest of mankind."[15] Similar criticisms appeared in France, and not only from those defending Catholic orthodoxy. Pierre Leroux, a disciple of Saint-Simon and Condorcet who developed an ethical doctrine known as the "religion of humanity," an early version of "liberal Protestantism," opposed Malthus on parallel moral grounds.[16]

Still a half-century later, booklets were being put out with titles like *God or Malthus? Is Over-population the Cause of Poverty? An Exposure of Malthusianism,* with the unambiguous message that "Malthusianism is atheism of the worst kind." Lord Shaftesbury, who tried to apply the spirit of Jesus to every element of life, believed that the principle of population was being "utilized to justify every type of social calamity." Most criticisms of Malthus, a French commentator pointed out, had concentrated on his product as "a man of science," but his crucial weakness was as "a man of faith." His "theological pessimism" led him to an "ethical pessimism"; lacking faith in the full beneficence of God because of his "rationalist deism," Malthus accepted as all but inevitable the vice and misery associated merely with particular conditions in one historical era.[17]

On the other hand, one clergyman published anonymously a series of nine sermons, each on a passage from the Bible newly interpreted to confirm the principle of population. Among Malthus's ecclesiastical supporters, the most influential was John Bird Sumner (1780–1862), who eventually became

Archbishop of Canterbury. His principal work in relation to Malthus was entitled *A Treatise on the Records of the Creation, and on the Moral Attributes of the Creator, with Particular Reference to the Jewish History, and to the Consistency of the Principle of Population with the Wisdom and Goodness of the Deity.* It won the prize in a contest set by John Burnett, a Scottish gentleman, for a disquisition on "the evidence that there is a Being all-powerful, wise, and good, by whom every thing exists, and particularly to obviate difficulties regarding the wisdom and goodness of the Deity." Obviously the existence of moral and physical evil—or, in Malthus's phrase, vice and misery—posed a newly urgent problem to theologians. As a reviewer (possibly George D'Oyly or John Weyland) remarked, "Although Mr. Sumner has brought himself to admit the truth of Mr. Malthus's principles, he yet [has] derived from them the same conclusions respecting the wisdom and goodness of God which we have ourselves derived from what we conceive to be a refutation of those principles." The main benefit to be derived from the universal tendency of population to increase, as Sumner understood Malthus, is that "every inhabited country [will have] as many persons existing as it will support," but there were also "collateral benefits" of various types.[18]

Higher education retained from an earlier era close associations with both the Anglican church and the state, and by the time Malthus attended Cambridge these ties were mainly encumbrances to the secular education that was becoming the universities' main function. In the very first sentences of his fascinating *Unreformed Cambridge,* Winstanley summed up the result of this conflict between past and future missions: "The University of Cambridge in the eighteenth century has been convicted of violating its statutes, misusing its endowments, and neglecting its obligations. It is impossible to dispute the substantial justice of this verdict." Cambridge operated under a set of Elizabethan statutes that regulated its government, curriculum, and discipline "with absurd minuteness." Though the vice-chancellor, the university's chief officer, usually had no prior experience in finance or administration, he typically managed to use his right to interpret any ambiguity in the statutes so as to expand his actual power considerably.

For much of the teaching staff, Winstanley continued, the academic dilemma of whether to teach or to undertake research was solved with a remarkable simplicity: do neither. Many fellowships were reserved to those in orders, and even lay fellows were forbidden to marry. Many of either type were ignorant, lazy, and uncouth, as boorish when they left Cambridge as when they had arrived. The professors ranked above fellows in status but not necessarily in other respects. "As a class they stand condemned of scandalously neglecting their duties, however clearly and meticulously those duties were defined, of failing to advance knowledge by study and research, and even of sometimes being unacquainted with the rudiments of the subject they had undertaken to teach."[19]

The stipulated duties—say, to deliver four lectures a year and to publish one of them—were hardly onerous, but they were sometimes ignored or carried out in a sloppy fashion. For instance, the lectures published by one W. F. Lloyd, a professor of political economy, consist in a mere summary of Malthus's *Essay* and similarly elementary disquisitions on three other topics, all bound together in a work lacking originality, interest, or scholarly purpose.[20] The actual instruction was by tutors, who were expected to be guardians and friends as well. Many tutors lectured or hired others to lecture on subjects they were not familiar with. These exacting and varied duties were remunerative, interesting, and not limited in tenure; tutorship was low in status, but in other respects it provided much of what most men desire from academic life.

The student body under the guidance of this faculty was no less diverse. Most of the students were "pensioners," who generally had to earn part of their living, or—with fewer resources—"sizars," who paid smaller fees and until well into the eighteenth century acted as servants. Around 1750 the students arriving at Cambridge from the best schools were well trained in English and classical languages, but so deficient in elementary arithmetic that many had to take extracurricular lessons from the master of a day school. The constant charges of favoritism were well based. The university's statutes authorized it to confer degrees on young men of stipulated ranks without their even being in attendance. In a farcical examination, a candidate could receive a bachelor's degree by answering a single question with one word. With no requirements at all, a master's degree was granted upon application from anyone who had received an A.B. at least a year earlier. Most of the graduates, lacking anything better, became clergymen, and for the less affluent students this was often a step up from their father's position.

According to an 1850 report of a royal commission, the "chief abuses" still at that time were "the absolute character of the governing bodies, the inadequacy and the inefficiency of the teaching, the system of 'close' [that is, restricted] fellowships and scholarships, the expensiveness of a university course, and religious tests" to determine who might receive a higher education.[21] At Jesus College the requirements that entering students be Episcopalian and that fellows not marry were abandoned only about a century after Malthus was a student there. During this long transition to modern norms, many in the universities declared themselves openly as Unitarians, and some went further either in their private thoughts or in their willingness to forgo the prerogatives of a fellowship or professorship. University politics was largely about the multifarious inhibitions to what we would term academic freedom; and one of the most famous victims of this growing contradiction between formal regulations and incipient university policy, as we shall see, was William Frend, Malthus's tutor.

With the universities unreformed, Britain's intellectual life developed also under other auspices, particularly the quarterly reviews. The first of these in both chronology and quality was the *Edinburgh Review,* founded in 1802 by Sydney Smith (aged 31), Francis Jeffrey (29), and Francis Horner (24). Some contributors were even younger, students at the University of Edinburgh, especially of Dugald Stewart, the distinguished disciple of Adam Smith. Most of the participants were Whigs, and at first the magazine was bound in blue and buff, the party's colors. Each issue, as large as a medium-sized book, summarized in full detail important new works on political economy, parliamentary papers, and a wide miscellany of diverse publications, all analyzed with great competence as part of a continuing struggle against the mercantilist tradition. A modern scholar, presumably with tongue in cheek, termed it "for its day and generation, a *Reader's Digest* of economic literature."[22] The two were similar at least in their phenomenal success. Beginning with only 750 copies of the first issue, by 1818 the *Edinburgh Review* reached a circulation of over 13,500, or more than any previous serial publication.

Until 1912 all its articles were anonymous, but the authorship of many of them can be deduced with greater or lesser probability. Beginning in 1808, Malthus published some half-dozen papers in it. Though challenged by a number of competitors—the Tory *Quarterly Review* (founded in 1809), *Blackwood's Edinburgh Magazine* (1817), and the *Westminster Review* (1824)—the *Edinburgh Review* retained for a full half-century its leadership in quality of content, size of circulation, and influence on men in high places and thus on public policy.

The quarterlies were the top of the vast mass of printed material flooding Britain during Malthus's lifetime. The separation of printing, publishing, and bookselling into different enterprises was just beginning; in many cases a small proprietor would buy an author's work, print it, and offer it for sale from the same premises. The products of this system comprised, to quote the subtitle of a work on "street literature," "broadside ballads, chapbooks, proclamations, news-sheets, election bills, tracts, pamphlets, cocks, catchpennies, and other ephemera."[23] On every disputed subject pamphlets circulated among the middle classes, and for a halfpenny or a penny those in the lower classes bought "chapbooks," or uncut booklets of from eight to thirty-two pages, on the same subjects. Relative to the adult population, the circulation was sometimes almost unbelievable; Paine's *Rights of Man,* as an outstanding instance, was certainly not a fugitive piece; it sold almost half a million copies in the British Isles. From the beginning of printing to the end of the nineteenth century, one can reasonably suppose, these publications often—or sometimes—had more influence on public policy than the books that have been preserved in libraries.

The present distinction, however imprecise, between professional and popular writings hardly existed. The shift that I have noted from "moral philosophy" to "political economy" was in process, but even those giving greater attention to empirical evidence and systematic theory hardly espoused a value-free formulation of their conclusions. "Economics" or "political science" did not yet exist; rather, both of these were combined in order to discover the optimum policy concerning "the economy," then conceived far more broadly than at a later time. Malthus's career, as he moved from curate to professor of history and political economy, included both end points of this change; and the debates in which he engaged reflected it even more pointedly. With someone like Ricardo, he disagreed sometimes sharply but always amicably, for their disputes were in a rational discourse within the discipline's developing boundaries; but Godwin's attacks were in the style of a Calvinist moralizer, with a disdain for factual evidence that set him off from the canons of modern scholarship.

Moral philosophy, becoming unfashionable in the social disciplines, reverted in part to the religious tracts from which it had derived and also moved into belles lettres. The shift in all the arts from Classical to Romantic occurred during Malthus's lifetime. Beethoven's Third Symphony, the definitive break with Haydn and Mozart, was published in 1804. The new style in literature, reflected in the search of Walter Scott or the Grimm brothers for stimulation in the history and myths of ordinary folk, fitted in well with the period's democratic slogans. From this political coloration there eventually arose a grandiose pretension that the ability to write knowledgeably about literary style gives a critic the right, even the moral duty, to judge the professional analysts of society. One would hardly describe Samuel Johnson, as an example of a prior standard, as a diffident man, but typically his opinions were closer in subject matter to his literary skills than the wide-ranging, utterly irresponsible, and generally acerbic writings of a Byron, say, on whatever struck his momentary interest. The point is important here, for much of the hostile commentary on Malthus came from Coleridge or Hazlitt, who like their many successors never felt they should temper their nastiness with carefully weighed evidence.

That public debates were conducted so inchoately both reflected and reinforced the relatively formless politics of the Hanoverian era. There were two parties, Whigs and Tories, and almost everyone interested in the issues was associated with one or the other. But the society was changing too rapidly to permit an agglomeration into two well rounded positions. Earlier, at the time of the "glorious revolution" of 1688, and again after Chartism outgrew its early sectarian limits, men took stands basically related to human liberties. During the long interim the main purpose of politics was the pursuit of office. The one sharp watershed during Malthus's lifetime, it might be argued, was the French Revolution, but this proved to be far less simple than *Liberté, égalité, fraternité.* As its course went from such slogans through the Jacobin terror to Napoleon's despotism, the nameless in their thousands and Europeans as distinguished as Beethoven or Wordsworth moved from enthusiastic support through painful doubt to horrified opposition. According to the most conscientious review of the evidence, the terror comprised 16,594 sentenced to death (excluding those condemned in absentia), perhaps as many as 400,000 imprisoned, and still more sentenced by revolutionary courts to fines, the pillory, deportation, or the galleys. "It is probable that between 35,000 and 40,000 persons [or about 7 percent of the population], including those who succumbed in the prisons and those killed without any form of trial, lost their lives as a consequence of terrorism."[24] From those who continued to endorse the alleged principles of France's revolutionary regime—the fellow-travelers of that time—a pernicious dishonesty pervaded the discussion of every question. Self-proclaimed moralists applied a double standard whenever they addressed a public issue: the imposition of mass terror in Paris was a salutary expression of revolutionary will, but the killing of eleven persons at Peterloo was a "massacre" that Shelley denounced in verse.

When Malthus was born in 1766, his country and France were in the middle of a long intermittent war of which initially the issue was, unambiguously, imperial power. In both India and America, Britain established and extended its colonial dominion and succeeded in maintaining it against repeated French challenges. The period from 1783, when the Peace of Versailles spelled out this British victory, to 1789, when the beginning of the French Revolution started a new phase of French expansion, was hardly a significant interruption. Battles were fought under new slogans and, in the case of France, with a drafted national army rather than mercenaries. Combat shifted from other continents mainly to Europe, though Napoleon's campaigns in Egypt and Russia suggest that his appetite was larger. This continuity during more than half a century of Anglo-French hostility should be balanced against the notion that Britain led the "reactionary" coalition against "progressive" Paris. Even if one accepts Emperor Napoleon as a carrier of social advance, this was not the only meaning of British opposition. The old order was breaking up in any case, as indicated by the fact that, long before the arrival of French troops, serfdom was ended in one country after another. And the momentum continued in

England—to cite one crucial example—by Parliament's motion
to abolish the slave trade (1791) and the prohibition of the
trade throughout the British Empire (1807) to the abolition
of slavery itself (1833) and the ensuing fight to end it wherever Britain could exert its might. It is a simplistic rewriting
of history to denote men like Burke, who supported the American revolutionaries and opposed those in France, as no more
than defenders of the old order.

The role of Malthus in this drama can be understood only
after we have assigned to ideology its fundamental significance. That he spent his professional life in the Hertfordshire
countryside, busy with teaching and writing and family matters, can give a false impression. Malthus was fully engagé, to
use the current cant; in his teaching, his books and pamphlets,
even his correspondence, he participated day by day in the
struggle to establish the factual and conceptual bases of social
disciplines and, as part of the same exercise, to extend human
freedoms.

Both proponents and opponents of his ideas take Malthus
as the watershed in the development of modern demography;
earlier theorists (from some of whom he borrowed ideas and
arguments) are designated as pre-Malthusian, and later ones
are analyzed in their relation to his system. The assignment
is just, for he saw population problems in the round and,
rightly or wrongly, pointed to issues that a century and a half
later are still the central ones in an ongoing debate. From
the foundation that Smith had laid, he helped develop the
essentials of classical economic theory, and in two respects he
was Ricardo's superior in this joint enterprise. Ricardo incorporated Malthus's principle of population into his conceptual framework, but with far less finesse, with almost a certain
crudity, compared with Malthus's thoroughly interlinked association between population and economy. Malthus deviated
from the other political economists of his day also in that his
theory pertained not only to production—then the central
problem—but also to consumption, which in classical theory is
typically assumed to be the limitless propensity of a reified
Economic Man.

As both William Otter and William Empson, the two main
sources concerning his personal life, pointed out in their
obituaries, Malthus was a pious man. That throughout his life
he was a faithful member of the Anglican community is less

pertinent for us, however, than that his career exemplified the separation of religious and nonreligious into discrete elements, which is what we mean by secularization. He did much to establish political economy as an honorable academic discipline; his professorship was not at Oxford or Cambridge, where archaic links to the church persisted long into the nineteenth century, but in a newly established college where the education was both markedly different and unambiguously of this world. Not surprisingly, this position at the edge of social change attracted brickbats from both sides: he was attacked both as "Parson Malthus" and as an atheist propounding immoral precepts. The same critics who have insisted on forgetting that professionally Malthus was a professor and have denoted him obsessively as "Reverend" (in at least one case even in a book's index[25]) have often expounded his theory from its preliminary version in the First Essay and denounced it as exclusively biological. Similarly, the stands that Malthus took concerning political questions were also unpopular at both ends of the political spectrum that was then taking form. Opposition to the Poor Laws marked him for many as utterly reactionary. And the truly radical proposal that Britain should institute universal free schooling, on the other hand, some conservatives saw as an invitation to anarchy. On balance, Malthus fitted in with his times, if we remember that in his times everything was moving; and the characteristic that best defines him is that he helped things move toward what he conceived to be a better society, with greater chances for happiness based on wider freedoms.

2

His Life and Work

MALTHUS'S DATE OF birth is given as February 13 in Keynes's *Essays in Biography*, as February 14 on the memorial tablet that the Royal Economic Society has placed in Bath Abbey,[1] and as February 17 by Leslie Stephen in the *Dictionary of National Biography*. Others who cited the fourteenth could not resist adding a witticism about Saint Valentine's Day. As can be determined from extant records, he was born on the thirteenth at "The Rookery," in Wooton, Surrey, and baptized the following day.[2] His full name was Thomas Robert Malthus, but the "Thomas" was never used; he signed his works and letters either "T. R. Malthus" or, in a slightly more familiar style, "T. Robt. Malthus." To designate him as "Thomas Malthus" is not formally incorrect, of course; it is no more an error than calling the twenty-eighth president of the United States "Thomas Wilson."

Robert's father was Daniel Malthus, whom no less a scholar than Walter Bagehot called "David."[3] He is reported to have been a gentleman of good family and independent means, a man of considerable culture, a friend of Hume and Rousseau, and one of the latter's literary executors. Some of the details in such characterizations seem not to be accurate. It is sometimes said that Daniel Malthus translated books from the French and German, and the *Dictionary of Anonymous and Pseudonymous English Literature* gives him as the translator of an essay on landscape, *Paul et Virginie*, and Goethe's *Die*

Leiden des jungen Werther; but this is all myth.[4] Certainly he knew Rousseau, whom he visited at Motiers and who (together with Thérèse, his common-law wife) visited the Rookery when Robert was an infant. But neither some of the standard biographies of Rousseau nor even a paper specifically on his visit to England mentioned Malthus as an executor of Rousseau's will.[5]

Even Payne's monograph on the Malthus family, a privately printed work on a rather narrow topic, mentions Robert's older brother Sydenham and only one of his five sisters. They were Henrietta Sarah, Eliza Maria, Ann Catherine Lucy, Mary Catherine Charlotte, and Mary Ann Catherine—four older than Robert and the last younger.

Such critics of Malthus as Cobbett and Marx condemned him especially as "Parson Malthus," a designation comparable in a current American context with labeling one of the thousands who have received a Ford Foundation grant the "Flivver Professor." In religion as in all else, Malthus was a moderate, attacked by fanatics at both poles. His principle of population was denounced as sacrilegious, and in his later writings he began to preface his name with "Reverend," presumably in an attempt to defend himself against such attacks. Marx's epithet might have been appropriate if he had attempted to show—as he did not—that Malthus's ecclesiastical tie biased his writings on secular themes. Indeed, according to Marx, "most of the population-theory teachers are Protestant parsons . . ." —Parson Wallace, Parson Townsend, Parson Malthus and his pupil, the arch-Parson Thomas Chalmers, to say nothing of the lesser reverend scribblers in this line." However, in contrast to these other Protestant clergymen, who "generally contributed to the increase of population to a really unbecoming extent," Malthus, according to Marx, "had taken the monastic vow of celibacy."[6] That Marx did not know that Malthus was a married man and the father of three children—Henry, Emily, and Lucy—indicates how little he tried to learn of the man whose character and motives he impugned. But Marx was not the only one to display ignorance of Malthus's family; the introduction to the Everyman edition of the *Essay* informs us that the author "practiced the principle of population to the extent of eleven girls."[7]

The routine inaccuracy about elementary vital statistics, perhaps unique concerning a personage of Malthus's prominence, might be dismissed as a curious aberration of scholarship except that the misrepresentation also pervades accounts of his work and ideas. In the following chapters I shall have recurrent occasion to note some of these lapses. As the most general one, consider the meaning we ascribe to the adjective *Malthusian*. The "Malthusian" (later, "Neo-Malthusian") Leagues sometimes took several generations to discover that the person whose name they used had been opposed to the contraception they advocated. This connotation of the word continues, and to it there has been added another false usage. In demographers' professional writings one often finds the phrase "Malthusian checks" used to denote what he called "positive checks"; thus, some of those who by their academic discipline should know Malthus best assign a label that follows the first edition of the *Essay* but ignores the other six.

YOUTH AND EDUCATION

A notoriously negligent father in real life, Rousseau compensated by spelling out an ideal upbringing in *La Nouvelle Héloïse* and *Émile*. Education should include no discipline or constraint; a child must be allowed to develop into what he is capable of becoming. (The original edition of *Émile*, consequently, was printed by a Dutch publisher, for its message was not one that the French censor would have readily passed.) Reportedly Daniel Malthus followed these precepts in raising his own children, but we have details only about his indirect influence: it can hardly be coincidence that all three of the tutors who dominated Robert's education made important sacrifices for their radical principles.

Robert's first tutor, who took over from his father when Robert was 10, was Richard Graves (1715–1804), who until illness forced him to change his plans studied medicine, then took a master's degree, became a fellow of All Souls' College, and was duly ordained. Subsequently, against the advice of family and friends, he married a lower-class girl, thus both losing his fellowship and offending his conventional relatives. After a period of abject poverty, he obtained a living at Claverton, near Bath, where for thirty years he took pupils whom he taught together with his own children. The literary work for which he is best remembered is a semi-autobiographical novel, *The Spiritual Quixote, or the Summer's Ramble of Mr. Geoffry Wildgoose: A Comic Romance*, a rather coarse satire on Methodists. That Malthus kept in touch with him is suggested by the fact that he visited Graves during his final illness and administered the last sacraments.

As a young boy Malthus attended Warrington Academy, an institution based on liberal religious and political principles. His tutor there was Gilbert Wakefield (1756–1801), whom the *Dictionary of National Biography* characterizes succinctly as "scholar and controversial writer." A graduate and fellow of Jesus College, he was ordained and, after several minor ecclesiastical posts, became a curate in Liverpool, where he tried to improve the condition of prisoners and to arouse the public against the slave trade. He read widely in an attempt to repair the gaps in his scanty theological knowledge, finally adopting Arian, or Unitarian, views. Unlike many who shared these opinions, Wakefield was honest enough to resign his curacy, and when he married he also lost his fellowship. It was then that he took a position at Warrington, where he taught classics from 1779 until the school shut down four years later. Malthus studied under him at the academy and continued as a private pupil for several years thereafter. During this period Wakefield was working on his *Silva Critica,* a two-volume study designed to unite biblical learning with that of ancient Greece and Rome. Later he edited various classical works and translated the New Testament. In a reply to a tract defending the war by one Richard Watson, Bishop of Llandaff, Wakefield asserted that the poor and working classes would lose nothing by a French invasion, and went on to denounce abuses in the Church of England and to condemn much of its liturgy. Together with his printer and publisher, Wakefield was convicted of libel; during his two years in prison, he kept himself busy corresponding on points of scholarship.

With this educational background, Malthus entered Jesus College in 1784. Among the later-prominent men who attended Cambridge at about the same time were William Pitt the Younger; William Wilberforce, a swashbuckling collegiate type whose interest in slavery developed only later; Thomas Clarkson, who even as a student wrote a prize essay in opposition to slavery; Charles Simeon, later vicar of the Holy Trinity Church in Cambridge and one leader of the evangelical revival; Richard Porson, a famous Greek scholar. In 1787

Wordsworth enrolled at St. John's, where according to his description in *The Prelude* he most resented the compulsory chapel. It was Coleridge's fortune "to come to Jesus at a time [in 1791] when the College counted among its graduates some men of marked individuality and magnetic influence. Among men immediately his seniors were Malthus, William Otter, . . . and E. D. Clarke, . . . [who] had formed an intellectual circle which gave an energy to the College strongly contrasted to the inertness of Saint John's."[8]

Malthus's tutor was William Frend (1757–1841), who also supervised the education of the Otter brothers and Clarke. With a degree from Christ's College, Frend was almost immediately elected a fellow and tutor at Jesus. After his ordination, he obtained the living of Madingley, near Cambridge, and with this double income could live in modest comfort. At the age of 30, however, he announced himself a Unitarian and had to resign his living and his tutorship, though permitted under the rules of the university to retain his fellowship. Over the following years he wrote a series of pamphlets reflecting his growing religious, political, and academic dissent. Three of these were particularly important. *Thoughts on Subscription to Religious Tests* (1788) attacked the ruling that only members of the Anglican church were eligible to get degrees at Cambridge: "I am far from thinking uniformity in opinion, whether philosophical or religious, a desirable object." *A Second Address to the Inhabitants of Cambridge and Its Neighbourhood, exhorting them to turn from the false worship of three persons to the worship of the one true God* (1789) followed a first address on the same theme. *Peace and Union* (1793) expressed still stronger disagreement with the church's doctrines and discipline.

Particularly as a result of the last pamphlet, steps were taken to remove Frend from the university. Opposition to him culminated in an eight-day trial, of which Frend published the proceedings with an introduction defending his actions:

I call on you, not only on my own account, . . . but . . . that by a timely interference on your part an abominable spirit of bigotry and fanaticism may be crushed in our seminaries of learning . . . The first thing . . . is the folly of making [a university's] members subscribe to a religious creed . . . To require men to go into orders is a relic of popery . . . Make the universities, in short, proper to qualify men for the situations which they are hereafter to occupy in life, and remove those ridiculous statutes which in the present days no one can obey.[9]

After Frend's trial a statement of recantation was drawn up, but he refused to sign it. As a consequence he was "banished" from the university; this meant not that he was expelled but that he was forbidden to reside within the university's limits. In 1806 he moved to London, where he became actuary of the newly formed Rock Life Assurance Company; and until illness forced him to resign some twenty years later, this was his main work.[10]

An idea of the range of Frend's interests can be given briefly by listing the full titles of some of his other short works:

The Effect of Paper Money on the Price of Provisions, or the point in dispute between Mr. Boyd and Sir Francis Baring examined, the bank paper money proved to be an adequate cause for the high price of provisions, and constitutional remedies recommended (1801). A year earlier Malthus had also written a pamphlet on the high price of provisions.

The Principle of Taxation, or contribution according to means, in which it is shown that if every man pays in proportion to the stake he has in the country, the present ruinous and oppressive system of taxation, the custom house, and the excise office may be abolished and the national debt gradually and easily paid off (1804). To recommend a system of progressive taxation was a proposal out of joint with the time, combining opposition to mercantilist duties with a law that would be enacted only a century later.

The National Debt in Its True Colours, with plans for its extinction by honest means (1817). This pamphlet repeated some of the ideas expressed in *The Principles of Taxation*.

A Plan of Universal Education (1832). "The advantages possessed by this kingdom if its leaders should establish a plan of universal education are great. Ample funds are at its disposal: . . . let the revenues of all the cathedral and collegiate churches be appropriated for this purpose." Malthus also advocated a system of universal free education. It is generally assumed that he derived this radical proposal from Adam Smith, but his espousal of it may have been reinforced by talks with his tutor.

Frend's forte was mathematics, but even in that field his papers combined intelligence with a certain eccentricity. As the obituary by a spokesman of the Astronomical Society noted, his unwillingness to accept unproved theses in science may have derived from his difficultly learned skepticism in religion. "Having been led to conclude that he had been betrayed by authority into the belief of propositions both inexplicable and false, the tendency to think that the inexplicable must be false . . . was a necessary ingredient of his future reflections on all subjects." Thus, he was never able to accept the hypothesis of gravity, which made him "the last of the *learned* anti-Newtonians."[11] His major work in mathematics was the two-volume *Algebra* (1796, 1799). In *A Letter to the Vice-Chancellor of the University of Cambridge* (1798) he solicited support for a professorship by means of a treatise on the roots of algebraic equations: "Negative or impossible roots, . . . like the epicycles of Ptolemy, were introduced into science from the same cause, the indulgence of an hypothesis instead of a rigid adherence to truth." Some of his mathematical pieces were almost playful—for example, a defense of Arabic as against Roman numerals entitled *On the Greatest Number That Can be Expressed by Three Figures*, $9^{(9^9)}$ (1831). More significant was the manual on life tables that he wrote as an actuary (1815). This was essentially a table of premiums for single lives and for two joint lives, at various ages but with no differentiation by sex. Applicants were to be asked whether they had had gout, a rupture, or spitting of blood. He recommended an 11 percent increment for persons who had not had smallpox or been vaccinated—an interesting indication of the importance of this one disease in the mortality of the period.

If some of these skills and ideas were passed on to his most famous pupil, there also was a wide divergence on both sides. From the time of the first appearance of *An Essay on the Principle of Population,* of which Malthus presented a copy to his former tutor, almost to the end of his life, Frend expressed disagreement. Since "men were guided by reason," population "would increase with decreasing increment, so that at the conclusion it would terminate with an equality of births and burials, each generation possessing the maximum of happiness adapted to its state that the earth can provide." In 1837, after he had suffered a slight stroke, Frend recalled the name of his pupil as "Malthouse"; but then Frend's biographer, presumably without that excuse, refers to him as "Richard Malthus."[12]

At Jesus College Malthus won prizes in Latin and in English declamation. His principal subject was mathematics, following the advice that his father gave him: "I recommend Sanderson's Optics to you, and Emerson's Mechanics; Long's Astronomy you certainly have. There are papers of the mathematical kind in the Royal Society transactions which are generally worth reading . . . I suppose Sir I's Principia to be your chief classical book after the elementary ones."[13] With Frend as a tutor and with this kind of regimen, Malthus graduated as Ninth Wrangler. The term, certainly unfamiliar to most Americans, derives (like *tripos* and *optime*) from the college disputations of an earlier age; it means that he graduated with honors in mathematics, the only one of his class at Jesus to do so. In 1793 Malthus was elected to a fellowship at Jesus and, as such, was one of those who "made an order" that the name of S. T. Coleridge should be taken off the boards unless he paid his tutor's bill. Also in 1793 he became curate at Okewood, Surrey, a village "truly remarkable throughout the eighteenth century for its enormous number of baptisms and its small number of burials."[14]

As William Otter summed up this education, "It is difficult to believe that a youth like Robert Malthus, naturally sensitive and intelligent, could be brought in frequent contact with men of such qualities and attainments without deriving great advantages, and incurring some danger. From the last, however, his natural good sense, and his early habits of observation, happily protected him . . . He began very early to judge for himself, even in matters relating to his education."[15]

William Otter (1768–1840), one of Malthus's closest friends at Jesus, wrote a memoir that is one of the two main sources for details of Malthus's personal life. Of all the men closely associated with Malthus, Otter fitted in with his times most conventionally. His career was in the church, in which he rose through a succession of posts to become Bishop of Chichester, where he was especially active in promoting education. His oldest daughter married Malthus's son Henry, then Vicar of Effingham. Otter wrote a biography of Edward Daniel Clarke (1769–1822), traveler, antiquarian, and mineralogist, and also a friend of Malthus's. Apart from a number of technical works, Clarke's main publication (in six volumes) was *Travels in Various Countries of Europe, Asia, and Africa,* which incorporated portions of Malthus's travel notes, not always entirely accurately.

Malthus's first written work, *The Crisis,* was never published. No copy of the manuscript is extant; quotations of several paragraphs are all that we know of its content. Two years later, in 1798, there appeared *An Essay on the Principle of Population, as it affects the future improvement of society, with remarks on the speculations of Mr. Godwin, M. Condorcet, and other writers.* Though published anonymously, it would soon bring its author widespread fame and notoriety. In 1803 he wrote a much expanded version of the *Essay,* which established his scholarly reputation. Some ten months later he married his cousin, Harriet Eckersall, thus forgoing his fellowship. In 1805 Malthus was appointed professor of history and political economy in the newly founded East India College. This was the first professorship in political economy established in Britain (and probably in the world), and he filled the post with distinction until his death.

PROFESSOR T. R. MALTHUS

In 1795 British India comprised Bengal plus small areas along the two coasts. In 1823, after the Maratha Wars, the territory designated as either British or British-protected included most of the subcontinent. With the extension of their control, the new administrators instituted some political reforms (for example, human sacrifice and suttee were outlawed), but essentially their rule began as a commercial enterprise, operated for the first decades by the East India Company. In order to train the many new employees required by the expansion, the company needed some sort of educational facility. Lord Wellesley, the Governor-General, established the College of Fort William in Calcutta, presenting it as a fait accompli to the directors of the company, who were hardly pleased with this addition to their responsibilities. Eventually Fort William's function was whittled down to teaching Indian languages only to those who were to serve in Bengal, but in the protracted dispute the directors became committed to setting up an alternative school with a broader scope. The East India College opened in 1806 at Hertford Castle and moved three years later to Haileybury.[16]

The new college's curriculum included a considerable training in Indian languages, beginning with Sanskrit, then Persian, and usually Hindustani, with other languages as optional supplements to this minimum. Students also had courses in the standard British subjects (classical languages and mathematics, in particular), as well as the English legal system, general history, and—a discipline not yet recognized at Oxford or Cambridge—political economy. All of this was crowded into two or three years, and the professors had to work much harder than at the universities to train their charges.

Students lived in pleasant rooms, large enough to hold a four-poster bed and a dining table at which friends could be entertained. Their day started at seven, when a bedmaker woke them and lit a fire. After a cold bath, they attended eight o'clock chapel and then returned to their rooms for breakfast. At first there was no lunch; later it was a casual affair in the buttery—bread and cheese and beer served by two girls that students during the first years remembered as very pretty. Dinner was in the Hall initially at three, later at five or six; evening chapel was at eight. Most of the time between these breaks was taken up with lectures and studying. There were never more than a hundred students, sometimes as few as thirty; on admission they ranged in age from 15 to 22, and they engaged in the adolescent diversions one might expect. Games were played for enjoyment and exercise rather than as a main school activity; and the discipline, though far stricter than at the universities, was lax enough to permit recurrent juvenile escapades. At the end of each term, however, students were given an examination lasting a fortnight and then placed in numerical order of relative overall merit. The prizes that could be won were valuable, for they could start a young man off to a better career.[17]

The contention that marked the college's beginning not only continued but spread to Parliament. Malthus wrote two pamphlets defending Haileybury, the first answering charges by a Lord Grenville in the House of Lords (1813) and the second a more general and important justification (1817). Some of the charges, such as that sometimes the students behaved like rowdies, were apparently valid in the abstract,

though not when their behavior was compared with that at
the universities. One issue was an allegedly insufficient training in the standard British curriculum. But before being
admitted, students were required to pass examinations in
Latin, Greek, and arithmetic, thus ensuring—in Malthus's
words—that they had received "the usual school education of a
gentleman." Moreover, this was continued in the "Europeans,"
the portion of the curriculum that more or less balanced the
"Orientals."

The principal charge, it would seem, was that some students
were favored in admission, grades, or graduation. Even raising the issue was a little preposterous considering the amount
of influence that the church, men of title, and those in the
government exerted at Oxford and Cambridge. In all likelihood an important reason for the hostility to the East India
College was that, on the contrary, it represented a partial break
with both the prevalent favoritism and the obsolescent regulations and curriculum. Students were accepted from any kind
of school in England, Scotland, and Ireland. By today's standards compulsory attendance at chapel twice a day would seem
to denote a considerable overemphasis on what was seen as
moral training, but as early as 1824 Roman Catholic students
were excused from attending. In particular, the unabashedly
secular purpose of the education set the college apart from
the universities. Undoubtedly students who had strings to pull
followed the custom of the age, but favoritism was held in
some check by a division of authority. The College Council
was subject to control by the directors of the company, who in
turn could not, for example, expel a student except by going
through the India House, where a student might hope that
"his personal interest would prevent any serious inconven-
ience." Only after some disturbances were the principal and
professors given the customary power to exercise discipline.
But such negative controls were less important than the examinations; and Malthus held that the ranking based on them
was done "with scrupulous care and, I firmly believe, with
singular impartiality."

Though it was run by a quasiprivate company, the college
in fact was training civil servants, and it did so far more effi-
ciently than competing institutions. As a reviewer wrote of
Malthus's pamphlet, "The East India Company in its com-

mencement was a corporation of merchants, occupied in augmenting the profits of its commercial monopoly; yet it has grown, by a progress of unparalleled prosperity, to be the sovereign of a mighty empire. The duties and conditions of its servants have undergone a corresponding change. From being clerks, factors, or writers, they are now advanced to the situation of judges, ministers of state, and governors of provinces."[18] In spite of its manifest lacks, the college was able to adapt to this change. Much of what we know about Sanskrit, the ancient society described in that language, or the India of the nineteenth century pictured in a series of remarkable censuses was due to the efforts of British civil servants; and this outpouring of scholarship started from the initial impetus of education under the East India Company's auspices. Most of the students came from relatively comfortable homes and might have been expected to ally themselves with the Indian aristocracy or at least, in terms of practical politics, to woo its support. But "whether because of the sermons of LeBas and Jeremie or the political economy of Malthus and Jones, they were most of them when they reached India on the side of the yeoman rather than the noble."[19]

For some leftist critics, the fact that Malthus was associated with the college instituted to train agents of British imperialism confirms their negative opinion of him and his works; but in fact the East India Company was a utilitarian stronghold. Bentham offered his services in framing a system of law for India; and though his offer was not accepted, his indirect influence on the company's administration was considerable. As Assistant Examiner and then Examiner in the company's London office, James Mill was able to draft dispatches that the directors accepted without demur. John Stuart Mill also worked for the company and, as he reported in his autobiography, was "in a few years practically the chief conductor of the correspondence with India in one of the leading departments, that of the Native States." At Haileybury, William Empson taught his course in "general polity and laws" using Bentham's writings to instruct his students. At a farewell dinner before he left to become Governor-General of India, Bentinck remarked to James Mill that "it is you that will be Governor-General." To Bentham it seemed "as if the golden age of British India were lying before me." In James

Mill's *History of British India,* one of his main aims was to dispel what he saw as "the silly sentimental admiration of Oriental despotism" that such philosophes as Voltaire had expressed.[20]

We know very little about Malthus's life at the college. Though the second major biographical source (together with Otter's memoir) was written by a friend and colleague on the faculty, William Empson, it barely mentioned his day-to-day activities there. The essay is rather a judicious and penetrating analysis of Malthus's mind and its products, and with such a subject the emphasis was entirely appropriate. For Malthus's life was his scholarship, his teaching and writing; and if we knew something of his office routine, his manner of teaching, or whatever, this would merely embellish the central core. From 1796, when he wrote the unpublished *Crisis,* to his death in 1834 can be taken as the period of his maturity, and the corpus that he produced during those not quite four decades is impressive. The two major works, the 1803 edition of the *Essay* and the *Principles of Political Economy,* were more or less fixed, so that subsequent emendations were not fundamental. The continuous activity was in a steady flow of pamphlets, articles in reviews, and correspondence with other scholars. His constant involvement with the application of theory to political questions can be seen in two pamphlets on the Corn Laws, for instance, or in the testimony he offered to a parliamentary committee on emigration. *The Nature and Progress of Rent* (1815) marked an important contribution to economic theory, on which Ricardo based his broader, and better known, exposition of the subject.

Malthus was elected a Fellow of the Royal Society in 1819. In 1821, the year that the Political Economy Club was founded, he became a member, joining there such distinguished scholars as Ricardo, James Mill, and George Grote, author of the notable history of ancient Greece. At the beginning of 1824 Malthus was elected one of the ten royal associates of the Royal Academy of Literature. When the Statistical Society was founded in 1834, he was one of the first fellows. He was a member of the French Institute and of the Royal Academy in Berlin, and one of the first five foreign associates elected to the Académie des Sciences Morales et Politiques. All these honors suggest that his contributions to political economy, what Empson called "the science of civilization," were widely recognized.

MALTHUS THE MAN

Linnell's portrait of Malthus pictures him as a handsome man, with a nobly high forehead, moderately short hair, very sharp eyes, and a humorous mouth on which the harelip that Harriet Martineau mentioned[21] is barely visible. Appraisals of his personality and temperament, if we discount the malice of uninformed critics of his works, were almost routinely positive. Empson's effusive comment was typical: "Mr. Malthus could hate nobody—which considering the strength of his feelings, public and private, and the provocations which for forty years he was perpetually receiving, was almost as wonderful a circumstance as that anybody could be found capable of hating him." Otter's memoir has similar passages: "Such was his diffidence and habitual disregard of self that he has left nothing upon record intended directly as a memorial of his life . . . The great, we had almost said the only, fault of Mr. Malthus with the public was that his opinions were in advance of his age." In short, as his niece Louisa Bray remarked, "no one could know him without loving him."[22]

These friendly comments from friends can perhaps be discounted as exaggeratedly positive, intended to balance the scurrility to which Malthus was subjected from the time of the *Essay*'s first appearance. But similar sentiments, sometimes a bit tempered, appeared also in opinions of those farther from his personal circle. Note, for instance, the anonymous reviewer of Malthus's pamphlet on the East India College: "The pamphlet . . . throughout exhibits a clear good sense and calm ability, . . . and with these qualities are united . . . great fairness and sincerity, . . . good faith and honesty as a debater." Or, as another example, consider the comment of Francis Horner, one of the founders of the *Edinburgh Review*, who after his election to Parliament continued to offer advice to the editor: "Since Malthus has begun to contribute, I hope it will not be for want of solicitation on your part if he does not continue to supply you with articles . . . Though his general views are sometimes imperfect, he is always candid and an advocate for what he believes to be most liberal and generous." Or, even more pointedly, in a letter that Horner wrote to John Archibald Murray, a Scottish judge: "There is no man with whom I like better to converse upon controverted subjects; not that he is remarkably original in such ex tempore exercises, or even satisfactory always in his manner of communicating his views, but then he has the mere love of truth, for which I would willingly exchange . . . versatility, dexterity, and eloquence." One must recall that Horner was a Whig and that Malthus, though also one, was a thinker too independent to fit comfortably under any party label. "He stood alone simply because at all times he was his own man."[23]

Indeed, Malthus's writing for the *Edinburgh Review* was hampered by this very independence. By 1821, when in all probability he contributed the anonymous review of Godwin's *Of Population,* he felt himself to be excluded from the magazine's analysis of economics. As he wrote to Sismondi in that year, "*The Edinburgh Review* has so entirely adopted Mr. Ricardo's system of political economy that it is probable that neither you nor I shall be mentioned in it. I know indeed that a review of your book was written and sent [by Malthus himself?], but it appears to have been rejected through the influence of the gentleman who is the principal writer in the department of political economy"[24]—that is, John Ramsay McCulloch, who had taken on himself the task of defending, with great vehemence if no marked originality, every syllable in Ricardo's works.

More generally, the great contrast between Malthus's benign stance and his position at the storm center of every important controversy during his lifetime poses a conundrum to the present-day analyst. There must be more to this paragon than an almost namby-pamby lovableness. One should note, as a start, that the squeamishness concerning sexuality that prevailed later in the century was certainly not absent during this proto-Victorian period, and that it took courage for a serious writer to base his thesis on "the passion between the sexes." Respectable people found it more comfortable to agree with Godwin that if sexual intercourse were stripped of "all its attendant circumstances, . . . it would be generally despised." In Malthus's travel diary, he observed at length whether women were pretty or not, contrasting national types and remarking specifically on the women and girls he and his companions met, describing in detail the color, fabric, and style of each article of female clothing. For all this lively interest in the other sex, Malthus led a decorous married life;

in contrast, Godwin, who paraded his licentiousness before the world, speculated that in the utopia of the future men would become sexless angels.

Supposedly the child was father of the man; to understand Robert Malthus better we ought to look at how he was brought up. His three tutors, to stress that important fact again, were all remarkable for their forcefully expressed radical opinions; but in the main they failed to convert their charge, as we know from the content of his own writings. Presumably they did, however, teach him how to maintain a consistently respectful attitude toward one's opponent (hardly exceptional in a boy toward his tutor, not to say his father), while trying to hold honestly to one's point of view and to present it clearly and forthrightly. This was excellent training both in polemical adeptness and, more important, in character.

As one common device for exploring the mind of a man long dead is to peruse his library, I was delighted when I heard that Sydenham Malthus, Robert's nephew, had donated his uncle's books to Jesus College. Setting aside several days in December 1976 for what I anticipated would be a profitable and pleasant bit of research, I arrived in Cambridge and, by appointment, met one of the librarians. She took me through several locked doors along a corridor to the end of one building's wing, where in a cold and gloomy room there were stored, uncatalogued, the literary remains of one of the college's most famous graduates. A few small bulbs hung from the ceiling, and to read the title of a book taken at random from the shelves, I had to carry it over to one of these skimpy lights. It was impossible to reach the top shelves, for no stools or ladders were available. Bundled up in my overcoat, I asked the librarian how one could work under such conditions, and she suggested that I might return on a pleasant summer day. The anecdote, I feel, is worth recounting not merely for the reader's amusement but as one indication of how little Malthus is honored even by his alma mater.

The one trophy I brought back from that expedition was a catalogue of the books, apparently drawn up in 1891, when the donation was made. It contains many titles published after 1834, when Robert Malthus died, and of the several tens of thousands published before that date there is no way of knowing which he owned and which were added later to the original collection. Some idea of the range is given by the topics under which the titles are arranged in this list:

Agriculture, botany, horticulture, forestry, etc.

Biography, memoirs, letters, etc.

Classics (Greek, Latin, and translations of them), antiquities, art, etc.

Divinity, theology, sermons, Bibles, the Koran, religious sects, ethics, etc.

Encyclopedic, educational, and general. Magazines, dictionaries, lexicons, etc.

Fiction, the drama, novels, poetry, etc.

Geography, travels, voyages, etc.

History (exclusive of Classics), astronomy, geology, philosophy, physiology, and general science.

Natural history, the animal kingdom, field sports, pastimes, etc.

Politics and political economy, commerce, money, tracts relating to the foregoing.

That Robert Malthus was well read in his professional specialty we know without circumstantial corroboration, and the more interesting lists are those that have nothing to do with political economy—say, the next to last. With publication dates prior to 1834, this includes works like the following: *Thoughts on Hunting, History of British Birds,* Buffon's *Histoire naturelle, Introduction to Entomology* in four volumes, *The Naturalist's Calendar,* and three books on chess. Was Malthus a bird watcher? He did play chess. He did enjoy shooting as well as having thoughts about it. Perhaps some other researcher, working on pleasant summer days, may find new clues to such details of his personal life. I must be content to concentrate on his professional career.

3

The Principle of Population

N O FULL COPY OF *The Crisis* exists, but Empson in particular quoted extensively from this earliest work of Malthus. In a short book mainly on a different topic altogether, Malthus had one comment on population: "I cannot agree with Archdeacon Paley, who says that the quantity of happiness in any country is best measured by the number of people. Increasing population is the most certain possible sign of the happiness and prosperity of a state; but the actual population may be only a sign of the happiness that is past." In several respects this is an interesting passage. Though Robert Malthus's differences with his father have been emphasized in every account of their relation,[1] in fact they were one in their concern with "happiness." For all his independence from political parties and schools of thought, Malthus throughout his life accepted without equivocation the utilitarian axiom that the function of political economy or of statesmanship is to improve the lot of humankind.

Second, these two sentences from Malthus's first work at least suggest a dilemma that has plagued modern demographic analysis—namely, that the growth of numbers may be the consequence of prosperity (or, as we would be more likely to put it, of development), but that the effects of population increase are sometimes to impair that prosperity or in the worst cases to destroy it. Even in sympathetic exegeses, Malthus's thesis on population growth is sometimes presented so

38

narrowly as to seem almost simple-minded; it is worth stressing that even this earliest, preliminary, and very brief statement implies something of the actual complexity of the empirical world.

THE PROVOCATION

That the *Essay* of 1798 was written in a polemical context is evident from its very title, which denotes it as "remarks on the speculations of Mr. Godwin, M. Condorcet, and other writers." The first comparison to be made, then, should be with the theories, explicit or implicit, in the works that Malthus disputed.

As noted earlier, some of the beliefs and practices that we associate with the mercantilist system persisted until well into the nineteenth century. During the heyday of mercantilism, its theorists were remarkably consistent in their advocacy of pronatalist policies; "an almost fanatical desire to increase population prevailed in all countries."[2] Of course, during most of human history the usual effect of ethical norms and particularly of family systems has been pronatalist, for as long as life was precarious the high mortality had to be balanced, if the group was to survive, by fertility at least as high. The situation during the mercantilist era differed in two important respects: the encouragement of a rapid increase in numbers was not implicit, buried in moral codes typically justified on other grounds, but explicit, the conscious policy of a powerful state; and in many places population growth was becoming an economic and social burden even before the full transition to the modern period.

Adam Smith's *The Wealth of Nations* was the first and most effective general attack on mercantilist norms; but Smith was little interested in demography. Skeptical of the view that Britain's population was decreasing—by as much as 30 percent since 1688, according to Richard Price—Smith furnished William Eden with some Scottish data with which to buttress a counterargument.[3] *The Wealth of Nations* itself, however, has only one considerable passage on population:

Poverty, though it no doubt discourages, does not always prevent marriage. It seems even to be favorable to generation . . . Luxury in the fair sex, while it inflames perhaps the passion for enjoyment, seems always to weaken, and frequently to destroy altogether, the powers of generation. But poverty . . . is extremely unfavorable to the rearing of children . . . In some places one-half of the children born die before they are four years of age; in many places before they are seven; and in almost all places before they are nine or ten . . .

Every species of animals naturally multiplies in proportion to the means of their subsistence, and no species can ever multiply beyond it. But in a civilized society it is only among the inferior ranks of people that the scantiness of subsistence can set limits to the further multiplication of the human species; and it can do so in no other way than by destroying a great part of the children which their fruitful marriages produce.[4]

As early as 1776, when these ideas were written down, Smith was aware of the inverse relation between the financial ability to rear children and the number actually born. And like many others both then and later, he ascribed this paradox to the deleterious effect of luxurious living on the physiological ability to bear children. In the second and following editions of the *Essay,* as we shall see, Malthus solved the paradox—correctly—by contrasting the ways of life of the upper and lower classes. The first edition, on the other hand, was essentially a considerable elaboration of the second of the paragraphs I have just quoted from *The Wealth of Nations.*

The new concepts of humanity developed during the eighteenth century affected remarkably little the population theory and policy of the mercantilist era. Though, as before, particular writers differed among themselves, typically growth in numbers was still taken to be an indisputable index of a nation's good health. Montesquieu recommended that Colbert's laws, which had rewarded only the prodigiously fertile, be broadened into a more inclusive pronatalist policy; Voltaire thought a nation fortunate if its population increased by as much as 5 percent a century; Saint-Just, later one of the instigators of the Jacobin terror, proclaimed that one could depend on nature "never to have more children than teats," but that to keep the balance in the other direction needed the state's assistance.[5]

Marie-Jean-Antoine-Nicolas Caritat, Marquis de Condorcet (1743–94), one of the two targets that Malthus specified, was a revolutionary of the Girondin faction whom the Jacobins tried in absentia and sentenced to death. For a while he remained in Paris, hiding in the home of a woman who knew him only by reputation; and over the next six months, while the tumbrils were rolling by almost under his window, he wrote his famous *Esquisse d'un tableau historique des progrès de l'esprit humain,* a history of progress from its earliest beginnings to its imminent culmination in human perfection. In order not to expose his hostess in Paris to danger, Condorcet left that asylum and, though without an identity card, managed to escape from the city. For several days he wandered in the Verrière forest, close to the residence of the Suarts, friends with whom he had previously lived. The manner of his capture and subsequent death, not given in most sources, was recounted in the memoirs of a friend, and it is a story interesting enough to be worth a short digression.

After passing some nights in the woods, the unhappy fugitive had the appearance of a pauper, with a long beard and dirty clothes, wounded in one foot and famished . . . Suart did not dare give him shelter, but he offered to go at once to Paris and . . . try to get an invalid's pass (which could take the place of an identity card) ; and they arranged that Condorcet should return the following day to pick up this safe-conduct. Condorcet asked for a copy of Horace and for some tobacco; these were his most pressing needs . . .

Suart managed to get a very old pass, . . . and he awaited Condorcet, whom he expected at eight that evening. It was necessary to get the servant out of the way, and at three in the afternoon his wife took her along on a visit to the village. Left alone, Suart waited. All evening he saw no one till his wife returned at half past nine. Neither that day nor the two following ones did anything happen; finally on the evening of the third day he heard . . . that a man had been arrested in Clamart [the adjoining town] . . .

The poor fellow, leaving the Suarts with a bit of bread, had returned to the Verrière forest, where he passed the night. The next morning he went to Clamart, where he gobbled up an omelet at an inn. His long beard, his untidy appearance, his air of suspicion, induced a zealot, one of those voluntary spies that infested all of France, to watch him. The spy demanded to know who he was, where he was coming from, where he was going, where his citizen's identity card was. Condorcet, too rattled to respond clearly, . . . was unable to give a satisfactory account of himself and was thrown into prison. The following morning he was found dead. He had taken stramonium [jimson weed] combined with opium, which (as he had told Suart when he left him) he always carried with him.[6]

According to the book that Condorcet wrote under these circumstances, mankind had moved upward through a series of evolutionary stages (somewhat like those later delineated by Comte or, in a different context, by Marx), starting with a mode of existence not dissimilar from that of other animal species, proceeding through social patterns like those of American Indians and other surviving primitives, and developing further through the advances of historical societies. The French Revolution had started the last stage of this progress, and soon the human race, freed from the chains of error, crime, and injustice, would attain universal truth, virtue, and happiness. All inequalities of wealth, of education, of opportunity, of sex, would disappear. Animosities between nations and races would be no more. All persons would speak the same language. The earth would be bountiful without stint. All diseases would be conquered, and if man did not become immortal, the span of his life would have no assignable upper limit. In this rational age to come, everyone would recognize his obligation to those not yet born and to the general well-being both of his own society and of all humanity, and "not to the puerile idea of filling the earth with useless and unhappy beings."

The same year that Condorcet went into hiding, a book expressing the same ideas was published across the Channel: *Enquiry concerning Political Justice*, by William Godwin (1756–1836). The son and grandson of Dissenting ministers, Godwin, in the words of his principal biographer, was "nursed in a very hotbed of forced piety." Before the age of 8, he had "a great familiarity with the phraseology and manner of the Bible," which in his own opinion "had a considerable share in the formation of his character." As a boy he was the sole pupil of Samuel Newton, another Dissenting minister, from whom he went to a Dissenting seminary. "I read all the authors of greatest repute, for and against the Trinity, original sin, and the most disputed doctrines, . . . and all my inquiries terminated in Calvinism." After graduation, Godwin also became a Dissenting minister, remaining in this family profession until he was 27 and "a sincere adherent" until he was 32.[7]

One who argues by epithets would find good reason for dubbing him "Parson Godwin," since effects of this training are clearly to be seen in his writings. From his Calvinist upbringing, he acquired an abhorrence of all emotion: "sensual pleasures are momentary; they fill a very short portion of our time with enjoyment, and leave long intervals of painful vacuity." The really good life is based entirely on reason, but reason conceived wholly as a quality of discrete individuals, Since any sentiment whatever linking one person to another Godwin saw as reprehensible, the emphasis on individuality general among classical liberals reached an ultimate in his writings. "Individuality is of the very essence of intellectual excellence . . . Everything that is usually understood by the term cooperation is, in some degree, an evil."[8] Even to participate in a concert, to act in a play, bordered on "a breach of sincerity." Godwin's anarchism was an elementary corollary of this distrust of any joint effort; one who refused on principle to belong to any political organization, in order that no partisan doctrine might interfere with his absolute freedom of judgment, would of course detest all forms of government. Unlike other radicals, he was opposed even to public schools. As a Calvinist minister he had joined with all Dissenters in resenting any slightest government supervision of church-linked schools, and when he left the church he opposed the supervision of schools by any authority. "All education is despotism. It is perhaps impossible for the young to be [instructed] without introducing in many cases the tyranny of implicit obedience."[9] He approved only of the incessant writing and talking by right-thinking intellectuals, who would thus gradually bring to the surface their neighbors' inborn virtue.

Godwin began by denouncing marriage as vehemently as any other human association not based exclusively on reason. The institution is "a system of fraud; and men who carefully mislead their judgments in the daily affairs of their life must be expected to have a crippled judgment in every other concern." Marriage is "the worst of monopolies," through which "philanthropy will be crossed and checked in a thousand ways."[10] Godwin held to this view until he himself fell in love. He lived with Mary Wollstonecraft and then, when she became pregnant, married her. When she died shortly after giving birth, Godwin published a memoir recounting their life together. Later, when their daughter had an affair with Shelley, Godwin thundered like a Victorian father—while at the same time continuing to "borrow" money from Shelley. Godwin wooed two other women and married a third, an ill-tempered widow who, had he known her then, might have stimulated his earlier denigration of the institution. This lapse from all principle, both society's and his own, became of course a favorite scandal in his critics' writings. A philosopher who advocates saintliness and implicitly points to himself as the model for all to follow is an irresistible target when he misbehaves.

The liaison with Mary Wollstonecraft was of fundamental importance also in the development of Godwin's philosophy. Man's capacity to improve indefinitely he had deduced from his postulate that "in all cases of volition we act, not from impulse, but opinion." From "the omnipotence of truth" it follows that "every principle which can be brought home to the conviction of the mind will infallibly produce a correspondent effect upon the conduct . . . The perfection of man [is] impossible [only because] the idea of absolute perfection is scarcely within the grasp of human understanding."[11] But when he became aware, like many another who fell in love, that even in his own case reason could not—indeed, should not—control passion altogether, the psychological premises on which *Political Justice* rested were thereby eroded. Godwin listed among "the literary productions which I am at present desirous to execute" a work to be titled *First Principles of Morals.* "The principal purpose of this work," he wrote in his diary, "is to correct certain errors in the earlier part of my *Political Justice.* The part to which I allude is essentially defective in the circumstance of not yielding a proper attention to the empire of feeling."[12] Not only was this book never written but in subsequent editions of *Political Justice* the offending passages were changed by only a few words. Undoubtedly the author came to recognize that if he were to forsake the postulate that every person can act completely rationally his entire edifice would come tumbling down.

In Godwin's view, "myriads of centuries of still increasing population may pass away, and the earth be yet found sufficient for the support of its inhabitants." Consequently, he thought it idle to be concerned about so distant a contingency. In the remote future, when a zero rate of population growth would become necessary, this would be realized in a world without births or deaths!

[Since] one tendency of a cultivated and virtuous mind is to diminish our eagerness for the gratification of the senses, . . . the men whom we are supposing to exist when the earth shall refuse itself to a more extended population will probably cease to propagate. The whole will be a people of men, and not of children. Generation will not succeed generation, nor truth have, in a certain degree, to recommence her career every thirty years.[13]

This dissipation of the sexual urge will be matched by a total conquest of death, brought about not, as in others' speculations, by improvements in medical arts, but by "the immediate and unavoidable operation of an improved intellect." Disease will be completely conquered by cheerfulness, which "gives new elasticity to our limbs and circulation to our juices," and by reason, which abolishes confusion, "in all instances the concomitant" of disease. In short, "the term of human life may be prolonged [simply] by the immediate operation of the intellect beyond any limits which we are able to assign."[14] Godwin was to write more on population, virtually all of it merely critical of Malthus's *Essay*. This vision of immortal castrati can be regarded as his main positive contribution to the science of demography.

Godwin did not, like Condorcet, commit suicide in prison, but the last years of his long life hardly substantiated the extravagant youthful dreams for which he is remembered. In 1833 he was appointed Yeoman Usher of the Exchequer, a post of which the nominal duties were performed entirely by menials. Thus it was that England's most important proponent of anarchism ended his life in comparative material comfort but as the object of government charity. How soured he became can be measured by recalling, in contrast, the often quoted passage from *Political Justice* on the inevitable bliss of the near future: "There will be no war, no crimes, no administration of justice, as it is called, and no government. Beside this, there will be neither disease, anguish, melancholy, nor resentment. Every man will seek, with ineffable ardor, the good of all." Compare this with the last entry in the old man's diary:

Everything under the sun is uncertain. No provision can be made a sufficient security against adverse and unexpected fortune, least of all to him who has not a stipulated income bound to him by the forms and ordinances of society. This, as age and feebleness of body and mind advance, is an appalling consideration. "A man cannot tell what shall be," to what straits he may be driven, what trials and privations and destitution and struggles and griefs may be reserved for him.[15]

THE FIRST ESSAY

Like most utopians, Condorcet and Godwin had focused their attacks on social inequities and looked forward to a time when these would disappear and, with them, all the ills of mankind. Malthus expressed strong sympathy with the sentiment underlying this exercise. He was struck, he wrote, by the spirit and energy of Godwin's style, the force and precision of some of his reasoning, and particularly the ardent, the impressive earnestness of *Political Justice*. But the result, however attractive, was no more than "a beautiful phantom of the imagination."

The great error . . . is the attributing almost all the vices and misery that are seen in civil society to human institutions . . . Were there no established administration of property, every man would be obliged to guard with force his little store. Selfishness would be triumphant . . .

[But] let us suppose all the causes of misery and vice in this island removed . . . With these extraordinary encouragements to population, and every cause of depopulation, as we have supposed, removed, the numbers would necessarily increase faster than in any society that has ever yet been known . . . We will only suppose the period of doubling to be twenty-five years, a ratio of increase which is well known to have taken place throughout all the northern states of America . . . Difficult as it might be to double the average produce of [Britain] in twenty-five years, let us suppose it effected . . . During the next period of doubling, where will the food be found to satisfy the importunate demands of the increasing numbers? . . .

It is a perfectly just observation of Mr. Godwin that "there is a principle in human society by which population is perpetually kept down to the level of the means of subsistence." The sole question is, what is this principle?

Malthus began with two postulates: that "food is necessary to the existence of man" and that "the passion between the sexes is necessary and will remain nearly in its present state." If one grants the validity of these "fixed laws of nature," then it follows that the "power" of population to increase is "indefinitely greater" than the "power" of the earth to provide food. "Population, when unchecked, increases in a geometrical ratio. Subsistence increases only in an arithmetical ratio . . . By that law of our nature which makes food necessary to the life of man, the effects of these two unequal powers must be kept equal." The two ratios were introduced as data rather than as additional postulates. The disparity between potential increase and potential food supply, Malthus argued, pervades the "animal and vegetable kingdoms," throughout which nature spreads seeds profusely and nourishment more sparingly.

Man cannot escape a law that applies to the whole of nature. He must eat, and his sexual urge drives him to generate offspring in numbers beyond the subsistence available over the long run. Compared with these fundamentals, all other factors are relatively unimportant. "No fancied equality, no agrarian regulations in their utmost extent, could remove the pressure of [the principle of population] even for a single century." Even so, the check on population growth is "more complicated" with humans than in the rest of animate nature.

Impelled to the increase of his species by a powerful instinct, reason interrupts and asks [man] whether he may not bring beings into the world for whom he cannot provide the means of subsistence . . . Will he not lower his rank in life? . . . Will he not be obliged to labor harder? . . . May he not see his offspring in rags and misery, and clamoring for bread that he cannot give them? And may he not be reduced to the grating necessity of forfeiting his independence, and of being obliged to the sparing hand of charity for support?

These considerations . . . prevent a very great number in all civilized nations from pursuing the dictate of nature in an early attachment to one woman. And this restraint, almost necessarily, though not absolutely produces vice. Yet . . . the tendency to a virtuous attachment is so strong that there is a constant effort towards an increase of population, . . . [which] tends to subject the lower classes of the society to distress and to prevent any great permanent amelioration of their condition.

If during a period of economic depression many postpone marriage, then the balance between people and food will improve. But with the consequent return of prosperity, more will begin families and help build up again the pressure of population on subsistence. The correlation between agricultural production and the number of marriages that Malthus suggested (which in more recent times has been demonstrated time and again) was partly hidden, he wrote, because it pertained mainly to the lower classes and "the histories of mankind that we possess are histories only of the higher classes."

But was it not possible to give the poor more? Redistribution of income through the mechanism of the Poor Laws, Malthus argued, would not increase the amount of any commodity; and "when an article is scarce and cannot be distributed to all, . . . he that offers the most money becomes the possessor." In other words, though the Poor Laws "may have alleviated a little the intensity of individual misfortune, they have spread the general evil over a much larger surface"; they tended to depress the living conditions of the poor both by encouraging them to marry earlier and thus reproduce themselves more plentifully and by reducing some of the independent working class to the status of poverty.

On the scale of the whole world over all of history, allowing for deviations in consumption norms, "population constantly bears a regular proportion to the food that the earth is made to produce." The general tendency is to breed up to the level of subsistence, and improvements in the supply of food means less that people eat better than that more people eat the same meager portions. And, indeed, despite all the enormous progress in agricultural and associated techniques, there are millions more living in destitution and misery in the last third quarter of the twentieth century than ever before in history. Even in the first edition of his *Essay,* with its overemphasis on biological determinants of population growth, Malthus was not totally mistaken in his vision of the future.

Transition to the Second Essay

The publication of the *Essay* immediately established its anonymous author as a controversial figure. The small book acquired the fame and notoriety that, paradoxically, it has retained to this day. For critics have often preferred to base their opposition to Malthus's system on this equivalent, in current American terms, of a master's thesis by a man who during his subsequent scholarly career was to revise it fundamentally.[16] As one critic put it, "The *Essay* leaves little doubt that economic progress must necessarily end in overpopulation. This holds especially true of its first edition, which is by far the best one to read, because in it Malthus does not temporize or encumber his argument with early demographic data of dubious quality."[17] In other words, after Malthus spent a lifetime laboring to improve the statement of his theory and gathering facts on which to base these emendations, those who would comment on the principle of population and find this greater complexity inconvenient should concentrate on the first edition as the easier target.

Obviously Godwin was interested in a book intended to undermine the foundation of *Political Justice,* and a discussion ensued on the points at issue between Malthus, then an unknown of 32, and Godwin, a man of 42 at the height of his fame. On August 20, 1798 (only ten weeks after the date of the *Essay*'s preface), Malthus wrote to Godwin continuing a face-to-face discussion and replying to an earlier letter from him.[18] An amicable interaction eventually affected the views of both. Godwin agreed to drop the word (though hardly the concept) *perfectibility;* and, as we have noted, he admitted at least to his diary that one could not presume human behavior to be wholly rational. Three years later, he published a little book in which he proclaimed an "unfeigned approbation and respect" for Malthus, for this adversary, unlike some others, "neither had labored to excite hatred nor contempt against me or my tenets" but had been motivated solely by "the investigation of evidence and the development of truth." Indeed, Malthus had "made as unquestionable an addition to the theory of political economy as any writer for a century past."

I admit fully that the principle of population in the human species is in its own nature energetic and unlimited, [but] is it necessary that we should always preserve the precise portion of vice and misery which are now to be found in the world, under pain of being subjected to the most terrible calamities? . . .

Another check upon increasing population . . . is that sentiment, whether virtue, prudence, or pride, which continually restrains the universality and frequent repetition of the marriage contract . . . Everyone possessed in the most ordinary degree of the gift of foresight deliberates long before he engages in so momentous a transaction . . . Is it not in the human character to reason after this manner in such a situation? The more men are raised above poverty and a life of expedients, the more decency will prevail in their conduct, and sobriety in their sentiments.[19]

From his side, Malthus accepted fully the proposition that the ability to reason differentiates human beings fundamentally from all other species. As we have seen, the idea had been expressed briefly in the first edition; in the second it was rounded out by adding "moral restraint" to the "positive checks" and vice and misery; and in the subsequent editions the development of the argument shifted more and more from biological determinants to the social settings that would engender the foresight through which population growth could be limited relatively painlessly.

Malthus's trip to Scandinavia in 1799 was another stimulus to the major revisions of the *Essay* that would soon follow. It took forty-seven hours to reach the mouth of the Elbe, and from there he and his companions went to "Hamburgh," across from Copenhagen into southern Sweden, then north and west into Norway as far as Trondheim. The diary that Malthus kept presents an engaging picture of an enthusiastic young man, earnest without being pedantic, interested in just about everything. His notes were scribbled and full of spelling errors; but even in this context he was decorous enough to change his remark that Copenhagen's canals "stink" to that "they are very offensive after hot weather," conscious enough of class structures to amend the designation of a Lapp from "the old gentleman" to "the old man." During the first weeks each day's entry began with a short note about the weather, followed by something like "Chestnuts in full bloom" or "The lilacs in Mr. Tank's garden were fully out." By modern standards the conditions of travel were primitive, but along the route the young Englishmen had access to local personages, who made them welcome with little side trips or lectures on the region. A professor of natural history at the University of Copenhagen showed them "some curious specimens relating to the formation of coal and amber." At the several mines they visited, Malthus took notes on production and profits. Like healthy young persons anywhere, the travelers were interested in what they were given to eat. They learned how to say "strawberries and cream" in Norwegian in the hope of getting that dish more often, but some oat cakes were "the coarsest that one could conceive to be eatable," more chaff than oatmeal; Robert took a small piece away with him as a sample. He was fascinated by the languages, noting that near where they landed in Germany a man seemed to understand many

English words though he did not know the language (undoubtedly he spoke Plattdeutsch and possibly also Frisian, which is even more closely related). Malthus wondered why what was named "Trondheim" on the maps was always called "Drontheim" by the people who lived there (the latter is the German form). He found it difficult to describe skis and fjords, for the words had not yet been transferred into English.

Like the good student of *The Wealth of Nations* that he was, Malthus jotted down at the beginning of his diary "Smith's Questions":

Interest of money.
Corn laws. Inland merchants and at the ports.
Recompense of laborer.
Relative prices of provisions and manufactures at different
    times.
Bills and bankers.
Religious establishments and sects.

This list was to focus his attention on matters to be investigated, and recurrently through the pages of the diary appear jottings about finances, economic trends, profits and wages, and the like. But the central question, for Malthus and also for us, was of course population, on which the notations were longer and more systematic. He had written to his father that he was trying to buy a wide range of demographic books— among others, Süssmilch's *Göttliche Ordnung* (but not in German, which he did not read), Muret's *Memoir* on population in the Pays de Vaud (on which there is a long discussion in later editions of the *Essay*), Haygarth on the population and diseases of Chester, Kersseboom on the number of people in Holland.[20]

The main stimulus to his demographic studies that Malthus found in Norway was a number of institutional arrangements to inhibit early marriage. A lower-class man drafted into the army "could not marry without producing a certificate signed by the minister of the parish that he had substance enough to support a wife and family, and even then it was at the will of the officer to let him marry or not." A similar check among agriculturists was more significant, for at that time Norway was essentially a country of farmers and farm laborers living together on virtually independent units. How slight was the penetration of a market economy is suggested by the fact, which Malthus noted, that one could not buy any butter in Christiana (now Oslo), for "all persons use what they make themselves or salt it for keeping." Farmers generally did not marry until they were able to get a holding of their own; those with no land generally became "servants" (or, as we would say, farmhands), and as such were generally forbidden to marry until they acquired a plot to work on a share basis. In other words, marriage was regulated according to the economic ability of the man to care for the family he would be founding.[21]

Malthus's observations on Norway have been subjected to a critical review by a modern demographer, who based his study largely on the census of 1801 (two years after Malthus's visit) and a series of studies done in the middle of the nineteenth century by Eilert Sundt, who with annual grants from the Norwegian government wrote a number of statistical volumes on the country's population. Against such benchmarks, one might have intimated that Malthus's conclusions were remarkably perspicacious, but the author concentrated on finding fault. He never noted that the glass is half full, always that it is half empty. It needs no emphasizing that Malthus's trip was a rather casual affair, that he knew no Norwegian, that he visited only a portion of the country (Sundt's studies also covered only 60 percent of the population), that his contacts were in no sense random. How then explain that on some main points Malthus was dead right? "Sundt argued that a farmer's son would not normally marry until he had a farm of his own." "Sons and daughters of the [crofter] . . . would normally leave the parental home some time during their teens to go as servants working and living on a farm. Rarely would they marry whilst in that position."[22] These were the central institutional checks to procreation noted in a retrospective analysis, and it took an exceptional intelligence to grasp their crucial importance from so slight a basis as Malthus had.

With the stimulus of new experiences, new reading, new ideas, Malthus returned home and wrote a second edition of the *Essay*, with a different title: *An Essay on the Principle of Population; or, a view of its past and present effects on human happiness; with an inquiry into our prospects respecting the future removal or mitigation of the evils which it occasions* (1803). It was in fact a new book, and some commentators (of whom James Bonar may have been the first) distinguished between what they labeled the "First Essay" and the "Second Essay." If Malthus had made a similar differentiation, some of the subsequent confusion might have been avoided.

In all there were seven editions of the *Essay,* six during Malthus's lifetime and the seventh, definitive version published in 1872. But the basic shift was from the First Essay, a mainly deductive book of some 55,000 words, to the Second Essay, in which the expansion of theory and of illustrative data increased the work to some 200,000 words.[23] No less an economist than Alfred Marshall rated the latter as "one of the most crushing answers that patient and hard-working science has ever given to the reckless assertions of its adversaries."[24] Subsequent editions included relatively minor changes, though with sometimes interesting appendices answering particular criticisms. *A Reply to the Chief Objections Which Have Been Urged Against the Essay on the Principle of Population,* appended to the 1806 edition, was also published separately so that it might be bound with earlier ones. With the 1817 edition there was a separate volume of 327 pages for owners of previous editions, entitled *Additions to the Fourth and Former Editions of An Essay on the Principle of Population.* In the seventh and final edition, an appendix of some 35 pages summarized these earlier rejoinders. From these details, which give only the barest suggestion of Malthus's continual effort to adjust his theory to criticisms that he deemed to be just and to answer those that in his opinion were not, the absurdity of basing one's judgment on the 1798 version becomes manifest.

The first four editions were published by "J. Johnson," the fifth and sixth by the more prominent John Murray. Murray was of Scottish forebears (his name was originally MacMurray), and he acted for a period as the London distributor and part-publisher of the *Edinburgh Review.* By the time he began to publish Malthus, however, he had broken this association and helped to found the competing Tory periodical, the *Quarterly Review.* Undoubtedly he added the *Essay* to his list not because of any particular agreement with its author but simply because he was publishing some of the best books of the period. For the modern reader, one advantage of the change of publisher is that the archaic long *s* disappeared from the text.

The designation of the author, which gives a very slight intimation of Malthus's self-perception, was revised from one edition to the next:

1798, anonymous.

1803, "T. R. Malthus, A.M., Fellow of Jesus College, Cambridge."

1806, "T. R. Malthus, A.M., Late Fellow of Jesus College, Cambridge."

1807 and 1817, "T. R. Malthus, A.M., Late Fellow of Jesus College, Cambridge, and Professor of History and Political Economy in the East India College, Haileybury."

1826 and 1872, "The Rev. T. R. Malthus, Late Fellow of Jesus College, Cambridge, and Professor of History and Political Economy in the East India College, Hertfordshire."

In other words, though he was formally a clergyman from 1788 on, he so designated himself only in 1826. This suggests that the clerical title that some critics have emphasized may have been a defensive gesture to counter the repeated charge that the *Essay*'s author was antireligious.

His reputation abroad is indicated by the remarkably rapid proliferation of foreign editions of the *Essay*. In 1809, three years after the third London edition, this was reprinted in the United States as the first American edition (Washington: Roger Chew Weightman). In the same year a French translation of the *Essay* by Pierre Prévost, professor of philosophy, was published in Geneva and Paris; and in 1823 there appeared a second French edition with Guillaume Prévost, professor of law, as joint translator. Appended to the latter were some remarks by the translators that helped to introduce the author appropriately to a francophone audience. For example, in contrast to a widespread contrary view, "the principal objective that Mr. Malthus set himself is to base the happiness of human society on a solid foundation, and in particular to place the lower classes in a happier state than the one to which they have been reduced in the most advanced nations."[25]

THE REVISED PRINCIPLE OF POPULATION

"In an inquiry concerning the improvement of society," Malthus began the revised version of the *Essay* (1872), the natural procedure is to investigate past impediments to "the progress of mankind towards happiness" and the probability that these will be partly or wholly removed in the future. He did not pretend to be able to discuss so large a topic in its entirety, but he claimed that "one great cause" has been "the constant tendency in all animated life to increase beyond the nourishment prepared for it." For population, "when unchecked," doubles once every generation. Among plants and "irrational animals," this potential increase is realized, and the "superabundant effects are repressed afterwards by want of room or nourishment." The matter, however, is more complicated in the human species, for man, a rational being, can consider the effects of his potential fertility and curb his instinct to reproduce. With man, thus, population growth is checked by two types of control, which Malthus termed the "preventive" and the "positive" checks. "In no state that we have yet known has the power of population been left to exert itself with perfect freedom."

The principal preventive check is "moral restraint," or the chaste postponement of marriage. Other types of preventive checks Malthus termed "vice," namely, "promiscuous intercourse, unnatural passions, violations of the marriage bed, and improper arts to conceal the consequences of irregular connections"—or, in today's language, promiscuity with prostitutes, homosexuality, adultery, and birth control or abortion. Positive checks include "wars, excesses, and many others which it would be in our power to avoid"; but in a country already fairly densely populated, lack of food is the decisive factor. If in Great Britain the average produce from the land were to be doubled over a generation of about twenty-five years, it "would be contrary to all our knowledge of the properties of land." That is to say, in contrast to the "tendency" or "power" of every species to increase at a geometric rate, under the most favorable circumstances usually to be found its subsistence increases at an arithmetic rate.

[Thus,] the human species would increase as the numbers 1, 2, 4, 8, 16, 32, 64, 128, 256; and the subsistence as 1, 2, 3, 4, 5, 6, 7, 8, 9. In two centuries the population would be to the means of subsistence as 256 to 9; in three centuries as 4,096 to 13, and in two thousand years the difference would be almost incalculable.

Lack of food, then, is the main ultimate check to population growth but "never the immediate check, except in cases of actual famine."

Apart from migration, the population growth in any area depends on the preventive and positive checks taken together, or, as we would say today, on practices affecting fertility and those affecting mortality. Moreover, "the preventive and positive checks must vary inversely as each other; that is, in countries either naturally unhealthy or subject to a great mortality from whatever cause it may arise, the preventive check will prevail very little. In those countries, on the contrary, which are naturally healthy, and where the preventive check is found to prevail with considerable force, the positive check will prevail very little, or the mortality be very small." Or, more simply put, fertility and mortality are, apart from transitional periods, generally either both high or both low.

Population tends to oscillate around its means of subsistence, as can be seen most clearly in primitive societies, whose control over the supply of food is at best very slight. If a hunter-gatherer tribe enjoys several years of superabundant game, typically its population will rise to absorb some of the greater amount of available food. But when this prosperous period is followed by shortages (partly perhaps because of the greater proportions of food plants and animals being consumed), then the population will be cut back to the size that can subsist in the more straitened environment. "When population has increased nearly to the utmost limits of the food, all the preventive and the positive checks will naturally operate with increased force . . . till the population is sunk below the level of the food; and then the return to comparative plenty will again produce an increase, and after a certain period its further progress will again be checked by the same causes."

In a country with a market economy, the interaction between population and its subsistence can be more complicated. To follow Malthus's illustrative example, if the number of people increased faster than the amount of food, then as a country of 11 million, say, grew to 11.5 million, on the average each person would get less to eat. Because of the consequent distress among the poor, more of them would put off getting married; and with the fall in the wage rate, farmers would hire more hands to improve agricultural land and turn up fresh soil, until the food available was again sufficient to supply everyone adequately. The oscillation seems on the surface to be similar to that in a primitive society, but note the two possible differences. The farmers who responded to low wage rates by extending or improving the land under tillage would probably raise the total amount of food harvested, so that the return to a new people-food balance would (or could) be at a higher level. That level, moreover, would not have to be at subsistence, for it could be raised by the aspirations of workers as reflected in the wages they demanded.

Discussing Malthus's principle of population in the context of his own emendations to the *Essay* (and thus treating him as one does every other writer) is still not enough for a just appraisal of what has been termed his "total population theory,"[26] considerable portions of which were expounded in other works. As we know from the article on population that in 1824 he contributed to the Supplement to the *Encyclopaedia Britannica,* he held to the end some of the ideas that he had started with; the biological-sociological theory in the *Essay* was combined with the mainly economic analysis in the *Principles* into a more complex amalgam. Indeed, Malthus's name is associated with the principle of population, but that principle became in his mature consideration the foundation on which to construct a grander edifice, which can best be explored story by story, wing by wing.

4

Minor Quibbles and Gross Misunderstandings

I F WE ADOPT the cynical definition of a classic, a work that everyone cites and no one reads, then the *Essay on Population* must be designated a superclassic—written by a man whose name has entered all the Western languages (with several false meanings, as I have remarked) but whose central ideas are often not accurately known even by professional demographers. Indeed, part of the difficulty lies in the subject matter and part in the confusions and half-contradictions that Malthus introduced as he developed his ideas over the whole of his lifetime. But the main basis of misunderstanding, now no less than a century and a half ago, is that there is hardly a cherished ideology, left or right, traditionalist or modernist, that is not brought somewhat into question by the principle of population. To argue, as even so fair and intelligent a critic as Flew did, that Malthus's schema was not "value-neutral" is almost silly.[1] As Malthus emphasized in the very titles of his books and throughout their texts, he wanted to analyze the determinants and consequences of population growth in order to contribute to "the future removal or mitigation of the evils which it occasions" and thus to encourage "the future improvement of society." To put his advocacy into a modern context, we can think of the conversion of his values into behavioral norms as "social policy." The question arises whether to judge his values against the standards of his day or, anachronistically, against our own. To discuss the issue, it is convenient to summarize the population checks in the form of a table.

TABLE 1. MALTHUS'S CHECKS TO POPULATION.

PRACTICES AFFECTING	APPROVED	DISAPPROVED
Fertility	Postponed marriage	Vice, e.g., contraception
Mortality	(Improved health)	Misery, e.g., malnutrition

Much of what Malthus wrote is still highly pertinent, but we should hardly expect every detail of his work to have escaped visible aging. Some twentieth-century commentators, for instance, have remarked on what they see as an excessive delicacy in his references to matters relating to sex, overlooking the fact that his contemporaries attacked Malthus for discussing such topics even euphemistically. Yet it is interesting how enduring some of his values have been. Our social policy, as did his, affects mortality only by decreasing it and thus aggravating whatever population pressure exists. Indeed, we have had to coin the word *genocide* to denote a twentieth-century phenomenon, and we are troubled by the implications of institutionalized euthanasia; but we are as far as Malthus was from advocating killing as a means of solving population problems. Though we would not be likely to use the word *misery* to label a category, we would not disagree that hunger, war, and the like belong in it. Attitudes and, more recently, laws in many Western countries have indicated a growing tolerance of the practices that Malthus termed vicious, but no one has yet proposed that children be trained in masturbation or homosexuality in order to cut the growth of population. The only really sharp difference, by the weirdest of paradoxes, pertains to the practice long dubbed "Malthusian" or "neo-Malthusian," and I shall return to how his stance on contraception has been consistently misrepresented.

A CATALOGUE OF CAVILS

Again and again, critics of Malthus's main thesis have buttressed their opposition with arguments—more or less irrelevant, more or less false—that sometimes have all but displaced

Malthus

the central core. To get at the trees, we must begin by clearing away the underbrush that has proliferated around the principle of population from 1798 to date.

"Plagiarism." It has become almost mandatory to include in any discussion of Malthus's population theory a remark that it was not wholly original. Even those who make the criticism typically indicate the narrow range of their own reading. Depending on their competence in languages and their prior training, some have noted partial anticipations of Malthus in the classics of ancient Greece and Rome, some in frequently ignored writings in German or even Swedish.[2] But usually the charge of "plagiarism" (as Marx put it, as always using the crudest epithet to overstate his case) depends on citing a few passages in English or French. Thus, from Condorcet's incidental observation that denizens of the imminent utopia that he envisioned would control their fertility, some have concluded that even in so antithetical a thinker one finds "the entire genesis of the Malthusian law of population, though in France these ideas remained unnoticed."[3] Among still earlier French thinkers who anticipated some "Malthusian" ideas, one might cite Sébastien le Prestre de Vauban (1633–1707), Pierre le Pesant Bois-Guillebert (1646–1714), and François de Salignac de La Mothe Fénélon (1651–1715). But Vauban, for instance, generally stressed—like the good mercantilist theorist that he was—"populousness as good in itself and as an index of the soundness of governmental arrangements." A more important figure in this context was Richard Cantillon (1680–1734), who linked population to both the economy and the social structure and who developed a theory of luxury somewhat similar to Malthus's.[4] Moreover, since Malthus is generally denoted the prime watershed in the development of demographic theory, surveys are likely to be entitled "Spanish Population Thought before Malthus" and accounts of individuals "A Seventeenth-century Malthusian," so that the seeming unoriginality of his ideas is constantly reinforced.[5]

Let it be stated unequivocally that many in the history of social thought had noticed, for example, that food and those who eat it must somehow balance; the wonder is that so obvious a point had escaped the attention of the others. According to Malthus. himself, before he wrote the first edition of the *Essay* he had read the works of only four writers on population

—David Hume, Adam Smith, Robert Wallace, and Richard Price. In his later studies Malthus found many more who had anticipated him, including in particular Benjamin Franklin, whose *Increase of Mankind* he seems to have read with great attention.[6] But by putting these ideas that other men had expressed into a larger framework and examining in detail the relation of population growth to economic, social, and political development, Malthus did more than any of his predecessors or all of them together. He wrote a book that, whether as guide or as butt, became for all the beginning of modern population theory.

"Jingles." That Malthus cast his theory as a contrast between two progressions, the geometric and arithmetic ratios, was undoubtedly due to his mathematical training at Cambridge. John Stuart Mill, a very sympathetic critic, remarked that "this unlucky attempt to give numerical precision to things which do not admit of it . . . is wholly superfluous to his argument." Edwin Cannan, decidedly less sympathetic, dismissed what he called "misleading mathematical jingles."[7] Perhaps one can respond to this kind of criticism of the form of the argument rather than its content by introducing (as with "social policy") another bit of modern jargon. When those in social disciplines construct a "model," they strip empirical reality to its essence and express this in mathematical terms in order to facilitate the analysis of how variables interact under specified assumed conditions. Malthus's model was truly very simple, but still too complex for the more simpleminded of his critics. The implication of growth by a geometric rate, by which a small starting figure soon assumes stupendous proportions, has become familiar to us from accounts, say, of how a dollar deposited to mark a person's birth could bring him a pleasantly substantial amount when he retires or, more pertinently, from estimates of the "doubling times" that are now sometimes included with population figures of the world's countries. Indeed, a number of recent calculations have been made only to demonstrate that population growth in accordance with its potential could not long continue. If the world population in 1956 were to double each twenty-five years, by A.D. 2330 it would reach $1,735 \times 10^{11}$, or the number of square yards on the earth's land surface.[8] Even more dramatically, if a population grew from a single couple

at an annual rate of only one percent (or about half the present rate of growth of the world's population), at the end of 10,000 years it would require $248,293 \times 10^{15}$ earths to furnish the material for the people's bodies.[9] But one reason that Malthus kept harping on the geometric progression was that he could not get the concept across to many of his contemporaries.

The arithmetic ratio, to which critics have paid less attention, is far more vulnerable. The charge most often leveled against it at the end of the nineteenth century, that Malthus had grossly underestimated the future improvement in agricultural techniques, is valid but not pertinent to a discussion of his theoretical framework; I shall return to it in a later chapter. Some of Malthus's contemporaries pointed out that the disparity between the potential for rapid growth and the realizable slower one pertains not only to humankind but to all species. Thus, they concluded, man's multiplication would generally be matched by multiplication of the foodstuffs on which he subsisted. However, when Darwin later generalized Malthus's principle to the whole of the biological world, he developed a model in which every species is bound by the same natural laws, including what Malthus called positive checks. Humans differ from other species only in the possibility of foreseeing, and thus if they will avoiding, the unpleasant consequences of rapid reproduction.

The contrast between potential and realizable growth can be expressed by two ratios, but the ones Malthus chose are not the best. John Stuart Mill later formulated some earlier ideas (such as the theory of rent, as well as the principle of population) as a "law of diminishing returns,"[10] with an implied model that comprises *two* geometric rates, one greater than the other. Certainly, Malthus's model also would have been far more elegant (though possibly subject to still more misunderstanding) if he had offered the generalization that all growth patterns are by a geometric ratio but that, if only because of the limit set by the land available, the rate for human reproduction is potentially greater than that for human food.

"Tendency." As Godwin wrote, "If Mr. Malthus's doctrine is true, why is the globe not peopled?" Or, according to a twentieth-century biologist, "Malthus's postulated increase of population is not the rule in nature; it is merely a potentiality,

rarely realized." This confusion about Malthus's meaning permeates discussions of the ratios. In a work accepted as a doctoral dissertation at the University of London, one finds the same specious point: "How could four millions of people be sustained on the food of three? The answer of friends and foes alike would be—they cannot. Therefore, since the [continuation of the series] can never come into existence, all the subsequent terms are false. They serve to bewilder the reader; . . . but since they do not represent fact, or even possibility, they obscure rather than illuminate the real problem."[11]

One difficulty has been the ambiguity in the meaning of the word *tendency*. As Nassau Senior wrote in his *Two Lectures on Population,* "The popular doctrine certainly is that population has a tendency to increase beyond the means of subsistence, . . . [and] I admit that population has the power (considered abstractedly) so to increase . . . What I deny is that, under wise institutions, there is any *tendency* to this state of things. I believe the tendency to be just the reverse." As Senior admitted in a letter to Malthus bound with his essays, he had mistaken Malthus's meaning. Yet the letters they exchanged became far better known than their content would seem to warrant; for example, no less a demographer than Mombert translated them into German.[12] During all of human history from the savage state to their time, Senior maintained, the food per person had in general become more adequate, and this empirical trend should be described as the "tendency" of the population-subsistence ratio.

What seems to be a minor terminological point (still being debated by linguists[13]) became a standard item in the Malthusian controversy. Thus, for example, "population has a natural tendency to keep within the powers of the soil to afford it subsistence . . . This tendency can never be destroyed and can only be altered or diverted from its natural course . . . by grossly impolitic laws or pernicious customs either accelerating the progress of population considerably beyond its natural rate or depressing the productive energies of the soil considerably below its natural powers."[14] Or, in another variation, "there is a tendency from the forces of gravitation for the planets to fall into the sun, but we do not on that account alarm ourselves with the idea of a general conflagration"; the important factor is not the "tendency" but the "actual power of increase."[15]

Malthus was willing to grant, as indeed he had written in the *Essay,* that in many instances food per capita had increased —especially, as he emphasized, where the preventive check of postponed marriage was widely observed. But, as he responded to Senior, he still preferred his meaning of *tendency:* "it conveys a more instructive and useful meaning than the one which you would substitute for it—namely, that food has a tendency to increase faster than population—a position which, without further explanation, seems to convey an incorrect impression of the laws which regulate the increase of the human race." However one decides on the correct or "more instructive" sense of the word, Malthus's readers had been given no reason to misunderstand him. For in his continual iteration of the same point, he had used a number of equivalent phrases: "population, when unchecked, increases in a geometrical ratio"; it has the "power" to do so; and so on. One might have thought that even an inattentive reader could hardly have missed the point, not to say an Oxford professor of political economy like Senior, whose own short work on population was little more than a commentary on Malthus's ideas. He might have noted, on the contrary, that the word *tendency,* like the two ratios themselves (or like *proclivity* or *propensity,* which a modern economist would be likely to use to express the same meaning), was one more indication of Malthus's shift from the certainties of moral philosophy to the probabilistic framework of the social disciplines.

Human Fecundity. For many decades the concepts of potential and actual reproduction were so confused that no terms existed to distinguish them. It was only in 1934 that the Population Association of America officially endorsed the developing distinction between *fecundity,* the physiological ability to reproduce, and *fertility,* the realization of this potential as measured by the number of offspring. Outside the professional writings of demographers the differentiation is still sometimes muddled; in what seems to be the current usage of physicians, for example, the two words are used more or less synonymously. (And in Romance languages the cognates have acquired the opposite meanings: French *fertilité* and Spanish *fertilidad* are translated by "fecundity," *fécondité* and *fecondidad* by "fertility.") In Malthus's time it took a considerable effort to communicate the seemingly uncomplicated proposition that the "tendency" or "power" of population to increase is considerably greater than its usual actual growth.

Once the concepts of potential and actual procreative power were properly understood, the far greater difficulty arose of how to distinguish between them empirically. Malthus simply took the highest fertility of which he was aware, that of the British colonies in North America, and hypothesized that fecundity must be generally at least this high, so that everywhere an unchecked population could double in twenty-five years. Though our example has changed, we still follow the same procedure. Ansley Coale, one of the most distinguished of American demographers, devised a new measure of fertility based on comparing the total fertility rate of any population with the highest rate ever recorded. If a woman married at age 15 and, throughout her fecund period, had the same number of children that Hutterites do in each age interval, she would bear an average of 12.6 children during her lifetime. If we take this to be the maximum physiological potential for a population (individual families have of course been larger), we can then measure the reproduction of less prodigiously fertile peoples against this norm.[16]

AMATEURS

That Malthus was a professor of political economy is pertinent in contrasting him with many of his critics. At that time it was customary for anyone of means to put out a pamphlet or even a book about anything, and to many the combination of sex and the Poor Laws was an irresistible topic. Moreover, the distinction now made, however vaguely and ambiguously, between responsible and ignorant commentary did not exist at all. It connotes no approval of the frequent pretentiousness in the social disciplines, their jargoned writing and opinions dressed up as science, to hold that nevertheless those with some training are on the average better equipped to analyze social questions than those who come unprepared to their subtle complexities. Concerning an era when this training hardly existed, when virtually every writer was to some degree self-taught, and when many professors at Oxford or Cambridge clearly saw their posts as sinecures virtually unencumbered by duties, the delineation of a professional stance is not easy. One differentiating characteristic was style: then as now, a dependence on personal abuse suggested that the logic needed bolstering. Though the available data were sparse and poor, with sufficient effort some could be ferreted out and used to make a point that either was or was not argued consistently. Perhaps the main criterion was seriousness of purpose: one who issued pronunciamentos on a number of quite diverse topics could hardly have thought very deeply about any of them. By such standards Malthus clearly passes muster as a professional scholar, but many of his critics do not.

Take David Booth as representative of one type. He was a self-educated brewer who wrote a number of works on brewing, education, and linguistics, including in particular the beginning of an "analytical dictionary of the English language." At Godwin's request, he wrote a pamphlet that Malthus dismissed as "solemn and absurd"; the solemnity at least is suggested by Booth's very title: *A Letter to the Rev. T. R. Malthus, M.A., F.R.S., being an answer to the criticisms of Mr. Godwin's work on population which was inserted in the LXXth number of the* Edinburgh Review, . . . (1823). According to the work's main point, Malthus's admission that the progressions need not be entirely regular constituted an abandonment of his principle of population.[17]

Another member of the new middle classes was William Edward Hickson. The son of a shoe manufacturer, he retired early from the family business in order to devote himself to philanthropy and literary pursuits, writing in favor of repealing the Corn Laws and of establishing a system of universal elementary education, especially in music. For twelve years he was editor of the *Westminster Review*. Malthus's theory, he wrote as late as 1849, "does not admit of the slightest prospect of any permanent improvement of the condition of the mass of the people from the progress of temperance, thrift, industry, intelligence, and skill . . . unless coupled with the condition of fewer marriages than at present or with some artificial means taken to reduce the average number of births to a marriage." Among checks to population that Malthus had overlooked were interclass or interracial marriages, which Hickson believed to be relatively sterile! On the other hand, "ignorance, improvidence, unwholesome dwellings and occupations seldom act as checks to population, because compensating by an increased fecundity for the mortality which they produce." Hickson deviated from the temper of his century by his lack of faith in progress: from his belief that all species have a natural term of life, he concluded that humans may well disappear before the problem of overpopulation becomes manifest.[18]

Or consider George Ensor, whose many works reflected, in the words of the *Dictionary of National Biography*, "very 'advanced' views in politics and religion." He wrote mostly about Ireland, where he had been born of an English father, and his attacks on the British administration read like a caricature of a nationalist pamphlet. His objections to Malthus, he wrote, arose from "his want of science; his infinite contradictions; his inhumanity; his loud abuse of the people; his silence respecting the hardheartedness of the opulent; his general indemnity to kings and ministers." That there was no reason to fear overpopulation he proved by a reference to Herodotus and a suggestion that any excess be shipped off to the colonies.[19]

Travers Twiss was a different type altogether, a scholar of classics and mathematics, a barrister, the Drummond Professor of Political Economy at Oxford, one of the few Oxford men of his day competent in German. His published lectures, dealing mostly with international law, were generally perfunctory, though those on population included a knowledgeable discussion of life tables with some historical examples. In his overall praise of the *Essay*, he showed a certain trepidation: "no one need fear to speak of Mr. Malthus's work with commendation." He suggested that a more appropriate designation of what Malthus had termed "positive checks" would be "diminutive" (indeed, "positive" had not been aptly chosen, but neither was this proposed substitute, for by definition both checks diminish the rate of a population's growth). His main criticism was that Malthus had classified vices as preventive checks; but "the more accurate statistics of the French police" and "the careful researches" of several French writers seemingly showed that "vice" increases mortality "infinitely" more than it reduces fertility. Nothing is given on precisely what these French researchers said nor even on whether one's supposition is correct that the topic of their research must have been the venereal diseases disseminated by widespread promiscuity. If one assumes that both Malthus and Twiss were in fact talking of intercourse with prostitutes, then Malthus was right in intimating that this almost never was permitted to result in a conception; on balance, those whose lives were shortened by a disease they had contracted would not shift this vice (not to say the others that Malthus listed) from preventive to positive.[20]

Thomas Jarrold was said to have taken an M.D. degree at Edinburgh, but according to the *Dictionary of National Biography* his name does not appear in the published lists of graduates. He wrote books on medical subjects, on the Poor Laws and education, and one attacking Malthus's principle. For a work by someone supposed to have some knowledge of physiology, this contains such remarkable assertions as, for example, "there is no physical cause of . . . famine, none of pestilence . . . Famine and pestilence are the consequences of indolence and selfishness." Thus, Malthus's contrast between number of people and amount of food had no point: "If Mr. Malthus had said that population is equal to the cotton or woolen cloth, the conceit would be laughed at; but really there is no difference in principle."[21]

The reader should not suppose that this list of commentators was selected only for the greater inanity of their remarks; they were in this respect typical of a considerably larger number. And though many of the criticisms were made by men known today only to the specialist, and in some instances even to him only for their relation to the Malthusian controversy, the total impact of their often ignorant and usually hostile reaction was such that it reverberates still in works published in the last quarter of the twentieth century. One reason for this extraordinary longevity may be that many of their comments were echoed by outstanding literary figures—what we would term the period's intellectuals.

LITERATI

In the sense of "a person possessing or supposed to possess superior powers of intellect," the first reference to *intellectual* in the *Oxford English Dictionary* dates from 1652; then there is a jump to a letter by Byron dated 1813 and a later excerpt concerning Coleridge. But the connotation of the word did not remain constant over this century and a half. With the erosion of religion during the eighteenth century, Western societies came to lack an authoritative moral guide, and during the latter stage of this dissolution the perception (and self-perception) of the writer and artist was changing from a person highly but narrowly skilled in one type of endeavor to one whose superior endowment, though expressed in novels or painting or scholarship, was in fact unbounded. As a literary or artistic movement, Romanticism had its term, but the concept of intellectual generated by the Romantics' self-aggrandizement continued to gain in importance. Today the word does not signify merely a poet or painter or professor, but often one of these who presumes to represent the national conscience on political issues of fundamental importance—in short, a secular priest declaring other men to be Good or Evil by criteria that require no specification beyond the judge's utter authority.

That Malthus should have become a particular target of intellectuals was in part no more than a craze, which spread from one to another like any other literary fad. But their knee-jerk reaction was also to several of Malthus's characteristics, or alleged characteristics. He was manifestly straight, in present-day slang, and to so well advertised a libertine as Byron what he termed Malthus's "eleventh commandment, 'Thou shalt not marry, unless *well*,' " was "turning marriage into arithmetic." "Without cash, Malthus tells you, take no bride, so Cash rules Love." To put it no stronger, Byron was uninterested in family or social responsibilities.

> All who have loved, or love, will still allow
> Life has nought like it. God is love, they say,
> And Love's a God.

And like most who disliked Malthus for whatever reason, Byron also helped disseminate such legends as that he "does the thing 'gainst which he writes." According to the editors' note, "Coleridge suggests that Byron may be referring to an apocryphal story that Malthus had eleven daughters," which, as I have remarked, survived to reappear in a biographical note by a twentieth-century professor.[22]

Shelley was associated with Godwin not only by his full acceptance of *Political Justice* but by his liaison with Mary Godwin. In 1818, when Godwin wrote his daughter that he was "over head and ears" in a new attack on Malthus, Shelley replied with an expression of his delight. In the same year, when he read a French translation of the *Essay*, Shelley saw for apparently the first time the actual writing of the man he called "a eunuch and a tyrant" and "the apostle of the rich," by implication an "arch-priest" and a "sow-gelder."[23] His principal commentary on Malthus, in *A Philosophical View of Reform*, concentrated the attack not on Malthus's economic or population theories but on his proposed social reforms. That the poor should practice marital restraint constituted in Shelley's view "new disadvantages" added to the injustices already oppressing them; to suggest that anyone should exercise a sense of responsibility in begetting showed a "hardened insolence."

Coleridge's opposition to Malthus was more political than Byron's, as venomous as Shelley's. As a young man, he was convinced that "the march of the human race" is "progressive" and not "in cycles," as the two progressions suggested. He reacted negatively to the first edition of the *Essay*, and he carried over his critique to marginal notes on the pages of the 1803 edition (which in his opinion was not significantly different from the 1798 edition), made to suggest to Southey how to write a review of Malthus's book. "The stupid ignorance of the man," he exclaimed in response to Malthus's intimation that annexing others' land for emigrants might be morally questionable; Coleridge did not think it "immoral to kill a few Savages in order to get possession of a country capable of sustaining a thousand times as many enlightened and happy men." As a man of letters, he felt impelled to denigrate the *Essay*'s style, but his attempt to condense Malthus's exposition of the two progressions resulted in a passage three times as long as the original, ending with the confession that "I have myself been uselessly prolix." How the epithets circulated among the small circle of literati is illustrated even from these jottings. One notation recommended that Malthus find himself a "sow-gelder," a phrase that reappeared almost two decades later in Shelley's *Swellfoot the Tyrant*. In his later years Coleridge came to agree with many of the positions (as on the French Revolution, for instance) he had spent his youth attacking. But for some reason his stance on Malthus became if anything more acerbic, as one can see from his *Table Talk* published in the 1830s. The "monstrous practical sophism" of the *Essay* he found to be "so vicious a tenet, so flattering to the cruelty, the avarice and sordid selfishness of most men that I hardly know what to think of the result." A comment in the *Westminster Review* noted that Coleridge's language conveyed "only the bitterness of hostile opinion without its energy."[24]

Robert Southey's essay "On the State of the Poor, the Principle of Mr. Malthus's *Essay on Population,* and the Manufacturing System," written in 1812, was a more substantial piece than the attacks by his fellow intellectuals. He began by noting the dimensions of poor relief:

Number of persons receiving parish relief	734,817
Those receiving occasional relief from poor rates	305,899
Vagrants apparently receiving assistance	194,052
Total	1,234,768

Out of the population of some 10.9 million, in other words, nearly one person in nine was on welfare, as we would say. In 1803 the parish rates (or local taxes) totaled £5,318,000, of which £4,267,000, or 80 percent, was expended on the poor. Although Southey held that "the laboring classes have a natural tendency to increase faster than the higher ranks," because "celibacy is much less frequent among them [and] they are more prolific," he characterized a similar statement by Malthus as "rubbish." The causes of the country's ills, he believed, were such factors as the Reformation, which had cut the charity of the church, and the growth of manufacturing industry, which had attracted the village poor to the towns. "Adam Smith's book is the code, or confession of faith, of this system; a tedious and hardhearted book, greatly overvalued even on the score of ability." Among the remedial measures he suggested were public works: "how many are the marshes which might be drained?" And with what result, Malthus might have responded; marshes had been drained by the score in Ireland, with a consequent growth of population and no lessening of the pressure on resources. On one point Southey agreed with Malthus: "National education is the first thing necessary . . . Lay but this foundation, poverty will be diminished, and want will disappear in proportion as the lower classes are instructed in their duties."[25]

William Hazlitt was a protégé of Coleridge, a partly self-educated son of a Presbyterian minister. According to Leslie Stephen's account in the *Dictionary of National Biography,* he never filled in the many blanks in his knowledge, for after the age of 30 he is said never to have read a book through. Even by the wordy standards of the Malthusian controversy, his *Reply to the Essay on Population* was verbose, comprising five "letters" of which portions had been printed earlier in one or another of the reviews. Hazlitt found the *Essay* to be "the most complete specimen of illogical, crude and contradictory reasoning that perhaps was ever offered to the notice of the public." Not only was Malthus not original, but on the issue of whether a utopia loomed just over the horizon Godwin had the better of the argument. As a sympathetic commentator remarked, Hazlitt was "diverted from Malthus's more valid arguments at least partly because some absurd inferences drawn from them seemed likely to, and apparently did, affect legislation."[26] To the present day this guilt by association continues to be an important basis of Malthus's denigration. Darwin seems never to have been blamed for the sometimes nonsensical, often outrageous, conclusions that other men drew from his theory; but Malthus has been made responsible for everyone who cited his name, often with little understanding of what he had written.

In 1821, when Hazlitt was an editor of the *London Magazine,* it published DeQuincy's *Confessions of an Opium-Eater* in its original version. This was so great a success that De-Quincy was given permission to publish anything he fancied under the running title, "Notes from the Pocket-Book of a Late Opium-Eater," including two attacks on Malthus, one pertaining to his measure of value and the other to population.[27] Hazlitt denounced the latter as virtual plagiarism, since the arguments, he claimed, were all taken from the articles he had written four years earlier. Tracing the origin of the attacks on Malthus is hardly possible, however, since they were common property, with each writer borrowing a phrase here, an idea there. For both Hazlitt and DeQuincy, for example, one of the main criticisms of Malthus was that his theory was not original with him!

William Cobbett also was seemingly unable to distinguish between what Malthus wrote and how others made use of what they thought he had said. As late as 1806, Cobbett's opinion was wholly positive: "Nor will it be denied that the tendency of the human species to multiply is much greater than the rapidity with which it is possible to increase the production of the earth for their maintenance." Malthus's principle was "a doctrine which can never be shaken." Then, in 1807, there appeared in Cobbett's *Political Register* three letters by "A.O." (in fact, Hazlitt) vigorously attacking the *Essay*'s thesis. Cobbett, never one to overvalue the virtue of consistency, thus announced another reversal in his opinion and the beginning of a tireless, and tiresome, campaign against the "monster" Malthus. According to George Bernard Shaw, himself an expert in dispensing vitriol, Cobbett ranked with Marx and Ruskin as one of the three nineteenth-century masters of invective; but from Cobbett's comments on Malthusian doctrine, this would hardly seem to be so. In *Surplus Population, A Comedy,* which Cole found "better fun and more actable" than an earlier satire,[28] a landowning M.P. hires a Malthusian economist to prevent the marriage of one of his laborers by carrying off the girl as his mistress. The rollicking comedy ends with the villagers throwing the squire into his own horse-pond. Cobbett's more serious argument focused on an interminable effort to show that England's population was declining, which he proved mainly by counting the churches of the medieval period and calculating the number of people that must have attended each of them. If not to fill them, he asked, "what should men have built such large churches *for?*" As the successive censuses proved him wrong, he countered by denouncing the enumerators as "impudent liars." "They assert that the population of Great Britain has increased from ten to fourteen millions in the last twenty years! That is enough! A man that can suck that in will believe, literally believe, that the moon is made of green cheese."[29]

In this survey of intellectuals' opinions we can conveniently come full circle and end where we started, with William Godwin. His *Of Population* (1820) is altogether a curious phenomenon. No other work except *Political Justice* itself so thoroughly commanded Godwin's attention; not a day passed without a record in his diary of pages written and rewritten. While at work on the book, he suffered a slight stroke, and during the ensuing period his journal recorded a "prevailing sensation of somewhat failing bodily powers." In this product of his old age, Godwin contradicted the generous praise that he had expressed in *Parr's Spital Sermon,* and this despite the fact that in the interim Malthus had adjusted his principle fundamentally to Godwin's earlier criticism.[30]

Of Population, 626 pages long, is prolix and difficult to summarize. Essentially it made four points: that Malthus had changed his position from the first edition (indeed!), that the world is not full (as noted in a dozen places in the book), that the ratios misrepresent the possible increase of mankind and of its subsistence (Godwin also had changed his view) , and that population statistics particularly for North America, which he interpreted as Malthus's crucial example, did not support the argument of the *Essay*. Godwin upbraided Malthus for having written "just as any speculator in political economy might have done, to whom the records of the Bible were unknown," not even referring to Adam and Eve as the first progenitors of humanity. Godwin, on the contrary, quoted at length from various books of the Bible to show that in ancient times a numerous progeny had been well regarded. More generally, *Of Population* showed a cavalier indifference to empirical data. China and India, Godwin asserted, "carry back their chronology through millions of years." After giving the enumerated population of England and Wales in 1801 and 1811, with the second 1.3 million larger than the first, Godwin concluded from a bare allegation that a first census must have been less accurate than a second that, after the decade had passed, "it is very conceivable that there was not one human creature more in the country." Indeed, "we have not the smallest reason to believe that the population of the earth is in any way more numerous now than it was three thousand years ago"—a conclusion from a collection of pseudo-data that do not warrant a discussion.[31]

Of Population was reviewed in the July 1821 issue of the *Edinburgh Review*. If we accept the general supposition that Malthus was the reviewer, it is the one publication of his that deviates markedly from his usual calm and reasonable manner of debate. Godwin's book he judged to be "the poorest and most old-womanish performance that had fallen from the pen of any writer of name since we first commenced our critical career," the product of an "enfeebled judgment." This last work of Godwin's "contains more nonsense, and more abuse, than any other answer to Mr. Malthus which we have met with; and whatever impression it may chance to make for a short time from the virulence of its language and the boldness of its assertions, the only permanant effect of it will be to establish more firmly the doctrines of the *Essay on Population*."[32]

MARX AND MARXISTS

Much of the current misinformation about Malthus stems directly or indirectly from Marx, who rejected him in language exceptionally vituperative even by the permissive standards of socialist polemics: "the contemptible Malthus," a "plagiarist," "a shameless sycophant of the ruling classes" who perpetrated "a sin against science," "this libel on the human race." Engels seemingly tried to find yet more expressive epithets: "this infamous, vile doctrine, this abominable blasphemy against nature and humanity, . . . the Economists' [that is, the physiocrats'] immorality at its lowest point. What are all wars and terrors of the monopoly system as against this theory?"[33] The constant hyperbole suggests a polemical weakness; verbal abuse is not a sign of strength in any social analyst.

Why should Malthus have been singled out for this immoderate attack? That the *Essay* was written in a political context, undercutting the extravagant hopes of the Condorcets and Godwins, is not the explanation; Marx did not typically defend the views of men that he and Engels dubbed "utopians." Nor is it pertinent that Malthus was a "bourgeois economist"; Marx treated Ricardo with great esteem. As I shall note in the next chapter, in some respects Malthus was closer than Ricardo to a Marxist position on how the capitalist system works—as Marx himself occasionally intimated. For example,

Malthus is not interested in disguising the contradictions of bourgeois production; on the contrary, he is interested in emphasizing them, on the one hand in order to demonstrate that the poverty of the working classes is necessary (it is necessary for this mode of production), and on the other hand in order to demonstrate to the capitalists that a well fed tribe of Church-and-State servants is indispensable for the creation of an adequate demand for their commodities.[34]

In order, however, to preserve the dogma that socialism is man's inevitable future, Marx had to discard Malthus's principle of population.

If Malthus's theory of population is correct, then I can *not* abolish this [iron law of wages] even if I abolish wage labor a hundred times, because this law is not only paramount over the system of wage labor but also over *every* social system. Stepping straight from this, the Economists proved fifty years ago or more that socialism cannot abolish poverty, which is based on nature, but

only *communalize* it, distributing it equally over the whole surface of society.[35]

Marx's main objection to the principle of population he
stated in a single sentence: "Every special historic mode of
production has its own special laws of population, historically
valid within its limits alone."[36] With the proviso that man is
an animal and that, at the biological level, transcultural generalizations are therefore pertinent, this is a valid point. Marx
himself, however, had nothing to say of what governed the
population growth of primitive, feudal, or socialist societies,
and what he termed his law of population for capitalist society was inadequate.

According to Marx's general theory of capitalist development, the competition in a free economy drives all entrepreneurs to increase their efficiency to the utmost by installing
more and more machinery. "Accumulate, accumulate! This is
the Moses and the prophets!" The growing stock of capital
goods, by the very fact of its greater efficiency, displaces some
of the workers that had been employed at a less advanced
technical level; the working population becomes "relatively
superfluous . . . to an always increasing extent." Moreover,
the composition of the labor force steadily deteriorates; the
employer "progressively replaces skilled laborers by less skilled,
mature labor power by immature, male by female, that of
adults by that of younger persons or children." No amelioration is possible under capitalism, for employers who do not
increase their capital stock will be driven into bankruptcy.
This line of reasoning, a generalization from Ricardo's argument that mechanization *may* lead to unemployment, cannot
be regarded as one of Marx's successful prophecies. But even if
one were to grant that increasing mechanization results over
the long term in ever larger unemployment, it still hardly
follows that this supposed trend operates "independently of
the actual increase of population." What Marx termed the
"industrial reserve army" pertains not to population as such
but to the labor force; and while the two concepts are related,
they are hardly identical. Over the short term, the proportion
of those seeking work who are able to find it obviously depends
in considerable part on the number of new workers entering
the labor force. As Marx himself pointed out in a different
context, "the demand for laborers may exceed the supply and

therefore wages may rise"; he cited as one example Britain in the fifteenth century after the extraordinary mortality of the Black Death had depleted both the population and the work force. But if wages rise because of such a relative shortage of labor, according to Marx the rate of capitalization will increase and the surplus will thus be reestablished. But since the analysis began with the assertion that under *all* conditions every capitalist is inexorably driven to accumulate capital as fast as possible, it was hardly permissible to develop the argument by holding that under *certain* conditions mechanization would be accelerated.[37]

If Marx freed Ricardo's theory of how capital growth affects employment from a "fatal dependence on Malthusian population dogma," as Sweezy declared,[38] this "great accomplishment" was at the cost of accepting as axiomatic the essence of what Marx took to be Malthusianism. In the 1930s demographers generally forecast that the population of the West would soon decline, and in the 1970s there has been a renewed speculation along the same line. But for Marx this was not even a hypothetical contingency; with the rapid population increase of the nineteenth century as his norm, he built his system around it without attempting to explain the growth in numbers by a Malthusian or any other model. If the population of any society were to decline at the same rate as (following Marx's argument) machines displaced workers, then there would be no industrial reserve army, no "immiseration," no Marxist system of capitalist development altogether. And no matter what the rate of population growth, Marx's analysis depends to one degree or another on this factor, which he passed over altogether.

The essential clue to understanding Marx is that, however little he liked the designation, he was more utopian than the predecessors that he sought to displace by founding what he termed "scientific socialism." To reject the thesis that one ought to work for the establishment of a perfect society, substituting the notion that the second coming is inevitable, hardly makes one less a perfectibilist. Malthus's arguments against Condorcet and Godwin applied also to Marx and, indeed, to socialists and utopians of all varieties. No less an economist than Edwin Cannan held that of the founders of the classical school—Adam Smith, Malthus, Ricardo, and John Stuart Mill—"Malthus is the only one who could ever be claimed as an antisocialist writer."[39] If it seems inappropriate to ignore, as one instance, Smith's vigorous defense of the free market, this concentration on Malthus has nevertheless been repeated in a score of variations. The French socialists of the nineteenth century, almost as important in the development of European thought as the philosophes from whom their ideas partly derived, held to the mercantilist view that a static population is a symptom of national degeneration. According to the Count de Saint-Simon (1760–1825), the growth of numbers is the best test of a country's prosperity. For Auguste Comte (1798–1857), Saint-Simon's early associate who is generally regarded as the founder of sociology, the principle of population was an amalgam of "irrational exaggerations," an immoral reflection of Malthus's support of the wealthy against the poor. In the reformed society that Étienne Babeuf (1788–1856) pictured in his *Voyage en Icarie,* the population would be doubled. In the opinion of Pierre Leroux (1797–1871), English economists were so ignorant of the moral and economic disaster caused by a declining population that they defended infanticide. As Proudhon (1809–65) summed up the doctrine, "There is only one person too many in the world, and that is Malthus." "For a long time socialists had to come out against Malthus—instinctively, spontaneously—and at the same time against the limitation of births."[40]

It is convenient to sum up many of the differences between Malthus and his critics in the form of a table adapted from a book called *Gray versus Malthus* written by "George Purves."[41] In fact, the author was Simon Gray, who with a fine show of objectivity showed that—it so happened—on every issue he was right and Malthus was wrong. Seldom has anonymity served an author so well, but apart from this interesting quirk the book stood above the level of its time. The format of the table emphasizes the fact that, when one poses the issues as either-or alternatives, both sides are typically partly right and partly wrong. If we have progressed in demographic analysis, it is by recognizing, for example, that in India much mortality derives from a lack of food but in the United States from overeating, that population growth in the West stimulated the demand for employment over the long run but in the 1930s aggravated the negative effects of unemployment. Struggling with such complexities, Malthus generally stated both halves of such

TABLE 2. SUMMARY OF THE DIFFERENCES BETWEEN
MALTHUS AND GRAY.

MALTHUS	GRAY
Population has a natural tendency to overincrease—that is, to increase faster than subsistence.	Population has a tendency to increase but not to overincrease, for any increase carries in itself the power of fully supplying its various wants.
The natural growth of population is according to a geometric ratio, that of subsistence only according to an arithmetic one.	The natural growth of population depends upon the circumstances, but uniformly results in a growth of subsistence nearly the same as its own.
The amount of subsistence regulates the amount of population.	Population regulates subsistence as completely as it does clothing, housing, and other goods.
Population increases more or less rapidly according to the abundance of subsistence.	Superabundance, or an excess of subsistence, has a defecundating and depopulating effect.
Population increase tends to overstock and thus to diminish the total employment to be divided among the available work force.	The increase of population tends uniformly to increase the demand for hands and thus employment.
The increase of population has a certain natural tendency to promote poverty.	The increase of population has therefore a uniform tendency to increase income and wealth, and over time by an increasing proportion.
The diseases and evils generated by the increase of population are chiefly those springing from a scarcity of food and from poverty.	The diseases and evils generated by an increase of population are chiefly those which spring from luxury, or an excess of subsistence.

Source: Adapted from Gray, 1818, pp. 10–12.

dichotomies but often left them as half-contradictory generalizations.[42] The more difficult task, to specify under what conditions each supposedly general proposition applies, neither he nor anyone else over the next hundred fifty years accomplished at all satisfactorily.

The most obvious reason for these loose ends in Malthus's population theory is the contrast between the First and the Second Essays, which was never entirely resolved. The emphasis on moral restraint as another type of population control shifted his attention from biological to social-cultural determinants, and he followed this new lead to the advocacy of those elements of political and social democracy that would conduce to greater marital responsibility. However, in "A Summary View of Population," published only four years before his death, the argument concerning the two progressions was restated with some embellishment but no essential diminution. We can suppose that Malthus, stubbornly resistant to the flood of abuse to which he was subjected, adhered to a theory that he himself had partly transgressed. Or, more charitably, we can suggest that he saw man as both a biological and a social being, and that, like ourselves, he was unable to coalesce the two kinds of environment into a single conceptual framework. This lack of total consistency in Malthus's corpus has been exaggerated in many accounts, for debates ostensibly about empirical or logical points have often been, half an inch under the surface, sharper disputes about fundamental political or moral issues.

A second reason for the discrepancies in Malthus's principle of population might be called chronological. Not only did Malthus live during a period of rapid change but the argument of the *Essay* pushed his analysis back into the past and far into the future. Until around the time that Malthus was born, the institutional checks to early and improvident marriage had still been working moderately well, and essentially his social policy was to adapt these legal and normative impediments to the new society coming into being. Unlike many of his critics, who with deep but hopeless nostalgia yearned for a return of the preindustrial age and its—for them—pleasantly simple social relations, Malthus saw economic development as the sine qua non of human advancement. He wanted not to turn the clock back, but to adjust it to a new time zone.

Malthus's population theory, finally, never fully jibed with his economic theory, which to some degree he developed independently. In contrast, Ricardo took over from Malthus an early version of the principle and placed it neatly in his analysis of how the economy works—at the cost of never developing the population theory from this preliminary statement. As expounded in the next chapter, Malthus's principal difference from Ricardo was that he did not rest content with discussing production, that era's crucial policy question. In his attempt to stipulate the determinants also of consumption, Malthus argued that a nonproductive (that is, "surplus") sector of the population may be needed to balance the one that produces much but consumes little. Again, the thesis is valid under some conditions, and the contradiction with a flat statement of the principle of population can be resolved only by specifying which conditions.

5

Economic Theory

BOTH IN THE modern view and in the context of this book, Malthus was primarily a demographer. But we can fully appreciate his analysis of the determinants and consequences of population growth only after we have woven in strands from his writings on economics, as we understand the word. Malthus's economic theory, however, is not at all easy to summarize within the compass of a single chapter. Even more than today, economics was then a disputatious subject, with bits and pieces being fitted into the eventual approximate consensus that Marx dubbed the "classical" school. In many of the works on how this doctrine developed, the task is simplified by tracing the main stream from Smith through Ricardo to John Stuart Mill, noting in passing whatever lesser works the particular author deems important. Such a presentation is not appropriate in this case, for Malthus both contributed some major portions to classical theory and dissented strongly from others. His *Definitions in Political Economy* (1827), for example, comprises chapters on how in his view some elementary terms were variously misconstrued by the Physiocrats, Adam Smith, Say, Ricardo, James Mill, McCulloch, and an anonymous author—in fact, Samuel Bailey (1791–1870), who wrote *A Critical Dissertation on the Nature, Measures, and Causes of Value* (1825) among works on such diverse topics as theories of reasoning and perception. What Malthus took to be the correct definitions make up only some 15 pages of the 261-page book.

There is also the problem that Malthus's thoughts on economics, like those on population, underwent sometimes important changes. For example, in the early editions of the *Essay* he cited the rent of agricultural land as one of the main factors in the price of grain; but in the third edition, following lectures he had prepared at Haileybury, he asserted that "universally it is price that determines rent, not rent that determines price." Then in the fifth and sixth editions he reworked the theme again, following the argument of his pamphlet published in 1815, *An Inquiry into the Nature and Progress of Rent.*[1] What is ordinarily called the "Ricardian" theory of rent was in fact, as Ricardo himself acknowledged, propounded first by Malthus and Sir Edward West.[2]

The difficulty of presenting a historical account is compounded, finally, by trying to relate Malthus to current concerns. That his deviations from Ricardian orthodoxy brought him closer on some important points (though, indeed, not on all) to Marx's revisions of classical doctrine is of sufficient interest to spell out in some detail, for it contradicts the conventional view. And according to Keynes's own account of how he arrived at the views presented in his *General Theory,* he was influenced by the more or less forgotten position of Malthus; this point is also worth a full discussion.

THE GENERAL ARGUMENT

The opening sentences of Malthus's *Principles of Political Economy* set its tone:

> It has been said, and perhaps with truth, that the conclusions of Political Economy partake more of the certainty of the stricter sciences than those of most of the other branches of human knowledge. Yet we should fall into a serious error if we were to suppose that any propositions, the practical results of which depend upon the agency of so variable a being as man, and the qualities of so variable a compound as the soil, can ever admit of the same kinds of proof, or lead to the same certain conclusions, as those which relate to figure and number.

Malthus wants to present a different point of view, he informs the reader, but on such matters as he is about to discuss neither he nor anyone else should presume to absolute knowledge. The passage is a good example of his engaging argumentation, a welcome contrast to the style of lesser men.

Malthus's *Principles* was published first in 1820 and then, posthumously, in a second edition in 1836. As with Godwin's critique of the first edition of the *Essay*, Ricardo's *Notes* provided Malthus with a detailed basis for rethinking the book's whole argument (though often referred to at the time, the *Notes* were long presumed lost and were then discovered by Ricardo's great-grandson and finally published in 1928 as a book of 246 pages). They provide perhaps the most succinct basis for comparing the two main strands of classical theory, the *Notes* as the orthodox reaction to Malthus's deviations in the *Principles*. Ricardo wrote to McCulloch of Malthus's *Principles*, "There is hardly a page which does not contain some fallacy."[3] But his continuing regard for Malthus is indicated also by the fact that he read every page at least twice and responded so fully, and so cordially, to this adversary.

In form and occasionally in content, the *Principles* of Ricardo and the *Principles* of Malthus are parallel works, each following the argument of *The Wealth of Nations* and amending it as the two authors thought necessary. Both men were stimulated in this endeavor by concern over such practical issues as the Corn Laws or the debate over bullion, and both tried to buttress their policy recommendations with a well rounded theoretical base—but not to the same degree. Ricardo wrote in an often quoted letter to Malthus, "Our differences may in some respects, I think, be ascribed to your considering my work as more practical than I intended it to be. My object was to elucidate principles, and to do this I imagined strong cases that I might show the operation of those principles."[4] According to Malthus, however, "the principal cause of error, and of the differences which prevail at present among the scientific writers on political economy, appears to me to be a precipitate attempt to simplify and generalize."[5] Schumpeter's *History of Economic Analysis*, the most magisterial work on its subject, has a similar but stronger criticism of Ricardo's work.

Ricardo's . . . interest was in the clear-cut result of direct, practical significance. In order to get this he cut that general system to pieces, bundled up as large parts of it as possible, and put them in cold storage—so that as many things as possible should be frozen and "given." He then piled one simplifying assumption upon another until, having really settled everything by these assumptions, he was left with only a few aggregative variables between which, given these assumptions, he set up simple one-way relations so that, in the end, the desired results emerged almost as tautologies . . . The habit of applying results of this character to the solution of practical problems we shall call the Ricardian Vice.[6]

As perhaps the main progenitor of modern economics, Ricardo bequeathed to it his limitations as well as his strengths. An important difference between the early nineteenth century and our day results from the rise in the interim of the various social disciplines, each with its own academic departments, associations, journals, and spokesmen intent on repelling potential intruders. As we now understand the word, Smith was not an "economist," but rather an economist-sociologist-psychologist-moralist who attacked the integrated system of mercantilism both piece by piece and as a whole.[7] Many also of Malthus's propositions pertain to types of societal analysis that can hardly be subsumed under either half of "political economy." But Ricardo "had no philosophy at all"; "he had not an inadequate sociology, but none at all."[8] By the narrowing of its subject matter, modern economics approached more closely than any of the other social disciplines the focused analysis typical of the physical sciences, and much of its success has certainly been due to this characteristic. But as it prospered within the bounds that Ricardo and others set, its practitioners were continually attacked for the discipline's exclusionary premises and the biases allegedly hidden in them —most significantly by Marx and in recent times by, among many others, Gunnar Myrdal. In their "methodology" in this broadest sense of the term, Marx was thus far closer to Malthus than either Marx or Malthus was to Ricardo and the other exponents of orthodoxy. Like Smith and like Malthus, Marx was no less a sociologist or moralist than he was an economist. This does not mean, of course, that either Marx or Malthus was interested in a mere chronicle of social events; for both, abstraction was the essence of science. Both believed that they derived their generalizations from the mass of empirical evidence they collated, and hostile critics accused both of collecting data to support their presuppositions. None of this applies to Ricardo; when members of the inductivist school among classical economists wanted an example of excessive abstraction, "they usually cited Ricardo."[9]

The nature and causes of the wealth of nations constituted the central concern both of Smith's masterpiece and of the many works based on it. Because Smith developed his argument in part negatively, by attacking such mercantilist theses as that wealth comprises gold, the works of the classical school contain "sweeping statements about the unimportance of money—even in the midst of explanations of its effects on real variables."[10] This negative judgment, which certainly can be supported from classical writings, perhaps understates the genuine contributions to theory that evolved from the famous "bullion debate." In 1797 the convertibility of paper money into gold was suspended, with a subsequent sharp rise in prices followed by a deflation, whose effects were aggravated in 1819 by the resumption of convertibility at the prior rate. This manifest and serious crisis stimulated a considerable debate on the relation between paper and gold. The so-called anti-Bullionists ascribed the rise in prices entirely to real rather than monetary factors, following the supposed logic of *The Wealth of Nations* to a position that no present economist could accept at all. D. P. O'Brien classifies the opposed Bullionists into two subschools, "rigid" (including in particular Ricardo) and "moderate" (including Malthus). Both agreed that the inflation followed from an "over-issue" of paper money, but the moderates

advanced a far more subtle and complex analysis of the relationship between the total stock of currency, the price level, the income level, the volume of transactions, the velocity of circulation, and the exchange rate . . . The Bullionists, especially the moderate Bullionists, provided an analysis of the main elements of the operation of an inconvertible paper money currency, including the role of liquidity preference, which laid the foundations for modern monetary theory.[11]

Malthus's main contribution to the debate was in three journal articles reviewing others' writings on the question—"Depreciation of Paper Money" (1811), "Pamphlets on the Bullion Question" (1811), and "Tooke—On High and Low Prices" (1823). In general, he supported Ricardo's tract, *The*

High Price of Gold Bullion a Proof of the Depreciation of Bank-Notes (1810), which had prepared the way for the deliberations of Horner's Bullion Committee in the House of Commons. But he noted also that Ricardo's view was too simple. A shift in prices, Malthus agreed, can be brought about by "a comparative redundancy or deficiency of currency" but also, and independently, by a "varying demand for different sorts of produce." "It is of the utmost importance to keep these two distinct causes which affect the course of exchange constantly in view, because they sometimes act in conjunction, and sometimes in opposition to each other; and the results produced by their sum, or their difference, cannot of course be accounted for by either the one or the other taken separately."[12] This initial exchange between the two men set the pattern: high respect on both sides for the quality of the adversary but an iterant complaint from Malthus that Ricardo tended to ignore empirical complexities.

Correlative with Smith's deprecation of the mercantilists' contention that wealth consists of gold was his alternative definition of "value." It is difficult for us today (unless we are infected with the Marxist virus) to appreciate how fundamental this concept was perceived to be. We tend to see the value of a commodity as what we are willing to pay for it, and the only corrective we make is to adjust for inflation from current to "real" prices. In spite of its importance in Smith's structure, his definition of value was not clear-cut, and it separated into the classical orthodoxy of Ricardo and Malthus's deviation from it—which (though it of course lacks the later addendum of marginality) is closer to the view of most economists today.

Where Adam Smith has most failed in the use of his terms [Malthus wrote] is in the application of the word *real*. The *real* value of a commodity he distinctly and repeatedly states to be the quantity of *labor* which it will command, in contradistinction to its nominal value, that is, its value in money . . . But he says that the *real* wages of labor are the necessaries and conveniences of life which the money received by the laborer will enable him to command . . . If the value of labor varies continually with the varying quantity of the necessaries and conveniences of life which it will command, it is completely inconsistent to bring it forward as a measure of real value.[13]

"The nature and measure of value," Jacob Hollander wrote in the introduction to Ricardo's *Notes,* were "the center of the doctrinal debate of Ricardo and Malthus."[14] Ricardo's definition, as Hollander noted, was "embodied labor" or "the quantity of labor required to produce the commodity valued." For Malthus, it was "the estimation in which a commodity is held, founded on the desire to possess and the difficulty of obtaining possession of it."[15] Suppose, Malthus wrote, that because of changes in the supply of shrimp a shrimper's daily catch rose from 800 to 1,600, or fell from 800 to 400. Though the input of labor remained constant at one day's work, the value would change with the supply relative to the demand. The hypothetical case was followed, as often with Malthus, with an actual example using such data as existed on the long-term trend in the production of grain per unit of work on the land.[16]

One important difficulty with the labor theory of value is how to relate "value" to the price at which a commodity is bought and sold in an actual market. Marx's attempt to reconcile the two was embodied in manuscripts that Engels compiled into the posthumous third volume of *Capital,* which in the view of hostile critics flatly contradicted the doctrine of Volume I. "Only in this vague and meaningless form" of market prices, Marx wrote, "are we still reminded of the fact that the value of the commodities is determined by the labor contained in them." In Schumpeter's view, "Marx . . . was under the same delusion as Aristotle, viz., that value, though a factor in the determination of relative prices, is yet something that is different from, and exists independently of, relative prices or exchange relations."[17] It was no accident, as Marxists say, that in spite of any difficulties in relating value to the empirical world Marx chose to adopt Ricardo's truncated version of Smith's more complex definition as the basis of his theory. For if workers create all value, then the "surplus" that entrepreneurs skim off as profit represents their exploitation of the working class. The theory gave Marx a scientific aura for his moral stance and political program; as so often happens, doctrinal disputes over seemingly remote abstractions led to practical consequences of devastating importance.

In summing up Malthus's general system of economic theory, one should note first of all his overall agreement with classical principles. The fundament of the classical school was the axiom that regulation by the state typically represents control by one special interest over the rest of the population. Mercantilist theorists had assumed that all men are usually in opposition; any person or social class, thus, could benefit only at the cost of another. With a division of labor and an unencumbered market, however, all could gain from the free exchange of goods. Laissez-faire is the most general and the most convincing argument against despotism, for the potential despot is offered not moralistic pieties but the proposition that it is in his own interest to cooperate in the market. In our day, when "liberal" has come to mean "with *more* state regulation and control," it is hard to recapture the exhilarating release from mercantilist bonds that the whole of the classical school represented.

Within this all-encompassing moral and analytical framework, there were of course important differences among political economists. As between Malthus, the deviant, and Ricardo, the prototype of classical orthodoxy, who comes out better? The exchange between them was far more extensive than Ricardo's *Notes* on Malthus's *Principles,* as is evident from Piero Sraffa's edition of Ricardo's writings. Throughout Malthus shows up as the insistent empiricist, countering Ricardo's "strong cases" with references to specific historical experience, without, however, ever losing sight of the importance of a theoretical structure by which discrete facts can be understood.[18] The difference in style still persists, represented in our day by the contrast, say, between model-building econometricians and such an economist as Simon Kuznets, whose works are always muddied by a far greater dependence on evidence. Which orientation is preferable to some degree reflects nothing more than taste: whether one is more impressed by elegance or a clumsier compromise with real-world complexity. As one who prefers the latter, I would say that, on the matters we have considered so far, Malthus the inductivist was also the better theorist. But I have still to discuss what in retrospect has become Malthus's most important deviation from classical orthodoxy, his rejection of Say's law.

Say's Law

Supply creates its own demand. This "law," derived from the circularity of the economic system, was postulated by the Physiocrats and taken over by Smith, thus becoming a fundament of both classical and postclassical analysis. Payment for all the factors in production—the costs of raw materials, wages, rent, interest, profit, and so on—furnishes potential purchasers with precisely enough to buy the goods produced. True, some entrepreneurs may offer commodities in amounts, or of types, not wanted by the buying public. Their poor judgment is corrected by the operation of the market; low profits induce them to cease making unwanted goods and to shift to those with an attractive rate of profit, reflecting the high demand relative to the short supply. But by its very nature the system cannot generate an overproduction across the board, an overall failure of demand to match supply, a "general glut," as it was termed in Malthus's day.

This forthright statement understates, however, the complexity of the supposed pattern. Twice in the development of economic theory, at the beginning of the nineteenth century and again in the 1930s, Say's law was at the center of doctrinal dispute; and continually it has been attacked from the sidelines by "underconsumptionists" outside the main stream. The dispute between Malthus and Ricardo was matched in France by one between Sismondi and Say.[19] Nor has the importance of the issue waned. In 1972 Thomas Sowell wrote an entire book on it; in 1977 William Baumol listed "at least" eight Say's laws.[20]

The crux of Malthus's criticism of the orthodox position related to Ricardo's premise that human wants are immediately and indefinitely expansible:

> An efficient taste for luxuries and conveniences, that is, such a taste as will properly stimulate industry, . . . is a plant of slow growth; . . . and it is a most important error to take for granted that mankind will produce and consume all that they have the power to produce and consume, and will never prefer indolence to the rewards of industry . . . Without an expenditure which will encourage commerce, manufactures, and personal services, the possessors of land would have no sufficient stimulus to cultivate well; and a country such as our own, which had been rich and populous, would, with too parsimonious habits, infallibly become poor and comparatively unpeopled.[21]

This deviation of Malthus from Ricardian orthodoxy, ignored for a hundred years or more, has been given increasing attention in recent years—less for its own sake than as part of the major shift from a Keynesian to what is termed a post-Keynesian framework. As early as 1933, when his biographical sketch of Malthus was published, Keynes was exclaiming, "If only Malthus, instead of Ricardo, had been the parent stem from which nineteenth-century economics proceeded, what a much wiser and richer place the world would be today!"[22] Also in his *General Theory* Keynes was effusive in his praise of Malthus. Ricardo, he wrote, "conquered England as completely as the Holy Inquisition conquered Spain . . . The great puzzle of Effective Demand with which Malthus had wrestled vanished from economic literature . . . It could only live on furtively, below the surface, in the underworlds of Karl Marx, Silvio Gesell, or Major Douglas."[23] Malthus was the most prominent, at least in Britain, of what Keynes called the "brave army of heretics . . . who, following their intuitions, have preferred to see truth obscurely and imperfectly rather than to maintain error, reached indeed with clearness and consistency and by easy logic, but on hypotheses inappropriate to the facts."[24]

In Keynes's view, of course, neither Malthus nor any of the other predecessors he discussed saw the matter as clearly as he did. But was the *General Theory* "essentially a rigorous exposition of Malthus,"[25] or, on the contrary, does "the claim of doctrinal precedence rest on nothing more than their common rejection of Say's law"?[26] There seems to be no risk of an early consensus on any of the disputed points. As one commentator remarked, "We seem to be in danger of reaching a position where Malthus can be 'all things to all men.' "[27] One of the more stimulating discussions reached the conclusion that in fact no good purpose is served by classifying Malthus as either Keynesian or not, for although Malthus analyzed the post-Napoleonic depression in a manner consistent with Keynesian analysis, his proposed solutions to unemployment were markedly non-Keynesian.[28] According to another paper on precisely the issue of the postwar unemployment, however, Malthus "was led to adopt and to develop to a remarkable extent the same line of approach which Keynes has made in our own day"; indeed, "there is more of Malthus in Keynes's *General Theory* than Keynes himself realized."[29]

One apparent difference is that Malthus stressed more the effective demand for goods, Keynes the relative lack of investment opportunities; but the distinction is not sharp. Here is Malthus on the relation between saving and investment:

> Adam Smith has stated that capitals are increased by parsimony, that every frugal man is a public benefactor, and that the increase of wealth depends upon the balance of produce above consumption. That these propositions are true to a great extent is perfectly unquestionable, . . . but it is quite obvious that they are not true to an indefinite extent, and that the principle of saving, pushed to excess, would destroy the motive to production . . . It follows that there must be some intermediate point, though the resources of political economy may not be able to ascertain it, where, taking into consideration both the power to produce and the will to consume, the encouragement to the increase of wealth is the greatest.[30]

Perhaps it is not extravagant to suggest that this argument resembles that of Keynes's *General Theory* at least in its attempt to generalize: Smith's thesis is rejected not as false but as too limited. Note, too, that for Malthus the lack of investment opportunities derives from the central issue—for him—of a lack of effective demand for commodities. In both theorists investment is obviously related to the market for goods, and whether there is a significant difference between them or only one of emphasis is debatable.[31]

The classical economists in general were interested mainly in analyzing production, the means by which the wealth of nations came into existence. Demand was expressed by a being later dubbed Economic Man, who used his reason to select among the goods offered and whose overall wants were indefinitely expansible. The reification of rationality has often been attacked, and even such a scholar as Schumpeter, who analyzed almost everything else dispassionately, was a bit impatient with these critics. Marshall's defense that the economist studies man in the ordinary pursuits of business life, if not a wholly adequate response, "went some way in the right direction."[32] The persistence of the problem is suggested by the fact that as recently as 1976 Harvey Leibenstein wrote a book devoted to the issue. In conventional microeconomics, he began, the unit of analysis is either the household or the firm; but individuals, the only ones to make decisions, are in fact the basic units, the atoms of which the usual molecules are composed. The postulate that individuals decide to purchase goods according to their utility is not true to the primary sense of "utility" in three situations: when a style or fad determines a commodity's attractiveness ("the bandwagon effect") ; when, on the contrary, a person buys in order to demonstrate that he is different from the crowd ("the snob effect") ; and when an effort is made to consume conspicuously ("the Veblen effect"). The "decision techniques" that an individual uses to judge the relative "utility" of alternative goods or services, then, can be viewed best not as a psychological constant but as a variable between "tight" and "loose" calculation. In sum, for Economic Man one should substitute "S. R. Man," with the initials standing for "selective rationality."[33] As a noneconomist, I find this to be a considerable improvement not only over the classical concept of demand but also over the broader "consumer behavior" that Wicksteed and others introduced in its stead. Paradoxically, however, some of these new insights were foreshadowed in Malthus—for example, in his analysis of fertility determinants. For him, as I shall spell out in a subsequent chapter, rationality was indeed a variable: the optimum means of achieving the unavoidable balance between population and resources was through a diffusion of the calculating foresight that he recommended.

According to the "correct" theory as defined by Schumpeter, "on the long-run trend (that is to say, neglecting the effect of temporary disturbances) there are no assignable limits to investment opportunity at appropriately falling rates of interest, except possibly institutional ones."[34] This rejects, of course, both Malthus and Keynes, and it represents a fair statement of the post-Keynesian consensus. How does this doctrine contrast with what Malthus wrote?

Malthus followed Adam Smith in dividing English society into three classes—landowners, capitalists, and workers. But "consumption and demand occasioned by the workmen employed in productive labor can never *alone* furnish a motive to the accumulation and employment of capital," and capitalists and landlords, on the contrary, have "agreed to be parsimonious, and by depriving themselves of their usual conveniences and luxuries to save from their revenue and add to their capital."[35] This last proposition was based on the standard classical doctrine, fully expounded in Nassau Senior's *Outline of the Science of Political Economy* (1836), that abstinence is the subjective cost of capitalization, paid for with profit. The impetus to deprive oneself of the fruits of one's labor in order to produce still more has been analyzed in several contexts. As I noted in the last chapter, for Marx the call to "accumulate, accumulate" was "the Moses and the prophets" of all capitalists; any deviant who neglected this first commandment would soon be driven from the market-place. From another point of view, Max Weber's familiar concept of the Protestant ethic was a specification of this characteristic capitalist behavior to members of Low Protest-ant churches—who were prominent, one should remember, among the craftsmen and petty merchants rising to become the owner-directors of England's new factories. In our time the inculcation of nationalism in less developed countries can be seen as a secular variant of the same theme: those induced to work hard for "their country" will be satisfied with collective rather than individual gains, so that in theory at least such states will be able to shift a greater portion of their national incomes from personal expenditure to capital accumulation.

If society consists of two broad types—those who above the level of subsistence prefer indolence to more goods, and those who try to build up a family property by consuming less than they produce—how can the disparity be brought into balance? According to Malthus,

> Every society must have a body of persons engaged in personal services of various kinds . . . It is perhaps one of the most im-portant practical questions . . . whether they furnish fresh mo-tives for production, and tend to push the wealth of the country farther than it would go without them . . . Menial servants are absolutely necessary to make the resources of the higher and middle classes of society efficient in the demand for material products.[36]

Nothing in Malthus's entire corpus, perhaps, excited a more negative response than this approbation of the unproductive consumer. "The part of your book to which I most object," Ricardo wrote Malthus on completion of his *Notes*, "is the last. I can see no soundness in the reasons you give for the useful-ness of demand in the fact of unproductive consumers."[37] And as the egalitarian demiurge became ever more dominant, the notion that the servants of the rich serve a useful general function was seen as not only factually wrong but ideologically blasphemous, a principal item in the case that Malthus was a spokesman for the landed class. Thus, according to Marx,

> Malthus represents the interest of the industrial bourgeoisie only to the extent that it is identical with the interest of the landlords, the aristocracy—that is to say, against the mass of the people, the proletariat. But when these interests diverge and are opposed to one another, then he puts himself on the side of the aristocracy against the bourgeoisie, as in his defense of the "unproductive worker."[38]

Even if we accept the notion that all adversaries of socialism, no matter how scrupulous their scholarship, are representatives of the ruling classes of the nonsocialist society, Marx's label still does not fit Malthus's specific argument that both landlords and capitalists tend to consume less than they produce and that the servants of both are therefore a useful stimulus to effective demand.

Marx's own theory of business cycles, expounded in small pieces over most of his writings, is difficult to appraise. Though he and Engels both condemned underconsumptionists explicitly, other passages have led a number of scholars, including Marxist partisans, to interpret him as also an underconsumptionist.[39] Paul Sweezy wrote concerning this as follows:

> It could be maintained that Marx regarded underconsumption as one aspect, but on the whole not a very important aspect, of the crisis problem. This appears to be the opinion of Dobb, and there is no doubt much to back it up. Another view is possible, however, namely, that in these scattered passages [which Sweezy had analyzed in detail] Marx was giving advance notice of a line of reasoning which, if he had lived to complete his theoretical work, would have been of primary importance in the overall picture of the capitalist economy; . . . and, on the whole, it seems to me the more reasonable of the two alternatives.[40]

It is perhaps a just interpretation to say that Malthus stressed more the tendency to underconsume, Marx the tendency of the rate of profit to fall, but that Malthus and conceivably Marx included both factors as reasons for their rejection of Say's law. That is, Malthus's defense of the unproductive consumer derived fundamentally from what may have been a significant improvement—in Marx's view—of orthodox classical theory. But for Marx it was less important that Malthus had analyzed the working of the capitalist economy "correctly" than that he had drawn "reactionary" political conclusions from that analysis.

Apart from the effusive approbation from Keynes and the partial approval that Marx possibly should have given him, was Malthus correct? The answer is no—provided all markets (including the labor market) operate instantaneously and entirely by the interaction of demand and supply. If men indulge their propensity to indolence, they will consume no more than they produce, until hunger drives them back to work. However, even at the beginning of the nineteenth century (not to say at the present time), markets functioned within the constraints of an institutional setting; and Malthus opposed the abstract classical model because he emphasized empirical reality. In arguing against John Stuart Mill's position, for example, Malthus remarked that the prices of cotton, wool, linen, and silk manufactures had *all* fallen below the cost of production; the estimated loss of £70 million was balanced during the same period by a rise in the prices of other goods by no more than £1 million. Mill's arguments against the possibility of a general glut, in short, seem to be "utterly without foundation." "If facts so notorious as these to which I have adverted are either boldly denied or considered as undeserving attention in founding the theories of political economy, there is an end at once to the utility of the science."[41]

One unrealistic element in the classical model is that it ignores any distinction between short- and long-term trends. Malthus not only granted that a gradual rise in the level of expectations was possible but (as I shall point out shortly) made of this potential a key element in his economic-demographic theory. As early as the First Essay, however, he noted that rigid wages are one reason why the oscillation between over- and underpopulation, those "retrograde and progressive movements with respect to happiness," is sometimes not readily apparent. It is typical that wages are "sticky": when the prices of foodstuffs are rising, the money that workers have to buy them seldom increases as fast.[42] In subsequent editions of the *Essay* and in such other works as *Observations on the Effects of the Corn Laws* (1814), Malthus generalized this argument to the whole of the economy.[43] When Keynes proffered the similar thesis that over the short run "hoards" would accumulate for lack of investment opportunities, he was asked what would happen when the interest rate fell to the level indicated by the investment market. He answered with the famous wisecrack, "In the long run we are all dead." But was this only a witticism, or should theory be concerned more with the short-term (and actual) deficiency of effective demand than with the eventual (and thus only potential) adjustment?

The second major flaw in the classical stance is that market adjustments are assumed to take place apart from institutional checks. Under the combined influence of Keynesians and Marxists, among others, Western countries have instituted "mixed economies" supporting "welfare states" in which—paradoxically—both the number of unproductive consumers and the proportion of the national income that they absorb are far larger than those represented by the servant class of the early nineteenth century. Those whose salaries derive from taxation (such as, in Malthus's example, "statesmen, soldiers, sailors, and those who live upon the interest of a national debt") do, in his view, "contribute powerfully to distribution and demand." In one sense, thus, they perform the same function in market relations as the servants of landlords and capitalists.

> To counterbalance these advantages, which so far are unquestionable, it must be acknowledged that injudicious taxation might stop the increase of wealth at almost any period of its progress early or late; and that the most judicious taxation might ultimately be so heavy as to clog all the channels of foreign and domestic trade and almost prevent the possibility of accumulation . . . Taxation is a stimulus so liable in every way to abuse, and it is so absolutely necessary for the general interests of society to consider private property as sacred, that no one would think of trusting to any government the means of making a different distribution of wealth with a view to the general good.[44]

We of the twentieth century have not only thought of it but have carried out the policy in practice. In Britain the punitively high taxes have in fact impeded (though, indeed, with a few interruptions) further industrial progress by clogging the channel to investment; and the United States, though lagging some decades behind, is marching stalwartly along the same road. That in modern economies the demand for goods matches or more than matches the supply is in itself no validation of Say's law, for the creation of unproductive consumers has been on a scale not imagined by any of its early critics.

The notion, summarized in so-called Phillips curves, that governments could choose between a rise in inflation and a rise in unemployment has foundered on the empirical trend of both to increase, a combination now termed "stagflation."[45] The failure of Keynesian policies is based in considerable part on the ever increasing proportion of the labor force working for governments, who are paid out of either the rising taxes or the more rapidly rising public debt. It is evidence of Malthus's prescience that he was able to analyze the main fault of the welfare state long before the term came into being.

Apart from the application of his economic theories to questions of population and to social classes—to which I shall return in subsequent chapters—how can one sum up Malthus's contribution to classical economics and its present relevance? Perhaps the best short statement is by Lionel Robbins. One should note first that the population theory was incorporated whole as an essential element of the classical doctrine; Robbins is certainly correct in rejecting Schumpeter's dictum that "if one were to remove the principle of population from the classical system, it would remain what it is." The theory of rent derived, as I have noted, as much from Malthus as from any other single theorist. Robbins believed that all would agree in praising Malthus's implicit contribution to the theory of international monetary relations contained in his discussion of the bullion issue. Though in Robbins's view Keynes was wrong in his sweeping denotation of Malthus as a forebear, "that is not all that there is to say in this connection."

> On the plane of practical judgment, I have no doubt that Malthus's position is preferable to Ricardo's. His instinct was against the rigidity—or assumed rigidity—of the Law of Markets [Say's law] . . . On this plane, how greatly superior in good sense is his attitude to that of Ricardo, bombinating away in a stratosphere of abstract logic which led him to attribute the postwar depression in part at least to agricultural protection.

Most appropriately, Robbins concludes this account of the differences between Ricardo and Malthus by quoting the last letter of the famous correspondence between the two friends: "And now, my dear Malthus, I have done. Like other disputants, after much discussion we each retain our own opinion. These discussions, however, never influence our friendship. I should not like you more than I do if you agreed in opinion with me."[46]

6

The Poor Law and Migration

NEITHER THE DIFFERENCES between Malthus and Ricardo over economic theory nor such narrower policy questions as the appropriate supply of bullion touch on what has become the main economic controversy concerning Britain in Malthus's period—namely, how industrialization affected "the standard of living." The debate has continued intermittently for a century and a half, and the labels ordinarily attached to the two sides, "optimists" and "pessimists," hardly denote the whole of the conflicting ideologies. In the earliest period the defense of the new economic system was undertaken in part by the industrialists themselves or their close spokesmen, the attack on it by such anti-industrialist poets as Southey. A more persistent theme has been the denunciation of capitalism by socialists like Engels, the Hammonds, and Hobsbawm; any evidence that a system defined as evil in fact improved the life of the working classes was not to be accepted easily. The present state of the controversy is well represented by a collection of papers compiled by Arthur Taylor, particularly the two summations by Hobsbawm for the attack and R. M. Hartwell and Stanley Engerman for the defense.[1]

On the narrow issue of whether average real wages rose in the postwar decades up to 1840, as Hobsbawm admits, the defense has won. He is able to continue the debate only by concentrating on supplementary points—that the rise in real wages was "relatively slight," that the higher average says nothing of the range, that the "way of life" did not necessarily get better, and so on. The essay by Hartwell and Engerman, titled "Models of Immiseration: The Theoretical Basis of Pessimism," focuses on what they see as the main point—the allegation that the capitalist system, at least in its initial phase, reduced the level of life of the lower classes. Similarly, in the introduction to the second edition of *The Long Debate on Poverty,* Norman Cash, its editor, summarized the favorable and hostile reviews of the first edition and found a good deal of agreement.

> It is conceded that not only in the long run but also in the short . . . industrialization substantially raised the standard of living of the British working classes; that only industrialization could have done this; and that relatively free industrial enterprise was the only possible method at that time of organizing the country's economic affairs. On the other hand, it is also agreed that progress in this matter was neither constant nor universal. People employed in domestic industries that were being outstripped by machine and factory technology, Irish immigrants, agricultural workers especially in the south of England, urban workers in time of prolonged unemployment or trade depression . . . afforded periodic or local examples of acute poverty and distress.
>
> What then is left to quarrel about? Three things, according to the critics of this book. First, that this analysis takes no account of the quality of life as distinct from material standards; second, that the problem of poverty, or of gross inequality of income between the richest and the poorest, was not solved as soon as it might have been; third, that in the short run the misery caused to a few might have outweighed the benefits to the rest.

Marx coined the word *Verelendung,* translated as "immiseration," to denote what he saw as an inevitable process; and in *The Condition of the Working Class in England,* Engels introduced his description of the industrial poor with an account of preindustrial life that is as spurious as an Olde Countrie Inne roofed with plastic thatch:

> The workers enjoyed a comfortable and peaceful existence. They were righteous, God-fearing, and honest. Their standard of life was much better than that of the factory worker today. They were not forced to work excessive hours . . . They had time for healthy work in their gardens or smallholdings, and such labor

was in itself a recreation . . . Most of them were strong, well
built people . . . In the absence of temptations to immorality
they lived God-fearing decent lives. There were no low public
houses or brothels . . . The workers' children were brought up
at home, where they learned to fear God and obey their parents
. . . Children grew up in idyllic simplicity and in happy inti-
macy with their playmates.[2]

Though Engels ended this fairy tale with the observation that
the workers of that period "remained in some respects little
better than the beasts in the field," it hardly detracted from
the several pages describing their bovine contentment. Presumably Adam and Eve also "vegetated happily," and for
Engels the counterpart of their fall from grace was the industrial revolution, which burst the rural isolation and brought
the happy craftsman into painful touch with the larger world.

The distinction between "optimists" and "pessimists," fatu-
ous in any case, is especially so when applied to Malthus. In
one of the best known histories of economic thought, we are
informed that Malthus and Ricardo, as the principal representatives of the school, "deserve to be classed as pessimists
because of their utter disbelief in the possibility of changing
the course of these inevitable laws [of social-economic de-
velopment] either by legislative reform or by organized voluntary effort. In short, they had no faith in what we call
progress."[3] And Malthus, according to another commentator,
"never cleared his mind entirely of the dismal theory with
which he began."[4] As we shall see in some detail, the drift of
Malthus's point of view through his lifetime was toward the
conviction that progress is both possible and amenable to
social intervention. The characterization of his thought as
pessimistic was based either on a dependence on the First
Essay as a definitive statement or on an acceptance of the
utopian expectations of Godwin as realistic, at least as contrasted with Malthus's denigration of them.

In the decades I am considering, two types of administrative
initiative were directly related to poverty: British emigration
policy consisted, in the graphic sense of its opponents, of
"shoveling out paupers"; and the seemingly endless debate
over the so-called Poor Law was about how to deal with those
still remaining in the bin. Both of these issues often involved
the Irish, and the interrelation between population and

economy in Ireland became an integral part of political debate in England. Most significantly in this context, Ireland was in several respects a "Malthusian" country, a prime instance of how a better food supply helped build up a greater population pressure, and, on the other hand, the only nation that reduced its fertility mainly by moral restraint.

IRELAND AND THE IRISH

The first Irish census was conducted in 1821, two decades after the English counterpart, and the first reasonably accurate and complete count, as in England, came only in 1841. K. H. Connell's analysis of the increase during the prior period has become the basis of all subsequent accounts. According to his estimates, the population rose from just under 2.2 million in 1687 (revised from Petty's figure) to around 3.2 million in 1750 to perhaps 5.0 million at the end of the century. According to the first three censuses, the population was 6.8 million in 1821, 7.8 million in 1831, and 8.2 million in 1841.[5] Though the early figures are not precise, no historian has quibbled about the approximate dimension of the increase.

The astoundingly rapid growth was not due to any significant change in mortality, fecundity, illegitimacy, contraception, or marital fertility; the impetus came almost entirely from a sharp fall in the age at marriage, which earlier had conformed to what Hajnal called the European pattern. By the latter decades of the eighteenth century, according to contemporary local estimates, most girls were "mothers at 16"; "an unmarried man at 25, or woman at 20, is rarely to be met in the country parts"; "couples marry whose united age scarcely exceeds 35 or 36." The country's subsistence base had been extended by the draining of swampland and by the substitution for grain of the potato, which became the poor people's staple. Until 1742 Catholics had been barred from owning land; a law of that year permitted them to hold fifty acres of bog together with half an acre of adjoining arable land, and to be immune from tithes for seven years. With a daily consumption of ten pounds (*sic!*) of potatoes and a pint of whole milk, supplemented occasionally and precariously by some meat, fish, or eggs, an adult got not only enough calories but a balanced diet. The potential growth of population was realized through an interaction with poverty. According to the testimony that Connell cited, "smallholders are induced to marry . . . [because] they know they can lose nothing"; "laborers get married under the idea that they cannot make their condition worse"; "a comfortable farmer's son . . . marries late in life, [waiting] until he gets a girl with a fortune."[6]

The economy on which the rapidly growing population depended suffered a serious deterioration during the eighteenth century. About two-thirds of Ireland's agricultural land was owned by English (often absentee) landlords; and the great majority of the Irish were "cottiers," who at exorbitant rents leased small plots, usually no more than an acre, and enough pasture for a cow or two. Restraints on Irish trade, which were in force until 1780, seriously damaged such industries as shipbuilding, woolen goods, and glass. The so-called Penal Laws, which gradually became inoperative during the century's latter decades, prohibited the employment of "Papists" as lawyers or manufacturers of weapons, for example (a Protestant who married a "woman of the Popish religion" was also barred from the law). No Catholic was permitted to work in "any trade, craft, or mystery" (except the manufacture of flax or hemp) with more than two apprentices. None was permitted to own a horse worth more than £5, and if any Protestant discovered such a horse he could legally acquire it by a payment of £5 5s. "The Protestants looked down on trade and, as a whole, took no part in it; whereas the Catholics, if ever so willing, were not in a position to take any part in it."[7]

Until 1793 Catholics were denied suffrage; the significance of their enfranchisement at that date is suggested by a letter from a County Down landlord who had made his Catholic tenants freeholders and was therefore able to promise a candidate their votes. The country was governed—if that is the proper term—by a portion of the Protestant minority. In 1795 the electorate was divided into three categories: resident owners of property worth at least 40s.; registered owners, not necessarily resident, of property worth £20 to £50; and owners of property worth more than £50, who could vote without either residence or registration. The Irish Parliament so elected did not, however, govern Ireland. Basic policy was set by Westminster and administered by an appointed Lord Lieutenant, who purchased the requisite majority of the Irish Parliament with a judicious distribution of offices, pensions, and other bribes—a practice that might have been designed to make the Irish M.P.s both independent and irresponsible.

Except for those who benefited directly, members of the English ruling class probably saw Ireland (then as now) as a burden. As C. T. Grenville wrote to a correspondent in 1784, "Ireland is too great to be unconnected with us, and too near to be dependent on a foreign state, and too little to be independent."[8]

The patchwork system began to ravel in 1795 with the disastrous viceroyalty of Earl Fitzwilliam, who until he was recalled after only two months in office aggravated every grievous fault in Ireland's administration.[9] There were outbreaks of violence by such secret societies as the Whiteboys. The widespread sympathy with the slogans of the French Revolution acquired greater significance with invasions of French troops in 1796 and 1798.[10] On the first day of the new century, January 1, 1801, an attempt was made to resolve the Irish crisis once and for all by the formation of the Union of Great Britain and Ireland.

Lord Cornwallis had written to Sir Charles Ross that he managed to bring about the Union by "negotiating and jobbing with the most corrupt people under heaven. I despise and hate myself every hour for engaging in such dirty work, and am supported only by the reflection that without a Union the British Empire must be dissolved." It is common to conclude from such evidence that the avarice of the Irish peers led them to kill their golden goose, but the issue was more complicated:

> To say that most of those who voted with the ministry were placemen was tautologous . . . I can find no more than twelve who voted against the measure [for Union] in 1799 and for it in 1800; . . . [and, apart from two apparent exceptions,] peerages and promotions within the peerage were not given to reward members who changed sides . . . It is a superficial and exaggerated view to assume that corruption was the main factor which carried the Union.[11]

The principal reason that opponents of the Union failed to prevent it, perhaps, was their own ineptitude, aggravated by public apathy. Some Irish supported it in anticipation that restrictions on particular parts of the Irish economy would be lifted (correlatively, opposition to the Union in the British Parliament reflected the lobbying of English woolen manufacturers, who feared the resurgence of Irish competitors). "It was just possible that a united government might handle Ireland's sectarian, commercial, and political problems more disinterestedly than the existing regime. It could hardly do worse."[12]

Irish Catholics did not oppose the Union because they had been given a more or less definite assurance that they would get more relief from the British than from the Irish Parliament. It was Pitt's intention to follow through with these ambiguous promises, and when George III blocked his policy he resigned as Prime Minister. The Union began, therefore, with the worst of possible relations with Catholics: expectations raised during several years of negotiations were brought to a dead end; and during the English crisis engendered by the king's insanity and the institution of the Regency, Ireland was hardly at the fore of London's concerns. Thus it was that dissolution of the Union soon became *the* goal of Irish politics. Steps toward this end focused on such issues as the abolition of tithes to the Anglican church, mass education and an expanded suffrage, an altered relation between landowner and tenant, and parliamentary reform. These constituted the platform of the Catholic Association reorganized in 1824 under Daniel O'Connell, an astute politician able to garner support both as a chieftain of the Kerry clan and as a member of the Catholic gentry educated in France and England. The association was financed by dues of a shilling a year, collected from peasants with the energetic assistance of the Catholic church. The struggle for reform in Ireland had half-hidden but fundamental repercussions in England, of which the most obvious was the Catholic emancipation finally realized in 1829. English Catholics could hardly have achieved this on their own; the bill was passed by a Parliament responding to pressures from Ireland against the wishes of England's largely anti-Catholic populace. Catholic emancipation thus "epitomized that separation of Parliament from people which was execrated by Radical reformers." It was not one strand of England's democratization but came about, on the contrary, in spite of that process.[13]

More generally, the state direction of Ireland's economy and society set a pattern for future developments in Britain. Even the most conventional Englishman, however determined to maintain local controls and laissez-faire at home, was willing to sanction for the new member of the Union an expedient centralization of governmental functions—a development that foreshadowed the later neomercantilist trend in British politics. As early as 1805, provision was made for Irish dispensaries (of which half the cost was met out of public funds) that in theory would furnish the poor with free medicine and medical services. A national police force, which still does not exist in Britain, in Ireland began to develop from 1825. In 1831 the state undertook a gigantic scheme of elementary education, with two-thirds of capital costs and operating expenses provided out of public funds; for all their crudeness (and the subsequent dispute over the religious content of the curriculum), these schools enabled a poverty-stricken population to achieve a level of literacy denied their English counterparts. The English Poor Law of 1834 was carried across St. George's Channel four years later. By 1841, the year that O'Connell was elected Lord Mayor of Dublin, Ireland's local authorities had lost most of their power, with the chief county officers appointed from the center. Thus, in the maintenance of order, the provision of welfare, the planning of the economy, and education, the Irish government was anomalous for its degree of centralization, uniformity, inspection, and professionalism —all brought about during decades when a combination of public-spirited amateurism and factional search for high office persisted in England.[14] Under these circumstances, emigration was also, as we shall see, partly under state auspices, not merely from Ireland but from Britain as well.

Apart from the references to the country in the *Essay* and *Principles,* Malthus offered his opinions on Ireland in several places, of which the most interesting perhaps are essays reviewing two books by Thomas Newenham.[15] The astounding increase in population had been possible because of the potato, which requires only a third of the land needed for the same nourishment from wheat; and Malthus speculated whether the spread of this staple might not stimulate a comparable growth in other nations. To the degree that Ireland's poverty derived from the ecological balance, it was in Malthus's view "beyond the power of the legislature directly to relieve it," but that did not mean that no measures were appropriate:

Every year that elapses under the present system tends to aggravate all the causes of discontent in Ireland . . . Every year fifty thousand youths rise to the military age in Ireland . . . The increasing strength of Ireland is the increasing weakness of England. Each passing year, while it adds both to the disposition and the power of Ireland to resist the wrongs she suffers, diminishes in a still greater proportion the power of England to enforce them.

In Malthus's opinion, Newenham was "much too fond of public grants and bounties" and in general gave the Irish government more credit than it deserved. "The great advantage of a free country," Malthus pointed out, "does not consist in its requiring higher qualities in its governors, but in its being better secured against their bad qualities . . . and having better means of removing a foolish or wicked minister." That Ireland's "great natural richness of the soil" had not provided the potential prosperity was due to the country's lack of capital and skill. The many commercial regulations that English traders had dictated, a "mean and pitiful jealousy of trade" into which Malthus did not bother to go in "disgusting detail," had been permitted "to crush the industry and repress the wealth of those who ought to be considered as friends and brothers." A tax on agricultural tenants is always onerous, he pointed out, for generally they can neither raise the price of their produce nor withdraw their labor to more profitable enterprises. And this truth applied especially in Ireland, where the extreme poverty of most tenants afforded them even less leeway. Since landlords acquired a "very great proportion of the whole produce" and tenants a correspondingly "very scanty proportion," Parliament should, "by every principle of justice and policy, remove the burden of the partial and oppressive county rates, and the still heavier and more oppressive burden of tithes, from the poor tenantry to the rich landlords."[16]

More remarkable than these comments on the Irish economy were Malthus's quite anomalous observations on religion. By their "dastardly, servile, and useless" acquiescence in the terms of the Union, Irish Protestants "had sacrificed their own wealth and honor by sacrificing their country"; emigration from Ireland was largely of Protestants, whose number was apparently falling off not only proportionately but in absolute numbers. On the other hand, "the humiliated Catholic, with no rank in society to support, had sought only . . . subsistence; and finding, without much difficulty, potatoes, milk, and a hovel, he had vegetated in the country of his ancestors and overspread the land with his descendants." The course set by Irish Protestants "must terminate either in complete emancipation or complete separation."

> This fruitful island . . . should be cherished by us as our richest mine of wealth, as well as our strongest pillar of defense. And yet this is the country the loss of which is daily risked by . . . the bigotry and littleness of one part of an administration, and by the tergiversation and inconsistency of the other . . . Let the Irish Catholics have all they have demanded; for they have asked nothing but what strict justice and good policy should concede to them.

Perhaps nothing one could cite from Malthus's work denies more forcefully the prevalent view of his theory. Even in the case of Ireland, where indeed the rapid growth of available subsistence had been followed by a no less rapid increase of population, Malthus did not view this succession as simple cause and effect. The underlying reason was the degradation of the Irish Catholic, who, seeing no escape from his lowly condition, spent his life proliferating. Even today, the emotional impact of Malthus's language is hardly to be found outside the writings of Irish nationalists. At that time, with Anglicans, Presbyterians, Methodists, and Radicals more or less united in their anti-Catholic stance, and with English Catholics somewhat embarrassed by their animalic coreligionists, Malthus's demand for responsible government, free trade, and elementary justice was more exceptional still.

The dependence of the lower classes on a single crop with little or no leeway for poor harvests led, as everyone knows, to the worst famine in modern European history. The potato blight appeared in some areas in 1845, while others still had abundant food. The following year it spread across the countryside. In fields covered with luxuriant green, every potato plant turned black almost from one day to the next. No poor person could afford to buy grain or meat; some cattle were slaughtered, others died from an epidemic of pleuropneumonia. As is typical in famine-stricken areas, the desperate peasants abandoned their hovels and swarmed to the soup kitchens set up in the poorest urban quarters, spreading destitution and disease as they went. Thousands died of typhus or relapsing fever, both spread by the louse and both thus favored by crowding in unsanitary conditions. According to a physician in one Galway dispensary, the ailments began with scurvy, followed by dysentery and famine dropsy; then by typhus, "very fatal," or relapsing fever, "fast propagated by contagion, but not so fatal" as typhus. As soon as the food supply improved, the diseases caused by a lack of nutrients subsided, but there was a sharp recurrence of typhus in 1848 and the following year an outbreak of cholera, imported from England and with no direct relation to the famine.[17]

The 1851 census listed some hundreds of thousands of deaths from various famine-related causes, but these data were compiled from such institutions as hospitals or from survivors in the least stricken areas. In a similar compilation by a medical journal, the editor noted that no reports had been received from several of the worst ravaged districts; "in many cases we regret to say that this has been caused by the lamentable mortality amongst our professional brethren." In comparing the censuses of 1841 and 1851, one notes large areas with a depletion by more than 30 percent over the decade, and only Dublin and Belfast showing an increase—but these figures reflect both mass mortality and the acceleration of emigration. The number who died of the famine and its direct consequences, though it will never be known, was certainly above half a million and perhaps almost as much as a full million.[18] Out of the population of 8.2 million in 1841, this represents a famine death rate of between 21 and 41—each an increment to the normal mortality of those years.

One consequence of the famine was that Ireland reverted to the earlier marriage pattern in its most extreme manifestation. Irish families have typically had as many children per year of risk as any of the Western world. The control of fertility was by the chaste postponement of marriage that Malthus had recommended, plus the usual concomitant that many put off a family commitment so long that they saw no point in assuming it at all. As late as the 1930s, 74 percent of Irish males and 55 percent of Irish females were single at ages 25–34 —far more than in any other Western country. (The comparable percentages for England and Wales were 35 and 33, for the United States only 29 and 18.) And in the same decade, of persons aged 45–54, about a third of the males and over a quarter of the females had never married. It has often been argued that this pattern derived in part from Irish Catholicism, but the cause-effect relation probably went as much in the opposite direction. With so high a proportion of celibates in the society, many sought careers in the church, whose influence was thus strengthened considerably. The effects of the famine persisted also because of the contrast between poverty at home and the far greater comfort that emigrants reported from the United States or even England. Since after the famine the Irish therefore aspired to a much higher level of living than most poor peoples, they chose—as Malthus would have predicted—to assume far fewer family responsibilities.[19]

THE ENGLISH POOR LAWS

If, as scholars of the period now agree, early industrialization effected a rise in lower-class real income, how can it be that one of the most urgent problems of those decades (and one in which Malthus was deeply involved) was the ever greater number of poor and the ever increasing burden on local taxes to provide for them? One reason was the large shift of villagers to towns. The Old Poor Law, as it is called (contrasted with the New Poor Law enacted in 1834), worked with tolerable efficiency so long as the population was mainly rural and almost static, but attempts to adapt it to radically changing circumstances brought more and more problems.

One reason for this was that most migrants to towns wanted more from life than the modest and often precarious supply of necessities that had satisfied their parents. The corruption of the term "standard of living" to mean level of living, though it is too well established to reverse, is particularly unfortunate in an analysis either of this period or especially of Malthus's recommendations. The crucial problem in Ireland, for example, he defined as the tendency of the lower classes to be content with too little; and the most significant amelioration would be, in twentieth-century jargon, a "revolution of rising expectations." As we can see from parliamentary hearings, the characteristics of England's industrialization that defenders of the old order found most disturbing were often changes that to us would suggest economic and social advance.

Thackrah lamented the fact that children were no longer contented with "plain food" but must have "dainties." The Reverend G. S. Bull deplored the tendency of girls to buy pretty clothes "ready-made" from shops instead of making them themselves, as this practice unfitted them to become "the mothers of children." [Philip] Gaskell saw decadence in tobacco, . . . moral decline in the growth of workmen's combinations [trade unions]. The men were no longer "respectful and attentive" to their "superiors."[20]

If for those witnesses tea-drinking and smoking were signs of lower-class degeneration, for Hobsbawm, on the contrary, the *slow* adoption of the same new customs proved that the country's levels of consumption were lagging.[21] The example indicates how difficult it is to distinguish what consumers wanted and could not buy from what they did not want. How many of the imprecisely recorded shifts reflected changes merely in taste?

Industrialization, however pervasive and important its influences, was not the only factor to be considered. If one attributes to capitalism or the factory system all the deleterious changes in the people's way of life, the conclusion is almost certain to be wrong. "For it is possible that employment in factories conduced to an increase of real wages but that the tendency was more than offset by other influences, such as the rapid increase of population, the immigration of Irishmen, the destruction of wealth by long years of warfare, ill devised tariffs, and misconceived measures for the relief of distress."[22] The dominant economic fact of the years from roughly 1790 to 1815 was that England was at war with France, and this set the rise in the real prices of imports and some foodstuffs. Homes in the new industrial towns were thrown together with whatever was left when the state deflected requisite materials and labor to the demand of military necessity. The word coined to describe these ramshackle houses, *jerry-built,* does not derive from a profiteer named Jerry but from the nautical word *jury* (as in "jury mast") , meaning "temporary," "emergency." The shortage of urban residences persisted, however, and the "temporary" dwellings were occupied for decades, in the worst cases becoming urban slums no better than the rural hovels of the preindustrial period.

The foundation of the Hanoverian welfare system was a codification of earlier practice in 1597–1601, especially the "43rd of Elizabeth" of 1601. For more than two centuries the principle remained constant that each parish should be responsible for the care of its own poor, but from this base there arose a structure that one might term either utterly inconsistent or marvelously adaptable. "One looks in vain for any fundamentally new idea in the Poor Law legislation following 1601; rather, the statute book is seen to contain more and more variations on set themes."[23] Many of the revisions in the Old Poor Law constituted humanitarian reforms under the impetus of such pioneers as Jonas Hanway (1712–86) and Thomas Gilbert (1720–98), such Members of Parliament as John Rolle (1750–1842) and Sir George Rose (1782–1873). Almost every one of the issues debated in later decades had been faced earlier, and benevolent reforms to improve the condition of the poor had been incorporated into English law.[24]

In any case, the specification of the "old" system in the statutes had little relation to the actual practice of many localities. In the 15,000 parishes of England and Wales, local control meant first of all great variation in every characteristic. The unpaid, nonprofessional administrators might exhibit humane feelings in the face-to-face relations with their charges or, on the contrary, a particular harshness. This lack of uniformity contributed greatly to the dispute over the effects of the system, for each commentator naturally selected cases that validated his prejudices; and this was true in particular of the largest works on which others depended for much of their argumentation and data—*The State of the Poor*, in three volumes, by Sir Frederick Morton Eden; the three-volume history by Sir George Nicholls, a member of the 1832–34 Royal Commission and strongly inclined to support whatever it recommended; and the four volumes devoted to the Poor Law by Sidney and Beatrice Webb, who spent their lives indefatigably propagandizing for socialism. "All investigators have been impressionistic in their conclusions, and none more so than the Webbs, whose comments on the Poor Law Commission and its aftermath subsist very largely on their own impressions of the Assistant Commissioners' impressions."[25]

When the Royal Commission on the Poor Laws was appointed in 1832, it dispatched twenty-six investigators (whom the Webbs believed to have been Benthamites) into about 3,000 parishes, or only one-fifth of the total of 15,000. To a questionnaire that the commission distributed on relief systems, parish economies, and labor relations, replies were received from one parish in ten; and there is no reason to suppose that these were typical of the whole. Some of the questions were poorly phrased, tending to call forth the responses that the commission expected. From the fifteen volumes of detailed data, two members of the commission—Nassau Senior, Drummond Professor of Political Economy at Oxford, and Edwin Chadwick, who until Bentham's death had been his private secretary—did most of the work of extracting a report. "There is little doubt that these two had already made up their able minds as to the remedies they would propose, and that they used the evidence collected by the Royal Commission selectively rather than analytically in order to stampede public opinion into backing the measures that they put forward."[26] In works on Malthus, he is often denounced as the main architect of the New Poor Law; but in works on how it came to be passed, the direct responsibility is likely to be assigned to such men as Senior and Chadwick—whose only relation to Malthus was to oppose him. Malthus's influence, because it was indirect, is harder to measure; but in some respects he left no doubt that he was opposed to the 1834 Act. A good example is the so-called law of settlement, under which a person applying for relief had to be a legal resident of the parish granting it.

During this period of massive and rapid economic development, it was important that laborers should be encouraged—or, as a minimum, not discouraged—in seeking new jobs in another locality, so that they would move not only from agriculture to industry, say, but also from village to town. Parish administrators, however, were fearful of accepting officially any newcomer who after a short interval might be added to their relief rolls; there was a constant scramble to dump paupers on another parish and to prevent any reciprocation. Gilbert's 1765 bill to incorporate parishes into Poor Law "unions" passed the House of Commons but was defeated in the Lords, and some two decades later a bill did pass permitting (but not requiring) rural parishes to combine into such larger units. The 1834 Act established a three-member Poor Law Commission with the power to group parishes and to supervise the boards of guardians that would administer these larger unions, and presumably this partial relaxation of local control lessened the interparish competition. But in its essence not only was the law of settlement retained after 1834 but its enforcement was probably stricter. As the Poor Law Commission noted, some of the larger unions employed full-time inspectors to investigate the status of applicants for relief and to effect their removal if possible.[27] As early as 1798, in the First Essay, Malthus had condemned the practice: "The whole business of settlements . . . is utterly contradictory to all ideas of freedom. The parish persecution of men whose families are likely to become chargeable, and of poor women who are near lying-in, is a most disgraceful and disgusting tyranny."

The 1834 Act did not specify how relief should be given, though this had become one of the most contentious issues. The workhouses under parish jurisdiction had become notorious as places where the young were corrupted and the sick or old could live only in misery. Sir George Rose was instrumental in changing the provision in the law of settlement under which parishes could remove paupers to their place of legal residence, and in arranging for "outdoor relief"— that is, not in workhouses. These were converted into poorhouses, to which only the aged or infirm were admitted. The types of persons eligible for relief were distinguished also by fostering the establishment of so-called Friendly Societies, which were supposed to provide the poor with financial assistance, life insurance, and fellowship. By another law "vagrants" were given a grace period and then, if arrested, were to be segregated from paupers, so as not to encourage the dissemination of antisocial attitudes and criminal behavior. Nothing of this variegated effort to inhibit the general merging of "able-bodied" poor, infirm, and aged into one hopeless mass reappeared in the 1834 Act.

The most important of the earlier innovations, also, had consolidated all of the lower classes into worker-paupers, with little or no distinction remaining between the categories. Several parishes set a scale based on the price of bread and the size of the worker's family, with the difference between that norm and his earnings to be furnished out of public funds. According to the famous scale that Speenhamland (in Berkshire) established in 1795, for example, for each price from one to two shillings for a "gallon" loaf, and for each marital state from a single man or woman to a couple with seven children, the minimum income was stipulated. The device was popular with almost everyone concerned. The poor were safe from extreme want under all market conditions; employers could find workers at almost any wage they chose to pay; and many members of the general public found it desirable both to give charity to those in need of it and to inhibit, so it was thought, the spread of revolutionary ideas from France. How the system worked in practice can be illustrated by one instance. According to the 1828 testimony of the over-seer of Ash parish, in Kent, each Thursday there was a meeting there at which paupers were "put up to auction." The best workers received the full pay of twelve shillings a week; if an employer bid eight or ten, the balance was made up out of parish taxes.[28]

The difficulties in estimating the number of poor relate not only to inadequate statistics but to the ambiguity of the con-cept. If we define the bottom tenth, say, of any population as "in poverty," then obviously the poor are indeed always with us. (So it was that a president of the United States, close to the wealthiest country in the world with a relatively narrow differentiation among the several income classes, found it ex-pedient to declare a "war on poverty.") According to "crude and impressionistic" data, the national income per capita of England and Wales rose from £8 or £9 in 1700 to £12 or £13 in the 1750s and about £22 in 1800. The £12 for the 1750s translates into purchasing power of about £70 in the 1950s, a figure to compare with national incomes per capita for the 1950s of some £30 for Nigeria, only £25 for India. Such data "strongly suggest that the levels of living enjoyed by English-men on the threshold of the first industrial revolution were distinctly higher than those which prevail in present-day Southern Asia or Africa."[29] A temporal contrast leads to the same rough conclusion. With an increase in population from about 5.5 million in 1660 to almost 9.2 million in 1801, the number of poor in England and Wales might have increased simply because additions to the work force could hardly be absorbed so quickly into the developing economy. The trend, however, was in the other direction. In 1660, according to Greg-ory King's classification, about a quarter of the population was poverty-stricken in the literal sense of having to spend more than they earned. This was both a chronic condition and one that in times of trade depression or poor harvest reached epidemic proportions of possibly more than half the total population. According to a count in 1802, on the other hand, the number of applications for relief (including a multiple count of the many who applied two or three times during the year) amounted to 11 percent of the population.[30]

This does not mean, of course, that the considerable rise in national income per capita removed all problems. Even for those who had employment, wages were often inadequate. In 1787 a family with five minor children spent more than it earned for food, soap, and candles, thus incurring day by day a deficit before paying for rent, fuel, and clothing. Under such conditions many in the work force were pushed down into pauperdom. With the growth of population and the constant migration, the local budgets used to finance aid were under constant and increasing pressure. The annual average spent on relief, £690,000 in 1748–49, rose to more than £1.5 million in 1776 (or much more than the rise in the price of grain) and to £2 million in 1783–85 (in spite of a fall in the price of grain). The renewed war with France generated another serious inflation, whose effects on living conditions were aggravated by several bad harvests. And after peace was established in 1815, the cost of relief continued to rise, reaching a high point of almost £8 million, or about 85 percent of the total collected in parish taxes.[31] In shillings per capita, the rise in the poor rate was also dramatic—from 2/6 in 1688 to more than 3/6 in 1714, 5/0 in 1784, 8/10 in 1803, 12/8 in 1813, and a high point of 13/3 in 1818.[32] There is a strong suggestion in the series that population growth was one factor in the rise of poverty, an interpretation that Malthus supported. It was not of course the only factor, and the downward trend in these per capita costs after 1818 suggests that the economy was successfully accommodating to the continued increase in population, as well as benefiting from the cessation of the wars.

The Poor Law of 1834 was based on the Benthamite principle that relief should be available to the able-bodied poor only under conditions deliberately set to be worse than those of the lowest-paid independent worker. The Act also, as we have noted, brought about a partial centralization of control, mitigating the effects of separate administration by each parish. Each union was under a board of guardians, elected by the ratepayers of the parishes included in it; and all guardians were supervised by a Poor Law Commission, who under the control of the cabinet had a wide degree of discretion. The 1834 Act had an initially favorable reception, but when the economic boom faltered, dispute over all the old issues was resumed with heightened bitterness. Two obscure anonymous pamphlets, *An Essay on Populousness* (1838) and *On The Possibility of Limiting Populousness* (1838), discussed how

117

one might offset the growth of numbers by killing off babies painlessly with carbonic acid gas. These turgid effusions were given wide publicity by two Chartist newspapers and reprinted by a Rev. Joseph Rayner Stephens together with a "refutation of the Malthusian doctrine." The identity of "Marcus," who authored one of the pamphlets, its attackers did not know, "but the style is tinged with that of the Malthusian sage."[33]

The Poor Law Commission, weakened internally by a public division between Chadwick and several of the assistant commissioners, was increasingly attacked by critics of all political orientations. Some local officials (mostly shopkeepers, proprietors of pubs, or, in the countryside, small farmers) lacked supervision altogether, and abuses allegedly proliferated. The commission's enemies delightedly reported one particularly savory scandal: the master of the Andover workhouse had cut the diet of able-bodied inmates so much that they gnawed at the rotten bones they had been assigned to crush. However inadequate the relief, however degraded its recipients became, its cost continued to drain a major part of taxes into a pit of apparently infinite capacity.

MALTHUS ON THE POOR LAWS

Malthus's criticisms of the Old Poor Law[34] were more hateful to his adversaries than anything else he ever wrote. "Christ says, or virtually says, 'Feed the hungry. Clothe the naked. Take the stranger in' . . . But Mr. Malthus has now taught us that the distressed poor are intruders, that they have no business where they are, and that the relief that is given them should be extremely scanty."[35] In Malthus's judgment, welfare payments may indeed have "alleviated a little the intensity of individual misfortune," and "in particular cases the individual good may be so great, and the general evil so slight, that the former may clearly overbalance the latter." The *main* effect of the Poor Law, however, was to "spread the evil over a much larger surface." While more and more money was poured into relief, the number of paupers increased and their distress often worsened. The reason was that the system, though founded on the best of intentions and generally administered by men of good will, was based fundamentally on "a gross error," a misunderstanding of the way the labor and commodity markets interacted.

Suppose, Malthus suggested, that every laborer were to be given three shillings a day extra, so that he might buy meat for his dinner. Most of the meat would continue to go to the well-to-do, who would still be able to buy it at the price to which it would rise with so large an increase in the demand. Because of the higher taxes needed to finance the additional relief, "the rich might become poor, and some of the poor rich," but the distribution of commodities would still depend on differences in purchasing power. If the production of meat rose, it would ordinarily mean a reduction in the grain harvested, and thus a higher price of the poorest sector's staple food. Neither justices of the peace nor even Parliament, however many believed this to be so, had the power merely "by publishing a particular edict to make the supply at once equal to or greater than the demand."

One effect of the Poor Law was to divert food to inmates of workhouses from "the more industrious and more worthy" members of the lower classes, of whom a larger number might therefore also become dependent. The goods made by the inmates of workhouses, moreover, deprived the free laborers of a portion of their market. Malthus quoted from F. M. Eden, "Whether mops and brooms are made by parish children or by private workmen, no more can be sold than the public is in want of." The impoverishment of those "whose only possession is their labor" was not only in their material consumption but also through their spiritual degradation. For if relief is given, someone must have the power to discriminate between those eligible and not eligible to receive it, and to manage the places where paupers are congregated.

Any great interference with the affairs of other people is a species of tyranny, and in the common course of things the exercise of this power may be expected to become grating to those who are driven to ask for support. The tyranny of church wardens and overseers is a common complaint among the poor; but the fault does not lie so much in these persons, who probably before they were in power were not worse than other people, but in the nature of all such institutions.

To this day several of the points that Malthus raised have remained constants in debates about the administration of welfare. How shall recipients of relief be distinguished, and what divisions shall be made within the pauper class? Again and again, attempts have been made to differentiate those unable to work because of their age or disability from the able-bodied, as they were called in Malthus's time. But the trend over the decades has been to challenge the rationale behind any such distinction: a person unemployed because of the slack labor market is no more at fault than one suffering from a physical infirmity. The difference, in Malthus's view, is that the inability is in one case absolute, in the other case partly contingent on such factors as the workman's pride. Society could inhibit the skid of respectable workers into dependent poverty by surrounding pauperdom with a sense of shame, helping each person on the brink to bolster his self-reliance and self-respect. "Hard as it may appear in individual instances, dependent poverty ought to be held disgraceful. Such a stimulus seems to be absolutely necessary to promote the happiness of the great mass of mankind." For if the line becomes blurred between worker and pauper, with all below the upper classes merging into worker-pauper, most will have lost in the process any will or ability to reinstate themselves once the conditions improve. For this reason the long-run effects of the English Poor Law were, in Karl Polanyi's word, "ghastly." "Although it took some time till the self-respect of the common man sank to the low point where he preferred poor relief to wages, . . . little by little the people of the countryside were pauperized . . . But for the protracted effects of the allowance system, it would be impossible to explain the human and social degradation of early capitalism."[36]

The second major point that Malthus made was, as John Rickman wrote in a letter to Southey, "We cannot make the poor comfortable without making them increase and multiply."[37] Payments of the Speenhamland type, in which wage subsidies and family allowances were confused, meant that the relief received by the pauper-worker depended in part on the number of his children. Employers could therefore pay lower wages to those with larger families and thus, according to evidence before several parliamentary committees, preferred to hire fathers. Farmers in many villages "will not employ single men at all. In others they pay them at a much lower rate of wages for the same work in the hope of driving them to seek work out of the parish."[38] "Men who receive but a small pittance know that they have only to marry, and that pittance will be augmented in proportion to the number of their children."[39] "The single laborer not only is *no better off,* but is in a *worse situation than the married man.*"[40] Such statements, only a sample from many others of witnesses testifying during these decades, constitute good circumstantial evidence that fertility rose as a consequence of the criteria by which relief was distributed. They are no proof of the relation, of course, but it is difficult to imagine what solid proof could be adduced from the data available.

Modern analysts have used the partial and inadequate statistics to arrive at opposite conclusions. According to Krause, in 1821 the four most industrial counties had 667 children under age 5 per thousand women aged 15–49, as contrasted with only 580 in the rest of England. Since infant and child mortality was probably greater in the most industrial counties, the higher child-woman ratio there is doubly impressive. Blackmore and Mellonie, with what Marshall termed "a touching faith in the sanctity of even the shadiest figures," proved to their own temporary satisfaction that the Speenhamland system had effected a *decline* in the birth rate. Some months later, however, they offered "a second analysis" showing that there was no relation between the subsidy and fertility. From the same data Huzel concluded that "the allowance system did not operate to increase birth or marriage rates, but possibly meant a reduction in infant mortality, although not substantial enough to affect the general death rate or to increase noticeably the rate of population growth."[41] Perhaps the most ambitious analysis to reach this conclusion was by Mark Blaug, who dismissed the contemporary evidence with a quip: "To a generation drunk on Malthusian wine, the population argument seemed irrefutable." He believed that the allowance system reduced infant mortality, thus distorting the level of fertility when this was measured by the child-woman ratio. The basis of his principal analysis was a division between "Speenhamland" and "non-Speenhamland" counties, according to returns from Poor Law authorities to a questionnaire distributed in 1824. In the question, "Do *any* laborers in your district employed by the farmers receive either the whole or any part of the wages . . . out of the Poor Rates?" the key word was the italicized "any." Not only is an analyst faced with the well known limitations of an ecological correlation, but the number of workers receiving benefits in each of the small number of parishes that responded could have ranged from a single case to all.[42] In other words, it is impossible to test Malthus's allegation statistically, for the data are far too poor to make even the most strenuous effort worthwhile.

Nor is the feasibility of analysis much greater with more recent data. During the 1930s many European countries enacted family subsidies or other types of pronatalist devices, none of which, it would seem, raised fertility.[43] However, the fact that, for example, those in Sweden who were given marriage loans still had fewer children than the national average[44] tells us nothing about how large the families of those particular couples would have been with no stimulus from the state. In other words, effectiveness should be measured not against the actual trend of another sector of the population, but against a hypothetical continuation of the fertility curve as it would have been under such circumstances. In any case, the several commentators who have used such pronatalist incentives to test the validity of Malthus's analysis of welfare recipients have ignored the radically different psychological settings of two types of family formation. Parents of small families matched the cost of bearing and rearing children against the probable satisfaction of having them; recipients of welfare typically did not govern their procreation by such a rational calculation.

Both Britain and the United States have adopted modern counterparts of the Speenhamland system of supplementing low wages out of taxes. When Britain's Family Income Supplement was first proposed in 1970, the Labour party and many academics opposed it—not, however, because it repeated the well established faults of the nineteenth-century pattern, but because it required a means test. As the law was eventually passed, families with a gross income less than a figure that Parliament stipulated received a supplement based on the number of dependent children; in 1977 the prescribed amount was £39 a week for a family with one child, plus £4.50 for each additional child. Not all households eligible for the additional income have applied for it, and many of those that have participated have understated their earnings in order to get larger payments.[45] As also with other systems, some of the poor are too proud to accept benefits, and some of those who do accept them are so lacking in self-respect that they try to cheat.

Under an American law passed in 1964, eligible families may purchase food stamps in a quantity based on their earnings and the number of their dependents. In a simple case, in 1977 a family of four with a monthly net income of $360 to $390 could buy for $104 coupons worth $166 in the purchase of food. But very poor families received their allotment free, and those near the upper limit of eligibility had to pay proportionately more, depending on not only current income but also the family's assets. In 1977 participants in the program numbered over 18 million, with a total subsidy of $6,000 million, or by far the largest item in the Department of Agriculture's budget. According to an analysis of a sample county, administrative costs at the local level amounted to an additional 23 percent of the payments made. The rules are so complex that, according to a survey by the federal department, the poorly educated among the participants do not understand them well enough to apply for all that they are entitled to under the law.[46] This complexity has undoubtedly also encouraged the widespread and well publicized fraud. In-kind transfers are inherently inefficient, and their very existence impedes the enactment of a more satisfactory welfare system.

To my knowledge no one has tried to analyze the effect on fertility of either Britain's Family Income Supplement or the American food-stamp program. In the rather few studies of similar programs, a typical beginning is to declare that there can be no conclusive evidence one way or the other. "Everything depends on the viewpoint a person or organization or government adopts"; "no rigorous scientific demonstration can be made that income maintenance will lead to a higher birth rate or that it will not."[47] Yet both of these authors proceeded to argue that in all likelihood social security has no effect on fertility—for to admit the contrary would mean that programs designed to alleviate poverty in fact help to aggravate it. One argument of modern liberals is that family subsidies are typically too small to pay for the cost of another child. In Canada, for example, "from the viewpoint of deductive logic, it is plainly 'bad economics' to bring a child into the world in order to receive a $6 per month allowance, even as a marginal matter."[48] But if the testimony before the parliamentary committees and Poor Law commissions accurately reported the situation in Malthus's time, the choice then was a bit sharper. A single man, or even a married one without children, had a smaller chance of being hired altogether; by limiting his fertility he would lose not a slight increment to his income but a job.

In an argument concerning fertility, however, the main fault of calculating the cost of another child against the additional payment received for it is the premise that those living in poverty typically behave rationally in begetting their offspring. As Malthus argued, one of the most deleterious effects of being poor is that, on the contrary, one is likely also to be fatalistic, feckless, irresponsible, without a belief in the future and therefore with no plans for it. Those at the bottom receive from welfare payments just enough to float along, but no genuine stimulus to exert themselves and become self-reliant. In that sense, income-maintenance programs may well become programs to maintain poverty. That Malthus was opposed to them was only half of his policy; he also advocated a public effort to foster the embourgeoisement of the poor, to shift them into the social class that does not depend on public charity.

Apart from the several chapters of the *Essay* that I have been discussing, the main source on Malthus's view of the Poor Law was an open letter to Samuel Whitbread. A Foxite Whig prominent in the Commons for ten years, Whitbread could be considered, in the words of the *Times,* "England's greatest and most useful citizen."[49] As overseer of the poor in his Bedfordshire parish, he became all too well acquainted with their condition, and he struggled to find ways to help them.[50] In 1807 Whitbread addressed the Commons in a speech on the Poor Law that attracted much attention. He proposed that a system of national education be established with a school in every parish. "I am confident that . . . every man in England and Wales will, as in Scotland, feel it a disgrace not to have his children instructed." Second, he proposed the establishment of a national institution through which the poor could invest without brokerage charges or taxes. Settlement in a parish would be fixed after five years' residence, with magistrates given the right to adjudicate disputed cases.[51]

Whitbread's opinion was that "a better man than Malthus

does not exist."[52] Though he found the general principles of the *Essay* to be "incontrovertible," and though Malthus's design and intention were "most benevolent," Whitbread disagreed with many of the conclusions—in particular, the view that the Poor Law not only had failed to achieve its objective but had produced more wretchedness than would have existed without it. Malthus's proposal, which he quoted, had been that "no child born from any marriage taking place after the expiration of a year from the date of the law, and no illegitimate child born two years from the same date, should ever be entitled to parish assistance." But even so gradual an abrogation of public assistance to the poor would, in Whitbread's opinion, convert them into "a most formidable body" of "dangerous enemies."[53]

In his response, Malthus also stressed his high regard for his adversary. Whitbread's plan for nationwide free schooling he found admirable. While "it is certainly true that a man who has brought himself and [his] family on the parish by his own idleness and vices deserves to be distinguished from those who have been only unfortunate," Malthus did not think it practical, as Whitbread had suggested, to make the "criminal poor" wear a distinctive mark. And Malthus was apprehensive about the clause empowering parishes to build cottages—which would have been the first step into the maw of tax-supported housing. Malthus had denied that the poor have a "natural right" to support because, in F. M. Eden's words, "it may be doubted whether any right, the gratification of which seems to be impracticable, can be said to exist." The state's role in ministering to the poor should be gradually reduced and replaced, in Malthus's view, by a "moral obligation of private, active, and discriminate charity," which he had supported in the "strongest language" of which he was capable.[54]

Dependent poor have remained a social problem, indeed often a growing one. Once children are born, it is good social policy to provide care for them, not only because a minimum humanitarian impulse demands it, but because long-run costs would be less if such children could become healthy and independent members of society. But there are families in the United States that have been on welfare for three generations, and nothing in social security has succeeded in getting such persons established as full members of society. Welfare programs, once initiated, typically grow without limit. Aid to Families with Dependent Children, which started during the interwar depression as a modest, seemingly temporary ameliorative, in 1977 was providing care for one child in every eight in the American population.[55]

If from the point of view of twentieth-century liberals Malthus stressed too much one side of a painful dilemma, he at least saw that it was a dilemma, and one not to be resolved with sentimentality.

URBANIZATION AND EMIGRATION

The two theories that demographers use to make sense of large differences over long periods, Malthus's principle of population and the demographic transition, both pertain to the relative balance between fertility and mortality. Both, thus, pass over the third basic element in population change. The omission of migration is an especially serious lacuna in an analysis of the hundred years centering on 1800. The remarkable growth of Britain's industrial towns was effected in large part by the in-migration of new factory workers from other parts of the United Kingdom; and from the end of the Napoleonic wars to the 1840s, emigration from Western Europe rose to unprecedented numbers. The conventional distinction between internal and international migration, which sometimes is less an aid than a hindrance to analysis, is particularly inappropriate in a discussion of movements within or from the United Kingdom in the early decades of the nineteenth century. The Irish or Scots who went to England, and the Irish who went to Scotland, were quasi-aliens; and presumably the motivations for their departure were essentially the same as those of migrants to the growing cities of their own countries or to overseas destinations.

Reliable statistics on internal migration, as on most social phenomena, began to be collected only after the period on which I am concentrating. After a partial count in the 1841 census, full data on the birthplace of each person in the population were first collected ten years later, or after urban growth had passed its highest rate. In 1851 there were almost three-quarters of a million Irish-born in Britain, plus perhaps almost as many born in Britain of Irish parents. For the prior half-century, migration within the British Isles can be very roughly estimated from comparisons of place sizes at successive censuses; and for the latter decades of the eighteenth century estimates must be even more approximate.[56]

In a later era rural-urban migrants would typically be self-selected for their greater adaptability, but the first of the factory workers had no craft tradition or other incentive to produce well; mostly casual laborers, they gave "factories" the same negative connotation as the allied "workhouses." In 1835–37 the Poor Law Commission itself removed about four thousand laborers and their families from agricultural regions in the South to the industrial Midlands, but when the new jobs dried up in the depression of 1837, the migrants were sent back to the parishes they had left. Anti-Poor Law committees were established to block, sometimes with riots, the influx of what were seen as potential or actual strikebreakers sent to the North in order to maintain wages at a low level. Improvements in conditions may have come less from the successive factory acts than from the introduction of steam power, which necessitated a higher level of skill in the operators. By 1838 a factory inspector noted that "the population connected with the works are much respected by the population of the neighboring country and associate freely with their own grade, and intermarriages with the agricultural population are not infrequent."[57]

The shift from water power to steam meant also that a widely dispersed industry became highly concentrated. Cotton manufacture around Belfast declined, and in Britain it grew mainly in Lancashire, where new cotton towns developed by a sizable in-migration especially from villages that earlier had had many handloom weavers. Cities became larger by the removal to them of many villagers rendered economically surplus in their home districts by both the more efficient agricultural practices introduced with enclosures and the increase in the rural population. By the time of the agricultural depression of the late 1830s and early 1840s, it was no longer possible to absorb the overflow of village poor into the still relatively prosperous manufacturing regions. Paupers were set to building railways, some 50,000 of them according to a contemporary estimate. But the irritant of rising costs and worsening poverty induced the government to try to generate a migration overseas as well.

European states operating under what Adam Smith called the mercantile system had hoarded not only gold but also population, which was regarded as a delicate plant that would flourish only under attentive care. In Malthus's view, to continue the metaphor, it was rather a weed that unless kept under control would overwhelm one's property. These generalizations, however, do not apply fully to emigration. Indeed, France under Colbert had shipped women off to the colonies and punished soldiers who refused to marry them; "in the same breath mention is made of shiploads of women, mares, and sheep, the methods of propagating human beings and cattle being regarded as roughly on the same plane."[58] Paradoxically, Britain's mercantilist policy developed fully after the end of the Napoleonic wars, together with the general rise of laissez-faire. And Malthus's position on the emigration schemes that the government devised was less negative than one might have anticipated from his general theory.

Earlier emigration from the British Isles, mostly from Northern Ireland, had been interrupted by the wars; and in 1817–18, when the total expenditure for poor relief reached £8 million, taxes in heavily burdened parishes amounted to almost half the rents collected. In the spring of 1815 British administrators planned to send to Canada 2,000 from Ireland, 2,000 from Scotland, and a smaller number from England. The execution of the scheme was delayed, and the 699 who finally embarked arrived in Quebec City too late in the year to journey to Upper Canada (now Ontario) and build shelters before the onset of winter. They were maintained in Quebec at government expense, then also for another year after their removal, and (because of a crop failure) some of the families for an additional two years. The unexpectedly high cost dampened whatever enthusiasm the Cabinet had had, and for a period efforts were concentrated on diverting to the British colony of Upper Canada some of the emigrants who landed in New York. Several hundred settlers were conveyed also to the Cape of Good Hope, whose Xhosa marauders found the large number of cattle protected by a small number of men irresistibly attractive. Though neither project was remarkably successful, the nuclei established in both Canada and Africa became the basis for promoting emigration on a larger scale. "The settlers experienced unnecessary hardship and disappointment, but those who were responsible were never compelled to digest their own mistakes."[59]

The man most responsible for developing further migration

schemes was Robert John Wilmot Horton.[60] Elected to the Commons in 1814, he became Under-Secretary for War and the Colonies in 1822. By his emigration plan, pauper families were to be sent from a British port to Upper Canada and maintained there until they were able to provide for themselves. Each family would be allotted a hundred acres as the basis of future independence. The cost, estimated at £35 per adult male pauper, would be financed initially by loans to parishes with local taxes as security and then, over the longer run, by low rents on the property of the established settlers. "Until all the colonies of the British Empire are saturated, and millions added to those who speak the English language and carry with them the liberty and the laws and the sympathies of their native country," the planned emigration could proceed indefinitely.[61]

One extension of Wilmot Horton's plan was a nameless corps consisting mostly of half-pay naval officers, who over several decades developed from an investigation of abuses in the passenger trade into a government agency to promote emigration. An ad hoc body of men with no particular training, no supervision, and very imprecise instructions, the agency was more in the eighteenth-century style than the bureaucratic counterparts that developed later.[62] The Colonial Office in London had no more than three dozen persons of all ranks on its staff in 1831, and its decisions concerning policy in New South Wales, for example, might take a whole year to communicate. In any case, its well considered plans were often vetoed by the far more powerful Treasury, for in those days the government showed a greater reluctance to spend a few hundred pounds than it now has in dispensing millions.[63]

A more important successor to Wilmot Horton was Edward Gibbon Wakefield, "builder of the British Commonwealth,"[64] who had a strong influence on Lord Durham's famous report on British North America. One recurrent theme in the report was the contrast between the United States, where "all is activity and bustle," and Canada, where "all seems waste and desolation." Canada's stagnation, Durham asserted in pure Wakefield language, was caused by "an erroneous land system, which scattered settlement and discouraged organized enterprise." Wakefield's followers denigrated Wilmot Horton's efforts to "shovel out paupers," but in fact the schemes the two developed had the same purposes and many common features. Their rationale has continued to our own day, with the passage of British emigrants to Canada or Australia paid out of public funds both to relieve Britain's economy of persons seen as surplus and to build commercial and sentimental ties among members of the former empire.

Whatever their specific details, the emigration schemes were not acceptable to many members of the British public. Some Irish scholars hold that efforts were routinely too little, too late: "a major scheme for state-aided emigration was not attempted."[65] But at the time some argued, on the contrary, that the state was trying to do too much. Opponents of what they termed "transportation" linked state-sponsored emigration to a word that had been used for the removal of criminals. English workers, Cobbett maintained, should stay in England, where for them conditions could only improve; but for those of the middle classes seeking to escape oppressive taxation he wrote his *Emigrant's Guide*. "It is not the aged, the infirm, the halt, the blind, the idots that go; it is the youth, the strength, the wealth, the spirit that will no longer brook hunger and thirst."[66] "Thank God," Sadler wrote of the asseverations in an emigration report, "these notions are as absurd and impolitic as they are selfish and cruel."[67] On the other hand, according to letters from emigrants to the United States or Canada (as filtered through a strong proponent of the schemes), "any laborer or mechanic who is willing to exert himself may be sure of obtaining full employment at high wages."[68]

Was the intervention of the government a necessary stimulus to emigration; did it benefit the British economy, the welfare of the emigrants, and the rise of the British Commonwealth? These are large questions to which answers can hardly be found by drawing a balance between the extreme statements on either side. At a time when passage on a packet from Liverpool to New York cost perhaps £30, one on a timber ship leaving from small ports throughout the British Isles cost as little as 26s.[69] Later, as land companies and Canadian railways competed for settlers, the fares sometimes fell even lower. Over these decades, no more than perhaps one in twenty of British emigrants received government assistance. In this era for the first time in history free migration became a mass phenomenon; individuals or families or groups bound by religious or other ties left of their own volition, repelled by conditions at home or attracted by those abroad, or, most often, inspired to seek a new way of life by the rising expectations that improvements in British society had engendered. It is paradoxical that, while this migration was rising to its maximum flow, political economists and statesmen were fussily arguing about whether and how to bring about the departure of a mere 5 percent of those leaving.

MALTHUS ON MIGRATION

Common sense tells us that if a thousand persons migrate from Country A to Country B, the population of Country A is cut by a thousand and that of Country B is increased by the same number. This simplistic equation is valid only in the short run, and how migration influences the growth of the two populations is in fact much more complex. Under some circumstances the effect of an outflow on the sending population is close to nil, for whatever relaxation the emigration brings about in the ecological balance results immediately in a lower infant mortality, a higher fertility, or both. However, if the movement is out of an area with an initially low population density, the subsequent growth can be much smaller than the commonsensical equation would suggest; for migrants are characteristically young adults who take with them, as it were, their future progeny. Thus, the departure of a proportion of Britain's villagers resulted *in some instances* in rural depopulation, for the residual elderly could not reproduce themselves.[70] At the receiving end, similarly, the long-term consequences of migration also depend on the particular circumstances, often being larger or smaller than the number of migrants would lead one to anticipate.

In short, the relation between migration and the size of the two populations depends on three components: (1) the direct movement of the migrants themselves; (2) the effect of the movement on the age structure of the two areas, which ordinarily increases the size of the transfer by raising the mortality and lowering the fertility of the sending population, and by raising the fertility and lowering the mortality of the receiving population; and (3) the effect on social-economic conditions in the two areas, which may enhance, reduce, or cancel the results of the transfer. In the abstract, one can say that all of these components are always relevant. In the concrete, their impacts are separately discernible only in such extreme cases as, for example, emigration from a very densely settled country like India or immigration to a relatively empty one like Britain's American colonies. But most advocacy of migration policy has been based on only the first of the three components. For instance, the fact that for some decades Australia denied admission to Asians (however objectionable this might have been on other grounds) did not in fact—as many alleged—help maintain the overpopulation and thus the poverty of India and China. As another example, when in 1945 the Netherlands was faced with a depleted postwar economy and a rapidly growing population, its institution of subsidized emigration was also based on false reasoning and thus was bound to fail.[71]

Malthus's doctrine on how migration affects population reflected some of the actual complexity of the relation, though commentators have sometimes taken his illustrative examples for simplistic points. The settlement of colonies, he wrote, was typically a precarious enterprise, partly because of the usual hostility of those already in possession of the land, partly because in any case the establishment of a new resource base required more than ordinary perseverance and luck. Once living conditions in a new colony became less rugged, the flow following the pioneers was likely to be far greater; but the effect on the sending population would still be "of short duration." Emigrants had left almost every European state in search of a better life, but their departure had not reduced appreciably the pressure of population on their home countries' resources. In sum:

> With any view of making room for an unrestricted increase of population, emigration is perfectly inadequate; but as a partial and temporary expedient . . . it seems to be both useful and proper; and if it cannot be proved that governments are bound actively to encourage it, it is not only strikingly unjust but in the highest degree impolitic in them to prevent it. There are no fears so totally ill grounded as the fears of depopulation from emigration . . . Emigration . . . at the present moment is well worth the attention of the government, both as a matter of humanity and policy.[72]

One might say that these general principles were supplemented in Malthus's testimony before the 1827 Committee on Emigration, but from the chair Wilmot Horton controlled the discussion so completely that his expert witness repeatedly responded with no more than "No doubt" or "Certainly," as well as often a paraphrase of "I do not know." The testimony pertained almost entirely to Ireland, and Malthus was asked to review some of the points I have already noted. By the estimate that he cited, its population had increased from 4.68 million in 1792 to 7.50 million in 1827, in spite of the slower growth because of the recent greater distress and probably higher mortality. The introduction of a poor law might bring some immediate relief but only at the cost of aggravating the problem. The movement of Irish to Scotland and England, Malthus believed, tended to reduce wages in those countries by intensifying the competition for low-level jobs. The dependence on the potato was pernicious; the Irish "are inclined to be satisfied with the very lowest degree of comfort, and to marry with little other prospect than that of being able to get potatoes for themselves and their children." What, he was asked, would "produce a taste for comfort and cleanliness?" "Civil and political liberty, and education."

Under Wilmot Horton's prompting, Malthus was willing to agree that both Britain and the colonies in North America would benefit from migration, though he added that "these colonies may not always belong to the British Empire . . . There might not for a considerable time be a particular wish on the part of the colonies to separate, but they may be conquered by the United States." "Do you not consider that the introduction of population is one of the best securities against that event?" "I think it is." This typical mercantilist argument is not one that Malthus advanced in other contexts. Without a leading question, he discussed migration in its relation to the population-resources ratio. Some expenditure was advisable to pay for a resettlement of Irish in Canada, but such an outlay could not be continued indefinitely. If without any financial pressure Britain could effect a constant sizable emigration, "you would no doubt keep the population in a better state. But if such a current emigration were to stop at any time, you would have a still greater tendency to a redundancy."[73]

A collection of Malthus's letters to Wilmot Horton, twenty in all dated from 1823 through 1831, was discovered in 1962 and subsequently published. In spite of the sometimes careless editing, they are a valuable addendum to the better known testimony, for without the insistently leading questions from the chair Malthus was able to develop some points that never came out before the Emigration Committee. His "principal objection" to Wilmot Horton's scheme, he wrote, was that "the character of the population which parishes are most inclined to get rid of would not in general make the most industrious and efficient settlers." The estimated cost of £35 to transport and settle one vigorous young emigrant might be a good guess, "but a person who had been for any time on a parish in England would probably have become somewhat indolent, and his habits of not depending on his own exertions would probably be carried with him into the new settlement." If something resembling the English Poor Law had to be transferred with the paupers whom the state assisted to emigrate, the project would obviously be somewhat more expensive. On November 8, 1827, several months after Wilmot Horton had summed up Malthus's evidence in a manner that showed that he agreed fully with the scheme, his star witness wrote to spell out serious doubts about its financial viability if applied to a "national system of emigration adopted as a permanent measure." Once the principal and interest of the cost of still more emigration reached a sufficiently onerous level, why should one expect Canadians to continue paying? Would not such indebtedness alienate them from the mother country, thus negating one of the supposed benefits of the scheme? These objections, Malthus repeated, did not apply to a temporary sacrifice incurred to encourage emigration over a short period in order to alleviate such a particular deleterious factor as a change in the management of landed property or in the application of the Poor Law.[74]

In sum, Malthus's stand on both emigration schemes and the Poor Law was based on his attempt to find a compromise between short-term benefits and the avoidance of yet greater harm over the long run. If the relaxation of ecological pressure was used to institute a more fundamental adjustment in the balance between population and food, it could have a permanently positive effect. But if this leeway was squandered, then eventually the problem would recur in a more intense form.

7

Population Growth

A COMMON ANACHRONISM in current appraisals of Malthus is to underestimate the difficulty in obtaining at that time the most elementary and —by modern Western standards—most routine facts about population. The state control of the economy that mercantilism connotes did include, it is true, the intention of keeping track of the state's subjects; but in the few scattered instances when this was done at all competently, the results were regarded as state secrets. Austria, for example, had a census in 1754, but the enumeration lay buried in the archives until this century, when it was rediscovered. There were eighteenth-century censuses in France also, and in 1694 a head count was ordered and a questionnaire distributed; returns from three districts are extant, but whether the forms were completed throughout the country and have since been lost is not clear.[1] The first enumeration of a total population may have been in the colony of New France (present-day Quebec) in 1665, and sixteen censuses were completed there over the next century. The earliest counts that any country made of its own population were probably in Scandinavia; like clergy elsewhere, Sweden's Lutheran ministers had long been keeping records of their parishioners, and at five-year intervals from 1749 on the government required the pastors to submit data from which population totals could be calculated. Gradually a similar secularization of ecclesiastical records was effected in Denmark and Iceland. These bits and pieces, however one appraises them individually, are seldom enough to lay a basis for a satisfactory record of even one country, and for the entire Western world we must make do with rather rough guesses.

POPULATION OF BRITAIN

Britain's first census was not taken until 1801, and earlier counts of particular cities or regions, made for such purposes as compiling lists of taxpayers, were doubly defective as a base from which to estimate the total population. The vital statistics collected by parish officials were not collated; and with the growing numbers both of Dissenters and of Anglicans unwilling to pay the fee for registering a marriage, birth, or death, more and more persons were left out of the church records. Proposals in the middle of the eighteenth century to establish a census and a comprehensive registration system came to nothing at that time.[2] It was against this background of sparse and poor data that a debate could flourish on whether Britain's population was growing or decreasing. In David Glass's reconstruction of the controversy, it fell into two stages, the first a relatively unnoticed confrontation between William Brakenridge and Richard Forster in the 1750s, the second a far noisier one during Malthus's lifetime with Richard Price and Arthur Young as the main antagonists.

Richard Price (1723–91) was the son of a Dissenting minister, "a bigoted Calvinist" according to the *Dictionary of National Biography,* against whom his son rebelled to become a nonconformist minister, "vaguely Unitarian but Arian rather than Socinian," and a writer on morals, politics, and economics. His plan to abolish the national debt opponents described as a "sort of hocus-pocus machinery" that would bring universal benefit with no loss to anyone. Opposed to the war with the American colonies, he was invited by the insurgent states to cross the Atlantic and take charge of their finances. In his cordial letter of refusal, he said that he looked to the United States as "now the hope, and likely soon to become the refuge, of mankind." As a friend of Benjamin Franklin, he wrote an open letter commenting on Franklin's pamphlet on the increase of mankind, and this can be regarded as a preliminary version of his *Essay on the Population of England* (1780). According to his data, the number of houses in England and Wales had decreased from 1,319,215 at the time of the Revolution of 1688 to fewer than a million. "While other countries are increasing, this country, in consequence of the causes of depopulation which have unhappily distinguished it, has for many years been decreasing."[3] The causes of this depopulation were three disastrous wars, the high price of food, the emigration of Englishmen, and, "above all," the increase of luxury and of public taxes and debts.

Arthur Young (1741–1820) was also the son of a divine, who wrote a book enchantingly entitled *An Historical Dissertation on Idolatrous Corruptions in Religion from the Beginning of the World, and on the Methods Taken by Divine Providence in Reforming Them.* His father died when Young was eighteen, leaving him, as he put it in his autobiography, "without education, profession, or employment."[4] For several years he farmed, not too successfully, a portion of the land he inherited, and then moved to farm in other regions. During his lifetime he wrote a number of books on agriculture and farm animals, four novels, and accounts of travels through the countryside of England, Ireland, and France. *Political Arithmetic,* the felicitous title of his book on population, is probably better known than its contents; Young described it as "one of my best works, which was immediately translated into many languages and highly commended in many parts of Europe." According to the sketch in the *National Dictionary of Biography,* Young "remains the greatest of English writers on agriculture," but "he contributed nothing of permanent importance towards the advancement of political economy"— perhaps a harsher judgment than is warranted.

The basic theses of *Political Arithmetic* were that "employment creates population" and that since the increasing national wealth had stimulated a larger demand for labor, the population must also have grown. "Who supposes that a country of warrens, heaths, and farming slovens, converted to well tilled fields, does not occasion an increased demand for hands? And was it ever known that such a demand existed without being supplied?" The argument could be validated by the beginning growth of cities in the industrial Midlands; Birmingham, by his reckoning, grew from 23,000 in 1750 to 30,000 in 1770. In America, similarly, "marriages abound, because children are no burthen." In short, England was "more populous than ever." But what of the lists of houses or of windows (on which there was also a tax), which showed a decline and, presumably, a falling off also in the number of inhabitants? Young's response is worth quoting as a striking example of how poor the factual base was for all these speculations:

> Sir W. Petty made the number [of people] in England and Wales in 1682 amount to 7,400,000. Davenant in 1692 made them 7,000,000, but in the same tract he makes them 8,000,000 and in 1700 he quotes and approves from Mr. King a computation of 5,500,000. Sir M. Decker supposed them in 1742 (from 1,200,000 houses, at 6 to a house) 7,200,000. Dr. Mitchel[l] says the number is 5,700,000, Mr. Wallace 8,000,000, Templeman makes it the same, another supposes it 6,000,000, another 5,480,000, Mr. Smyth 6,000,000, Dr. Brakenridge 5,340,000, another 8,000,000, Dr. Price 4,500,000.
>
> From the accounts we have had of former enumerations, there are reasons to think they were taken with much inaccuracy.[5]

The debate was carried on also in two short works by David Hume and Robert Wallace—respectively, *Of the Populousness of Ancient Nations* and *A Dissertation on the Numbers of Mankind in Ancient and Modern Times*.[6] From a theoretical analysis of potential growth, Wallace argued for the "superior populousness of antiquity," but even before his book was published, Hume had introduced a welcome note of empirical realism: "We know not exactly the numbers of any European kingdom or even city at present; how can we pretend to calculate those of ancient cities and states, where historians have left us such imperfect traces?" The controversy attracted much attention not only in Britain but also among such French philosophes as Montesquieu and Rousseau and the German theorist Johann Peter Süssmilch.

In retrospect, it may seem strange that so much energy was expended debating a straightforward question on which no satisfactory statistics existed. The controversy was stimulated, of course, by the interesting assortment of interpretations that could be assigned to the precensus data or even to the first censuses themselves; but that does not explain why intelligent and busy men thought the exercise to be worthwhile. The debate in actuality was not merely about whether the population of Britain was becoming larger or smaller but mainly about greater issues: Was a large and rapidly growing population a sure sign of a society's good health? On balance, were the growth of industry and of cities, the movement of larger numbers from one social class to another—in short, all of what we now term "modernization"—a boon to the people or the contrary? And in society's efforts to resolve such dilemmas, could it depend on the sum of individuals' self-interest or was considerable state control called for?

If we define *conservative* by what the word's etymology suggests, as desirous to conserve elements of the past, and relate this denotation to Malthus's period, the definition leaves ambiguous what portion of the past was to be maintained. To an extraordinary degree the university curricula of that day were built around two otherwise obsolete languages and the cultures in which they had flourished: every graduate was expected to know enough Latin and Greek to understand a phrase or two and to adorn his own conversation with an occasional tag. From the postulates (1) that a large and growing population is good and (2) that the ancient world had embodied a superior civilization, one could hardly avoid the conclusion that there had been a decline in numbers from ancient times. Not only did Malthus's professorship, as I have remarked, constitute an important innovation in curriculum, but his writings on political economy were quite free of the usual genteel affectations; he wrote in English and usually assumed that passages from French did not need translation, but he did not parade his knowledge of Greek and Latin. The "conservative" also looked back with nostalgia to the more recent past, when—according to the myth that grew even faster than the industrial cities—the ordinary Englishman had lived contentedly in a peaceful and pleasant world. There had been rural poor, but—as Southey and, as I have noted, Engels pointed out—unlike the new urban proletariat they had been rooted in their districts, with strong ties to their families and their employers.

With the whole of the educated class spiritually embedded in the Greek-Roman civilization, and with many persons of otherwise diverse political opinions looking back to prefactory days as a pastoral idyll, there was a strong disposition to see industrialization as degradation. And by the definition of well-being that Malthus was challenging, the degradation meant at least a slower growth of population, possibly even a decline in numbers. We also have no precise data, but the reconstruction of England's population growth summarized in the accompanying table is accurate enough to show the long-term rise and its acceleration during the first decades of the nineteenth

TABLE 3. ESTIMATED POPULATION OF ENGLAND AND WALES, 1086–1841.

DATE	POPULATION (MILLIONS)	SOURCE OF INFORMATION
1086	1.1	Domesday Book
1346	3.7	Poll tax, times estimated family size, times number of families
1377	2.2	Same, after Black Death
1545	3.2	Chantry lists
1695	4.8–5.5[a]	Gregory King's estimate
1801	9.2	
1811	10.2	
1821	12.0	Census returns
1831	13.9	
1841	15.9	

[a] The larger figure is King's; Glass has suggested the range given, with the most probable figure above its midpoint.

Sources: J. C. Russell, 1948; Glass, 1965.

century. The first figure is from the count that William the Conqueror had made of his new subjects. The estimates based on poll taxes or chantry lists are less accurate, for they depend in part on how well one can guess the size of the average household. In 1695 Gregory King estimated the population with a technical expertise well in advance of his day, and from that date to the first census just over a century later the population almost doubled. On this point at least Malthus was right, and his opponents were completely wrong.

The decline by 1.5 million out of a total of 3.7 million, the consequence of the series of epidemics known as the Black Death, was the most dramatic of the ups and downs over the centuries. In their reconstruction of these fluctuations, modern historians have in effect confirmed Malthus's thesis. Following a series of good harvests, the rates of marriage and fertility rose, and the population increased to above the level that could be supported when food became less abundant. According to an interesting hypothesis, the upswing in the English population during the eighteenth century constituted another of such long-term fluctuations. This "long wave," however, started from a higher level, and its momentum was maintained and, for a period, even accelerated. The transition to the modern period was under way: unless checked by a deliberate control of fertility, the population would continue to increase, it would seem, indefinitely.[7]

Though the first several censuses constituted a far better data base than anything that had preceded them, by modern standards they were markedly deficient. John Rickman, who supervised the first four counts, was competent and conscientious; but he started fresh with no specific organization. Enumeration was carried out by overseers of the poor, assisted by church officials and, if need be, by "constables, tithingmen, headboroughs, or other peace officers." With little confidence in the results so obtained, Rickman insisted that the schedule be kept short and simple. No question was asked even on age in the first two censuses, and in the next two the reply was on a voluntary basis; even with deficient data, it would have been possible to estimate the trend in Britain's fertility far more assuredly than with the statistics that were available. On the other hand, Rickman undertook pilot surveys to test alternative ways of determining respondents' occupations—a method of assessing questions that became routine a century or so later. Reviewing the results of the first census, he commented that "the total population of Great Britain must exceed the number of persons specified in the above summary, inasmuch as there are some parishes from which no returns have been received." Though the following counts were probably not so deficient, it was not until the 1841 census, carried out under a General Register Office on the basis of a fundamental change in procedure, that a reasonably complete and accurate enumeration could be assured.[8]

The final edition of the *Essay* has two chapters on the population of England, the first written just after the census of 1801, the second after the census of 1811 with an addendum written after that of 1821. That Malthus chose to present his material in this fashion rather than rewriting the whole has a certain advantage for the modern reader, for one sees vividly the contrast between the early speculations based on incomplete registrations of births and deaths and the later, more assured estimates derived from the censuses.

Increases indicated by census figures exceed by a considerable margin the estimates derived from the excess of births over deaths, which Malthus assumed to be grossly under-counted. He merely mentioned in passing alternative explanations of the discrepancy: that persons moving about were counted twice in the censuses, and that the population of England was increased that much by migration from Ireland and Scotland. In the portion of the chapter written after the 1811 census, Malthus compared two series of estimates, which I have adapted here in a table. Though he did not use the

TABLE 4. POPULATION OF ENGLAND, 1780–1810,
ACCORDING TO MALTHUS'S ESTIMATE (IN THOUSANDS).

DATE	ESTIMATED FROM UNCORRECTED BIRTH AND BURIAL REGISTRATIONS		ESTIMATED FROM NATURAL INCREASE, WITH CORRECTIONS FOR UNDERREGISTRATION AND DEATHS ABROAD	
	POPULATION	DIFFERENCE	POPULATION	DIFFERENCE
1780	7,953		7,731	
		63		267
1785	8,016		7,998	
		659		417
1790	8,675		8,415	
		380		416
1795	9,055		8,831	
		113		456
1800	9,168		9,287	
		660		550
1805	9,828		9,837	
		660		651
1810	10,488		10,488	

word *smoothing*, he followed the same technique to argue that the first series, derived from birth and burial registrations, was far less probable than the second, based on corrected birth and death registrations with an addendum also for the estimated number of deaths abroad. The jerky movement of the first series, with the initial increase less than a tenth of the second, would be acceptable only if it could be explained by some extraordinarily rapid shifts in the conditions affecting fertility and mortality. Lacking any evidence of such radical changes (which could hardly be hidden from even a casual view), Malthus concluded that the principal factor in the

irregular increase each five years was the inaccurate registration of births and deaths. And according to the consensus of
modern scholars, he was undoubtedly correct.

THE AMERICAN COLONIES

The pre-Columbian population of the Americas was so
small by European standards that the continent could be regarded almost as uninhabited. The main reason, as Malthus
pointed out in a chapter on American Indians, was that they
subsisted mostly from hunting, supplemented here and there
by "a most rude and imperfect agriculture." The low population density, however, was not merely the direct consequence
of food shortage, but also of "customs which operate sometimes with greater force in the prevention of a rising population than in its subsequent destruction." The Indian birth rate
was supposed to be low—according to Malthus's sources
(mainly William Robertson's *History of America*), because of
a "want of ardor in the men towards their women." As suggested in scattered reports also concerning other hunting and
gathering peoples, "the hardships and dangers of savage life"
diverted "attention from the sexual passion." In many tribes,
moreover, women did most of the hard labor, so that the danger of childbirth under primitive conditions was aggravated.
Among males, the high mortality from diseases was raised by
intermittent warfare. Nor did the beginning dissemination of
European civilization help matters. The introduction of guns,
for example, probably contributed to the destruction of wild-
life that several sources noted, thus making the dependence on
hunting yet more precarious. After a survey of other factors,
Malthus returned to the first of his positive checks: "in spite of
all the powerful causes of destruction that have been mentioned, the average population of the American nations is, with
few exceptions, on a level with the average quantity of food
which, in the present state of their industry, they can obtain."

This section on American Indians, also of interest in itself,
laid a foundation for the subsequent discussion of the white
population of what became the United States. In the four
northern colonies of New England, the population had
doubled each twenty-five years, rising from 21,200 in 1643 to
half a million in 1760. In New Jersey the period of doubling
was only twenty-two years, in Rhode Island still less. "In the
back settlements, where the inhabitants applied themselves

solely to agriculture, and luxury was not known, they were supposed to double their number in fifteen years." From the time of the first national census in 1790, the whole of the new country continued to grow by a doubling every twenty-five years. Supposedly, this increase derived mainly from the balance between births and deaths, only supplementarily from immigration.[9]

The best modern check on Malthus's estimates is a recent book by Robert Wells based on the 124 local censuses in the British colonies, 68 in North America and 56 in the West Indies. In London the Board of Trade continually used these counts to note the very rapid growth of the colonial population. In a report to the king in 1721, for example, the board suggested a number of imperial reforms, arguing from their remarkable increase in numbers that the colonists represented an enormous potential value to the home country. Earlier fears about whether the colonies could survive at all gave way to pride in their prosperity, a sentiment encouraged also by the defeat of the French in 1763. But in 1775 Edward Wigglesworth, a Harvard professor of divinity, concluded from his population projection that by 1825 more Englishmen would be living in the New World than the Old. "His message to his fellow colonists was clear—even if Great Britain wins the present struggle, we will win in the not too distant future."[10] The anomalous demography of the American colonies, in other words, had been well established, and Malthus needed but little research to document his statements.

According to Wells's summary, the demographic patterns of the English colonies varied greatly. Growth of population was generally relatively slow in the West Indies, only somewhat faster in Canada. From the first to the last censuses, the geometric rate of annual increase of the continental colonies ranged from 9.7 percent in Georgia and 9.4 percent in Nova Scotia down to 2.3 percent in Connecticut and in Newfoundland. This represented a doubling in, respectively, 7.49 and 21.35 years.[11] The most obvious differences that seemingly affected the rates of increase were the proportion black, which ranged from 90 percent in some of the smaller islands down to nil in several of the Canadian provinces, and the age and sex structure. Of the conservatively estimated 2.8 million persons in all of England's North American colonies in 1775, 78.7

percent lived in what became the United States, 17.3 percent in the islands, and only 4.0 percent in Canada.[12]

Malthus's explanation of the rapid growth of the mainland population was not based merely on the almost uninhabited land that the colonists took over.

> To the quantity of rich land which they possessed in common with the Spanish and Portuguese colonies, they added a greater degree of liberty and equality. Though not without some restrictions on their foreign commerce, they were allowed the liberty of managing their own internal affairs. The political institutions which prevailed were favorable to the alienation and division of property. Lands which were not cultivated by the proprietor within a limited time were declared grantable to any other person. In Pennsylvania there was no right of primogeniture, and in the provinces of New England the eldest son had only a double share. There were no tithes in any of the states, and scarcely any taxes. And on account of the extreme cheapness of good land, and a situation favorable to the exportation of grain, a capital could not be more advantageously employed than in agriculture, which, at the same time that it affords the greatest quantity of healthy work, supplies the most valuable produce to society.[13]

For Malthus, in short, the decisive factor was liberty, both economic and political; the potential prosperity implicit in the rich resources could be realized only through a social system that encouraged each producer to work hard by permitting him to retain almost all of what he produced rather than paying it out to church or state.

The importance of the American population in Malthus's theoretical structure is great. That the population doubled each twenty-five years was generalized in the geometric progression as the maximum potential growth under the most favorable conditions—a conservative estimate even from the smaller doubling periods that Malthus himself cited for several sectors of the colonial population. More important, the fact that in his view a population increase at this rate could benefit those concerned flatly contradicted the gloomy view commonly associated with "Malthusian" theory. In Europe the growth of population generally incurred economic costs, but in the relatively unsettled United States there were economic advantages. For each situation, then, there must be a best rate of growth, dependent on the development of the economy and the optimum relation of population to it. In spite of the classical economists' dominant concern with policy, they never developed the idea of a population optimum much beyond this beginning hint in Malthus. J. S. Mill took it one step further with his "law of diminishing returns," which was refined by Sidgwick. But the first clear statement of the concept of optimum population came from Cannan in 1888,[14] and not until well into the twentieth century was it refined—and then thoroughly muddled. But the underlying idea is to be found in Malthus's discussion of the American colonies: both the mercantilist dogma that population growth is always good and the popular "Malthusian" one that it is always bad must give way to a balanced view that its benefits depend on the circumstances.

The half-contradiction in Malthus's discussion of population policy is sharpened when we consider in that context the implications of his advocacy of nonproductive consumers, a point developed almost incidentally in Keynes's *General Theory*. If, as Keynes held, the marginal efficiency of capital is lower the greater the existing amount of capital, why should there not have been a long-term decline in its marginal efficiency during the nineteenth century? Because, Keynes wrote, "the growth of population and of invention, the opening up of new lands, the state of confidence and the frequency of war over the average of (say) each decade seem to have been sufficient."[15] In a review of *The General Theory*, Hicks picked up this point, which he called "Mr. Keynes's strongest card."

> It does become very evident, when one thinks of it, that the expectation of a continually expanding market, made possible by an increasing population, is a fine thing for keeping up the spirits of entrepreneurs. With increasing population, investment can go roaring ahead, even if invention is rather stupid; increasing population is therefore actually favorable to employment. It is actually easier to employ an expanding population than a contracting one, whatever arithmetic would suggest—at least this is so when expansion or contraction is expected, as we assume generally to be the case . . . This population point is enough in itself to establish the high significance of Mr. Keynes's theory of long-period unemployment.[16]

This became the dominant view of how population relates to the economy—expounded, for example, by a student of Keynes in a work called *The Economics of a Declining Population* and, in the United States, in a presidential address to the American Economic Association.[17] In the most grandiose extrapolation from Keynes's obiter dicta, Bladen proposed a "population interpretation" of modern capitalism. "Free enterprise may prove to have been a boom enterprise, and the modern trend to something like the old mercantilism may be a trend toward institutions appropriate to an era of stationary population."[18]

This dilemma is no longer at the center of demographers' attention. The very word "optimum" acted as an invitation to broaden the concept by introducing such factors as "general welfare," military strength, mean longevity, international trade, and even popular mood. And with the vast growth of social welfare, Keynes's analysis of unemployment has been superseded. But if we retain an economic definition of optimum and accept, at least for the sake of the argument, the idea that population growth can stimulate a capitalist economy, then there are two optima—what might be termed the Darwinian one relating people to resources and the Keynesian one relating consumers to the investment market. In nascent form both are in Malthus, and perhaps he can be excused for never having resolved the difference between them if one recalls that no one else has done it since then. The contradiction was closer to the surface in Keynes, who moved from a strong neo-Malthusian stance in the 1920s to the underpopulationist position of the 1930s, noting only that "when devil P. of Population is chained up, we are free of one menace; but we are more exposed to the other devil U. of Unemployed Resources than we were before."[19]

MATHEMATICAL ANALYSIS

Malthus's study of mathematics at Cambridge laid the base for the arithmetic and geometric progressions, which (as I have noted) many have found difficult to understand. In its final form, the *Essay* shows other indications of this training, though the presentation is often not what we would use today.[20] For example, his formula for projecting a population from a base figure and rates of fertility and mortality has different symbols from ours, though it follows the same principle.[21] Like all his contemporaries, Malthus used fractions rather than decimals, and to the modern reader such a figure as 1/79 (taken from this example) seems a bit archaic. In discussing the "unlimited" or "indefinite" improvement of human society that Condorcet had postulated as a law of nature, Malthus compared it to the concept of a mathematical limit:

> In the famous Leicestershire breed of sheep, the object is to procure them with small heads and small legs. Proceeding upon these breeding maxims [implicit in Condorcet and some cattle breeders], it is evident that we might go on till the heads and legs were evanescent quantities; but this is so palpable an absurdity that we may be quite sure the premises are not just . . . Though I may not be able in the present instance to mark the limit at which further improvement will stop, I can very easily mention a point at which it will not arrive.[22]

In the wide assortment of data that Malthus collected, there was a no less wide range of statistical competence, and he assayed his evidence judiciously. He noted, as one example, that in the 1760s a fear of depopulation had spread in Switzerland, and that Jean-Louis Muret seemingly substantiated this unease by showing that births had steadily declined over the past two centuries. But Malthus found it "strange" that Muret "should rest the whole proof of the depopulation of the Pays de Vaud on the proportion of births." Improved health had undoubtedly enabled the Swiss "to rear up to manhood a greater proportion of their children [and] had furnished the requisite population with a smaller number of births"—as one could conclude from Muret's own figures. And even Muret's interpretation of the birth data was faulty.

> He found that 375 mothers had yielded 2,093 children, all born alive, from which it followed that each mother had produced $5\frac{10}{12}$, or nearly six, children. These, however, were all actually mothers, which every wife is not . . . [Moreover,] on account of second and third marriages, the fecundity [in modern usage, fertility] of marriages must always be less than the fecundity of married women. The mothers alone are here considered, without reference to the number of husbands.[23]

Remarkably, this is a criticism highly pertinent today, for it has become usual to measure fertility by relating natality only to the women who bore the children—as though virgin births were routine throughout the world. In one exceptional study, the author showed that, of the females of fecund ages in one rural township of Taiwan, the percentage of widows had fallen by about half from 1905 to 1935. By the prolongation of *males'* life expectancy, thus, women's effective reproductive period was extended almost three years, and their completed family size by about one child.[24]

One mark of a professional demographer is that he subjects the data he uses to tests for internal consistency and accordance with the range expected from theory and other empirical evidence. The whole of the *Essay* is replete with analyses indicating that Malthus went far beyond the difficult task of compiling the widely scattered statistics. He applied his high standards first of all to himself. In a letter to Francis Horner, John Whishaw (who would soon become another influential Whig) enclosed a long statement from Malthus noting a mathematical error he had made in the 1803 edition of the *Essay* and requesting that the correction be printed in the *Edinburgh Review*.[25] In the third edition of the *Essay,* the whole passage was rewritten, but critics continued to attack Malthus on the point—the Rev. Robert Ingram, for instance, as late as 1808, after both the third and the fourth editions had been published.

In an interesting paper Boulding has translated the Malthusian theories into a series of models composed in the style of a modern economist. He begins with the thesis of the First Essay and then brings in preventive checks as an additional factor, noting that moral restraint is imposed as the standard of living is raised from bare subsistence to something more. Then he applies the model to a number of dynamic situations, and ends by asking whether the exercise has been useful: "The first claim which can be made is that the Malthusian system, especially as an *equilibrium* system, throws light on many historical situations . . . A population which is limited by 'physical' subsistence, say per capita intake, is a good example: . . . Ireland from 1700 to 1846, many South Sea islands, perhaps the Far Eastern populations today."[26] Emphasis might be placed on "*many* historical situations"; in contrast to the usual discussion of Malthus, the attempt here is not to condemn or justify his thesis as a whole but to distinguish where it is applicable.

MODERN THEORIES OF POPULATION GROWTH

Faster than the growth of any population has been that of articles, books, conferences, institutes, and discussions at all levels and of all sorts on population growth. It would take a book of this size merely to list the pertinent works that have appeared over the past several decades, and any short summary of dominant trends can hardly do justice to all points of view. The controversy is no less contentious today than in Malthus's day, and the empirical evidence, strangely, is probably less solid on the points at issue than at the beginning of the nineteenth century. Malthus's name is constantly used to designate one or another position in the debate, but almost never with full accuracy.

In his discussion of the relation between population and resources, Malthus defined the latter essentially as food, supplementarily as space. As I shall note in Chapter 8, the amount of food that can be grown per unit of arable land has risen tremendously since his day, largely as a consequence of the further development of science and industry. Industrial society, however, itself depends on a far wider range of natural resources than human nutriments. As early as 1865, the English economist W. S. Jevons wrote a book titled *The Coal Question: An Inquiry Concerning the Progress of the Nation and the Probable Exhaustion of Our Coal-Mines.* In the United States, Gifford Pinchot, generally regarded as the founder of the conservation movement, wrote in 1910, "We have timber for less than thirty years, . . . anthracite coal for but fifty years . . . Supplies of iron ore, mineral oil, and natural gas are being rapidly depleted"[27] In 1923, a book written under Keynes's guidance both quoted at length from Jevons and extended his argument to iron, cotton, wool, and, by implication, every other ingredient of industrial production.[28] In our own day the best publicized statement of this thesis was in *The Limits of Growth,* written under the sponsorship of a group of private citizens that calls itself the Club of Rome. According to its prognosis the highest possible level of living that the entire world could enjoy would be about half that in the United States. The authors recommended, therefore, that both population growth and capital investment should cease, so that the modest benefits of a reduced world industry could be distributed equally among all peoples.[29] Though some judged *The*

Limits of Growth as one of the more important documents of our age, the Club of Rome found it necessary to put out a much amended prognosis only two years later.[30]

These predictions of the imminent depletion of this or that natural resource, growing ever more ominous over the past century, have seldom been validated by the facts. Whether it is accurate to label the recurrent argument "Malthusian," as is usually done, is questionable. For Malthus, the extrapolation into the future implicit in the two ratios was intended only as an abstract model; his discussion of actual trends was based mainly on data pertaining to the immediate past, and one can suppose that a scholar with his empirical bent would not have been enamored of the irresponsible forecasts that the computer has so greatly facilitated. More importantly, those who would put a limit to growth derive less from Malthus than from his anti-industrial critics who—then as now—wanted both the products of an advanced economy and the supposed pristine quality of agrarian life.

The parallel campaign to eliminate pollution has been if anything more hysterical than that to preserve resources. Strangely, the United States has gone well beyond the socialist governments of Europe in this regard: according to a British planner, "the vast body of experience built up in America has been the starting point for research in this country."[31] Under the National Environmental Policy Act of 1970, the United States committed itself to "a national policy which will encourage productive and enjoyable harmony between man and his environment."[32] According to what may be the best appraisal of reducing air and water pollution in the United States to "acceptable levels," in constant 1958 dollars it would cost some 872.2 thousand million over 1972–76 and 956.9 thousand million over 1972–80. Unemployment would increase substantially, especially among such marginal types as workers in food-processing plants, with sometimes serious reverberations among the farmers supplying them.[33] Put in such cost-benefit terms, the elimination of pollution is not overwhelmingly attractive to the electorate of an advanced nation; and the governments of poorer countries, sharply focused on the development of their economies, sometimes perceive the world-wide propaganda to avoid pollution as a device to prevent the rise of competing industrial nations.

Malthus, of course, had nothing to say on this issue, and I

do not think one should regard it even as an extrapolation from Malthusian doctrine. The pollutants that anti-industrial enthusiasts denounce have nothing to do with population growth except in the obvious sense that any human activity is enhanced by a growth in numbers. Control is an engineering-fiscal-political problem, not a demographic one. Cities otherwise as different as Pittsburgh and London, for example, have been transformed from their prior notorious condition without the expulsion of a single inhabitant. The trend since Malthus's day, moreover, has been a marked reduction in the kinds of pollution most deleterious to humans—in particular, pollution of food and drinking water; and the science and industry that have made this past progress possible will also furnish the means of controlling new kinds of pollutants. As the London *Economist* remarked in a review of *The Limits of Growth* (March 11, 1972), "In 1872 any scientist could have proved that a city the size of London was impossible, because where were Londoners going to stable all the horses and how could they avoid being asphyxiated by the manure?"

One consequence of the campaign to conserve resources and eliminate pollution has been to put the population problem in a totalist perspective. "The planet earth," by this view, is becoming overcrowded; and the supposedly world-wide policy has been felt most in the United States, which has been saturated with antinatalist books and brochures, all as a strange counterpoint to the decline of the American birth rate to the lowest point in history. Of the American gross national product in 1970 of about $4,500 per capita, the raw-materials component was less than $100, or relatively no higher than at the beginning of the century.[34] Nothing in this bizarre campaign is Malthusian—neither the indifference to the population trends of particular countries nor certainly the anti-empirical style of the typical proponents.

Perhaps the closest modern parallel to Malthus's analysis is such a work as Coale and Hoover's book on the population of India. How would India's economic development be affected, the authors ask, if its birth rate, instead of remaining constant, fell by half during the next generation? The country's population was projected from 1956 to 1986 assuming that the probable sharp fall in mortality would take place together with one of three alternative hypothetical courses in fertility: (1) no change or (2) a decline by half between 1966 and 1981 or

(3) a decline by half between 1956 and 1981. The 357 million in 1951 would increase, depending on the trend in the birth rate, to 775, 634, or 590 million in 1986, and the respective rates of continued growth in that year would be 2.6, 1.0, or 1.0 percent per year. In a country like India, according to this analysis, economic development depends very largely on how much of the national income can be invested rather than diverted to the current consumption of food, housing, education, and general "social overhead" by a rapidly growing mass of people. Cutting the birth rate would raise total production, which would have to be divided among a smaller number. Thus, by their calculation, the real income per consumer of the low-fertility population would be at least 38 percent higher in 1986, and growing much faster than with the alternative projections.[35]

Apart from its relatively comfortable dependence on Indian censuses and plan estimates, how does such a work differ from a straight extrapolation from Malthus? Most obviously, of course, Coale and Hoover fully accept the legitimacy of contraception. They are entirely modernist also in their hope that the state would apply antinatalist measures wholesale, while for Malthus the responsibility for controlling the size of one's family was not corporate but personal. Less obviously, this difference connotes a more fundamental distinction. According to Malthus, as we shall see in a subsequent chapter, each person's decision whether to postpone having children derives from his moral convictions but also, in social terms, from the greater benefits he expects to get by reducing his family responsibilities. The new opportunities to rise in the English class structure were part of the transformation the society was undergoing. That is, for Malthus (but not for Coale and Hoover or most of the other demographers who have analyzed less developed countries), population growth was mainly a dependent variable, a response to change in the economy and the social structure.

The proposition that the growth of numbers is typically beneficial, accepted as axiomatic by mercantilist theorists and opposed by Malthus, never disappeared altogether; and recently it has been revivified in some challenging empirical studies. In poor agrarian countries, it is contended, the main direction of causation is the opposite of what Malthus argued: "population growth is the independent variable, which in its turn is a major factor in determining agricultural developments." That necessity is the mother of invention is suggested by the frequent instances of "the vicious circle of sparse population and primitive techniques";[36] but such correlations, of course, do not in themselves indicate a cause-effect relation in one direction or the other.

The most fundamental challenge to Malthus's analysis is in a recent book by Julian Simon. A faster population growth in developed economies results initially in a lower income per worker, in his view, but after a generation or two in a higher income. In less developed countries a moderate growth of numbers results over the long run in a higher income per worker than either a rapid growth or a static population. But since in a country like India the short-run negative effects of population growth are severe and the long-run benefits slow to appear, "the argument is stronger for a reduction in population growth in India than in other less developed countries." More generally, a moderate rate of growth is beneficial because of its stimulus to agricultural investment, especially in irrigation, and to such elements of the infrastructure as roads.[37] The conclusion is based on data that are subject to challenge, on a different measure of development (income per worker rather than per person), and on arguments that many other economists will not find convincing. An excellent statement of an unorthodox position, as Joseph Spengler notes in the book's foreword, it is bound to prompt critical responses and thus to sharpen the population debate.

The issue here is not whether Simon's general argument is correct but rather whether his interpretation of Malthus is. It is not. Very early in the book the point is made, as it often was made around the end of the nineteenth century, that the rapid rise of Western populations was accompanied by a substantially improved level of living. Over the long run of human advance, the prediction of disaster that Malthus allegedly made was wrong. Either progress may continue or man may return to near-subsistence living. The point is that "Malthus's analysis and prediction cannot be confirmed or falsified without specifying a place and time span, which Malthus did not do."[38] It is the same argument made in *Capital*, that "an abstract law of population exists for plants and animals only," and it is no more true now than when Marx made it. Man is an animal, subject to general biological laws, and *also* an animal with a culture that limits the impact of physiological imperatives. It is surprising that anyone who has glanced through one of the later editions of the *Essay,* with one chapter after another on particular peoples at particular times in history, could fail to note Malthus's effort both to generalize and to specify. "The most important idea in the analytical economics of population comes from Malthus and can be stated in a single sentence: *Ceteris paribus,* the more people the lower the per-capita income."[39] This is a fair summary of Malthus's doctrine concerning relatively densely settled areas but not concerning, for instance, the American colonies. As I noted earlier, Malthus was groping for a concept of optimum that would distinguish underpopulated countries, which would benefit from a growth in numbers, from overpopulated ones, in which more people would lower the level of living. Simon does the same, though he draws the line differently, with India rather than, say, the England of Malthus's day designated as overpopulated.

The most important misunderstanding of Malthus pertains to fertility. One of Simon's summary propositions is that "the long-run total impact of increased income level in less developed countries is to decrease fertility, though the short-run partial effect of rises in income above subsistence is to increase fertility."[40] This does not "refute" Malthus; one might say rather that it paraphrases him. As I shall show in full detail, Malthus not only indicated the dual effect of rising income on fertility but tried to show *why* an increase or a decrease took place. He made no "prediction" of disaster; on the contrary, the successive editions of the *Essay* suggest his growing conviction that in one country after another the necessary balance between people and food was being achieved by a decline in fertility rather than by a rise in mortality.

Why is it that in a thoroughly competent book, full of subtle argument and intelligent deduction from empirical evidence, the figure of Malthus is drawn not only crudely but incorrectly? One reason, perhaps, is that the contradictions between the First and the Second Essays, between the effects of the two kinds of checks, confound the reader. But the main reason, certainly, is that the dominant commentary over almost two centuries has been to erase the complications that Malthus struggled to explicate and to make of him a cardboard figure.

8

Mortality

A S FORMULATED some two generations ago, what is termed the demographic transition was conceived as taking place in three broad stages: (1) preindustrial societies, with high fertility and mortality and a consequent low natural increase; (2) societies in transition, with continuing high fertility but declining mortality and a consequent rapid natural increase; and (3) modern industrial societies, with both fertility and mortality stabilized at a low level and a consequent more or less static population. While some details and many implications of the theory have proved to be dubious, in overall terms the schema describes the main dimensions of population change from before Malthus's lifetime to our own. In particular, the *principal* cause of what has been termed the population explosion, whether in Europe at the beginning of the nineteenth century or in the less developed countries today, has been the improved control over death at early ages.

It is difficult today to imagine what the high mortality of earlier eras connoted, and the statistics that demographers cite do not conjure up the conditions of life that they imply. Jean Fourastié, using data on France that demographic historians had collected and analyzed in their fashion, imaginatively reconstructed the life of a person in a society where on the average one could expect to live only to age 25.

At the end of the seventeenth century, the life of the average family head, who had married for the first time at age 27, could be represented schematically thus: Born into a family of five children, of whom only half reached the age of 15, he also, like his father, had five children, of whom again only two or three were still alive when he died. This man, living to an average age of 52—which placed him among the venerable aged, for only 205 of every thousand males born reached 52 years—survived in his immediate family (not to speak of uncles and aunts, nephews and nieces, and first cousins) an average of nine persons: one of his grandparents (the other three having died before his birth), his two parents, three siblings, and three of his children. He had lived through two or three famines as well as three or four periods of high-priced grain, which were tied to the poor harvests that on the average recurred every ten years. Moreover, he had lived through sicknesses of his brothers and sisters, his children, his wife (or wives), his parents, and himself, having survived two or three epidemics as well as the more or less endemic whooping cough, scarlet fever, diphtheria, and so on, which each year claimed their victims. He had often suffered from such physical ailments as toothaches and wounds that took long to heal. Poverty, disabilities, suffering were constantly before his eyes . . .

Death was in the center of life, just as the cemetery was in the center of the village . . . A child's average age when the first of his parents died was 14 years . . . Men of 25 to 30—already scarred by harsh experience and motivated much more by enduring family needs than by superficial attraction of physique or intellect—contracted unions that, though broken only by death, lasted on the average less than twenty years.[1]

MORTALITY DURING ENGLAND'S TRANSFORMATION

As the world's first industrial country, England has been the subject of many studies on how industrialization and urbanization affected the life of its people. All the arguments for and against modernization, which are echoing still today, started in that context, and Malthus's analysis of the trend in England's death rate is of special interest.[2]

Malthus was well aware, first of all, of how inaccurate the available statistics were. For the period 1796–1800 the annual average number of burials related to the estimated population by a ratio of 1 to 49 (equivalent to a crude death rate of 20.4), but this was so low that "it cannot be considered as approaching to the truth." Judging from the estimated proportion of the population living in cities, he supposed the death rate to be about 25 per thousand. This, he thought, was not only below the mortality of most other countries but "the lowest proportion of deaths that can well be supposed, considering the circumstances of the country." He noted Richard Price's estimates (which I have converted into crude death rates) by size of place:

London and other large cities	44–53
Smaller towns	36–42
Villages	20–25

Malthus agreed that the differential was as stated, but he thought that Price had exaggerated the unhealthfulness of towns or that, alternatively, they had improved since Price had published these estimates. For "there certainly seems to be something in great towns, and even in moderate towns, peculiarly unfavorable to the very early stages of life," possibly "the closeness and foulness of the air." The growth of the urban population, thus, depended on a constant replenishment of villagers, but "we need not accompany Dr. Price in his apprehensions that the country will be depopulated by these emigrations, at least as long as the funds for the maintenance of agricultural labor remain unimpaired."

On the whole, Malthus's interpretation was not bad. He used the data available (national vital statistics started only in 1837), and he was properly skeptical of their probable accuracy. He accepted the generally held proposition that the new towns were more unhealthful than villages, but he did not exaggerate the difference and suggest, as many besides Price did, that urbanization was becoming equivalent to depopulation. On the other hand, though he surmised that some improvement in urban living conditions might be in process, he greatly underestimated the extension of average longevity that would take place in the century following his death. The supposition that the stinking cities of early industrialism could be the sites of a longer average life was a notion repugnant not only to the "nature poets" and Engels, not only to Chadwick[3] and Ruskin and the Webbs, but also to a very large sector of nineteenth-century British opinion of all political orientations. Yet to the degree that we can tell from various types of inadequate data, according to the universal judgment of modern scholarship life expectation rose appreciably during the development of the industrial system.

This was contrary to what one would expect from the concentration of a larger and larger proportion of the population in towns. Lower-class urban quarters were probably no more squalid than their rural counterpart, but their population density made the cities the graveyard of countrymen, to repeat that graphic aphorism. Both in England and elsewhere in the Western world urban death rates were higher than rural until the last quarter of the nineteenth century, when public sanitation had become efficient enough to cancel the physiological effect of crowding. From about 1750 on, in the better-class neighborhoods of English cities scavengers gathered human excrement, or "night soil." The "water closet," invented toward the end of the eighteenth century, emptied either into large vaults under the houses or, later, into sewers that flowed into a river. Until 1850 one of London's drinking-water companies still had its intake a few feet from the mouth of the Westbourne, which had become the Ranelagh common sewer! The cholera epidemic of 1831–32, which came just when urban sanitation was at its worst, may have been something of a blessing, for it helped physicians in their efforts to establish minimum norms of public health. In short, the efficient disposal of sewage, the purification of water, and the better control of food hygiene particularly with respect to milk were largely responsible for the remarkable decline of mortality from intestinal infections—beginning in the middle of the nineteenth century. However, during Malthus's lifetime hygienic conditions probably worsened or, at best, improved far too slowly to account for the decline in mortality from roughly 1760 to 1840.[4]

Indeed, the reasons for this greater longevity have remained something of a puzzle, on which scholars still disagree. They can be classified into four categories, listed in what may be the order of increasing importance or probability.

1. A different balance between the virulence of the infectious organism and the resistance of the human host. An important (though perhaps dubious) example was the bubonic plague, which during the eighteenth century was still endemic in Eastern Europe. In 1720 an infected ship brought the disease to Marseilles, where in a furious outbreak some 40,000 of the city's 90,000 inhabitants died. After spreading through Provence and a few adjoining districts with smaller losses, it petered out, and in a little more than a year the epidemic was over.[5]

Increased biological resistance or, more probably, a change in the virus itself was also the decisive factor in the transformation of scarlet fever from a frequently fatal disease to a relatively trivial complaint. The effect of such greater or smaller susceptibility on the long-term trend in the general death rate, however, would ordinarily be slight in societies with inefficient controls over other major diseases.

2. Specific preventive or curative therapy. It is hard for modern man to assimilate the fact that until the twentieth century the contribution of medicine and medical institutions to the reduction of mortality was so slight as to be almost insignificant. It is a moot question whether fever hospitals, for example, helped restrict contagion by the semiquarantine they imposed or, on the contrary, raised the death rate by the fact that many of the persons who entered them would be infected. So long as bleeding was the first treatment for illness, the contribution that physicians made to their patients' health was minuscule; so long as something like half of surgical patients died of infection, it can be questioned whether surgeons saved more patients than they killed. "It might safely be said," two medical historians concluded, "that specific medical treatment had no useful effects at all, were it not for some doubt about the results of mercury in syphilis, iron in anemia, cinchona in malaria, and inoculation against smallpox."[6]

Of the four diseases, the last was one of the more important in England of the eighteenth century. Inoculation with a small, nonfatal amount of infected liquid, it was discovered, could establish immunity. This practice was introduced in the 1720s and used intermittently through the rest of the century. In the 1920s it was generally thought that its effect on the prevalence of smallpox was considerable,[7] but most of the more recent analyses have questioned this conclusion. Administered without asepsis, the inoculation could infect the patient with other germs, and unless he was segregated during its course he could spread smallpox to others. In one instance, a single inoculated child infected seventeen persons, of whom eight died of the disease. In 1798 Edward Jenner established that vaccination with cowpox germs, which causes only a minor skin irritation, also effects immunity against smallpox. In part because of the ambivalent results of inoculation, there was some opposition also to vaccination, and it is hardly likely that it cut the general death rate very much during Malthus's lifetime.

"To summarize: except in the case of vaccination against small-pox (which was associated with 1.6 percent of the decline of the death rate [in England and Wales] from 1848–54 to 1971), it is unlikely that immunization or therapy had a significant effect on mortality from infectious diseases before the twentieth century . . . Immunization and treatment contributed little to the reduction [of mortality] from infectious diseases before 1935, and . . . it would be surprising if medical measures were more effective in the period which preceded registration of cause of death than in the century which followed."[8]

3. Changes in social norms or patterns of life. Most of these, associated with the migration to overcrowded cities, affected mortality mainly by increasing the risk of infection, but there were some changes also in the opposite direction. Although there are no precise data, of course, it is probable that infanticide was common in Europe during the period I am discussing. The most suggestive indication is the record of foundling hospitals. In 1756 Parliament ordered that an asylum for exposed or deserted children be established in every county, riding, and division of Britain; and in 1811 Napoleon decreed a similarly widespread system in France. These institutions, though supplementing the foundling hospitals that had existed under church auspices since the early modern period, proved everywhere to be inadequate to care for the flow of unwanted babies. According to a plausible argument, infanticide remained fairly common in Western Europe until the last quarter of the nineteenth century, when it was supplanted by contraception.[9] If the practice became less prevalent in the eighteenth and early nineteenth centuries, in all likelihood the decrease was not by itself enough to depress the general death rate.

It is more difficult still to assess the possible effect of new customs whose relation to the death rate was fortuitous and, in many cases, unrecognized at the time. Among the lower classes the fiber from which clothing was manufactured changed from wool to cotton; Engels, following his rule that every innovation shall be denoted a deterioration, cited this as one more step in the "immiseration" under way. In fact, the lighter cotton clothing was probably washed more frequently, and this seemingly was the main reason for the reduced prevalence of typhus.

4. Improved supply of food. If one accepts the proposition,

which many analysts now take as the fact to be explained, that mortality declined during the period of England's early industrialization, and if one is convinced also by the arguments of such historians as McKeown and his associates that the decline cannot be adequately explained by new medical procedures, altered physiological relations between bacteria and their human host, or most other changes in the way of life, then one comes to improved nutrition as the only remaining factor. McKeown quoted Sherlock Holmes to this effect: "When we have eliminated the impossible, whatever remains, however improbable, must be the truth." There is, of course, also a substantial positive basis for denoting a better food supply as the dominant factor in England's decline in mortality, for the country's agriculture improved astoundingly over the century from 1750 to 1850.

AGRICULTURE AND FOOD

Up to the first half of the eighteenth century, the cultivation of land followed practices made impregnable by tradition. A third of the land was left fallow each year, to rest from its exertions, and the other two-thirds was planted in coarse grains. Most of the small and scrawny farm animals, fed from stubble and heath, were killed off each autumn and eaten during the winter as salt meat. The inadequate pasture was often held in common, as was occasionally some woodland and water, which might include limited rights to snare rabbits and catch fish. Attached to most villages were squatters permitted to eke out a miserable living but without any legal right to the use of the joint property.

During the second half of the century, a series of individual acts of Parliament transferred the common land of villages to the private ownership of wealthy families, who invariably enclosed their property with hedges. Deprived of the use of the commons, squatters and cottagers often suffered a decline from even their modest living conditions; and some of the more substantial cultivators, unable or unwilling to maintain themselves in the new circumstances, also sank into tenancy or pauperism. If the social cost was high, the benefits were far greater. "The age of enclosure was also the age of new methods of draining, drilling, sowing, manuring, breeding, and a hundred other changes, all of them requiring capital."[10] Potatoes and other root crops became staples. New breeds of farm animals and plants were developed. About two million acres of waste land were brought under cultivation.

There is hardly a question, then, that the food supply increased enormously in both quantity and variety. But the population also grew; was the food per capita also better? The question pertains not only to the gross balance between people and subsistence but to the distribution of available nutriments among the various social classes. Reading of the amply stocked tables of the well-to-do, we might wonder how much was left over for those squeezed off the land into the new urban proletariat. Perhaps the best evidence that an improved diet became general is the lower incidence of food-deficiency diseases, and especially their virtual disappearance as causes of death. By 1830 scurvy had become so rare that an experienced physician was unable to diagnose its symptoms, and it would seem that rickets also was declining markedly.[11] And since a debilitated organism is less resistant to invading micro-organisms, the better food supply effected a decline not only in such nutritional diseases but also in those caused by infection.

Medieval Europe had suffered from severe famines, which recurred well into the modern era. At the end of the seventeenth century a succession of poor harvests created a subsistence crisis through most of Europe; in 1698 the death rates in two regions of Sweden rose to 90 and 160 per thousand population. The winter of 1708–09, long remembered in France as *le grand hiver*, brought to that country among several others intense misery and heightened mortality. William Alison, a reformist physician and a professor at the University of Edinburgh, wrote a short work on the famine of the 1840s, concentrating his attention not on Ireland but on the Scottish Highlands. This book can be regarded as a commentary on Malthus's observations concerning Ireland, written after the famine that Malthus had feared would take place.

All questions regarding poverty . . . are inseparably connected with the conditions by which population is regulated. The best system of management of the poor [is that resulting in the] least redundancy of population . . . [The best controls of population are] by keeping up the standard of comfort among the poor themselves; and by giving every proprietor of land a direct and obvious interest in constantly watching and habitually checking the growth of a *parasite* population, for whose labor there is no demand, on his property.[12]

Apart from the Irish case, these recurrent food shortages developed into true famines only occasionally, and then typically only in certain regions or countries. On the scale of world history Europe's food shortages have been relatively puny. The normal death rate of the great civilizations of Asia, on the contrary, "may be said to contain a constant famine factor." Between 108 B.C. and A.D. 1911, China withstood 1,823 famines, or nearly one per year during those two millennia.[13] Most were over only a portion of the country; the worst were nation-wide. But throughout China, every district experienced a famine at least several times during each normal lifetime. A well documented example is the province of Hupei; during the 267 years from 1644 to 1911, only 27 were entirely free of disaster, including those for which the record is known to be incomplete. In 1877–78 the famine that struck four northern provinces cut them off so completely that almost a year passed before news of it reached the capital. Cannibalism was common, and local magistrates were ordered to connive at the evasion of laws prohibiting the sale of children so that the parents might buy a few days' food. The dead were buried in what are still today called "ten-thousand-man holes." During just those two years an estimated nine to thirteen million perished from hunger, disease, or violence.[14] It was hardly necessary in nineteenth-century India, as another example, for "Malthusians among the Indian civil servants" to conclude that "if there was not sufficient land to sustain the population, the surplus should be removed either by emigration or by death."[15] On the contrary, the British brought the endemic famines under control partly by improving irrigation systems, mainly by building a rail net that provided the means of transporting food to areas where shortages started.

If in comparison with other civilizations Europe suffered far less from deficiencies in subsistence, and if Malthus witnessed the remarkable improvement in agricultural production taking place during his lifetime, why did he focus his attention so narrowly on food, repeatedly citing shortages as the most fundamental of the positive checks? The very fact that food supply was variable made it susceptible to analysis. It was hardly the case, as one opponent of Malthus argued, that "the Giver of all good and of fertile seasons never withholds from the hands of industry its proper reward—abundance."[16] The control of infectious diseases seemed fixed at what we would regard today as a very ineffective level; deaths from disease were like deaths from old age, a fact of nature subject to no more than minor improvement.

Indeed, every control of infection has come as something of a surprise, as can be exemplified by one of the best modern attempts to estimate the future growth of the American population. The major advances in reducing mortality, Warren Thompson and P. K. Whelpton pointed out in 1938, had been in the conquest of major contagious diseases, and it was unlikely that the death rate could fall much below what had already been achieved.[17] They were proved wrong much more quickly than Malthus, for they wrote on the eve of advances in diagnosis, medicine, surgery, and public health. Today, similarly, no expert can offer a valid prognosis concerning cancers or heart diseases, the two major causes of death in advanced countries, not to say automobile accidents or homicides, which have become increasingly important causes of death for persons under the age when those two disease complexes ordinarily strike.

Seemingly the paradox that I note in Malthus was to be found also in the attitudes of the typical Englishman. Among the symbols of patriotism common among the lower orders were such popular songs as "The Roast Beef of Old England" and the thickset figure of John Bull, an obvious contrast to the emaciated French.[18] Yet the same people who celebrated their better supply of food were likely to protest its lack. Attempts to maintain public order in Britain have sometimes been ascribed to a paranoid fear of a mob that might be stimulated by the French example. One should recall that urban police forces were a later invention and that "in eighteenth-century England the most characteristic form of popular protest was a riot."[19] The most common cause was a food shortage. A large proportion of the population had moved to cities, where they had to depend on inefficient transportation and market systems. Along the eastern coast much food was absorbed by the many soldiers stationed there to repel the French invasion that was being prepared across the Channel. Wheat had become a status symbol, and paradoxically the whitest bread, bleached with alum, was eaten in the poorest areas. Four times during the decades 1792–1818, when the harvest was relatively poor and the price of wheat relatively high, the shortages were enough to tip the balance. Four types of "food riot" can be distinguished: in a food blockage, a mob in a transshipment point prevented foodstuffs from being sent farther; in a retributive action, the mob attacked persons accused of profiteering and stole or destroyed their property, which usually included food; in a price riot, the mob seized food, set its price, and sold it openly; and in an agrarian demonstration, farmers dumped or destroyed their produce in a protest against one or another injustice.

The origin of such events was typically complex. Tilly argued against what he called the hydraulic model of explanation: "hardship increases, pressure builds up, the vessel bursts . . . Instead of being in any simple sense responses to hunger, serious conflicts over the food supply ordinarily occurred when groups of men felt their established right to a particular source of food was being violated by . . . merchants, officials, or holders of food."[20] Although many historians and most sociologists continue to teach that hardship generates revolt, the usual fact is the contrary. As man's level of living rises, his standard of living—the level of his aspiration, in the common phrase—usually rises faster, so that as things get better dissatisfaction sharpens. On every scale, from riot or strike to full revolution, the timing is ordinarily the opposite of what we would anticipate from the conventional wisdom of either Malthus's day or our own.

Malthus certainly could not guess how the availability of food would be extended in the century and a half following his death. Not only were such traditional extensions of arable land as by drainage and irrigation continued on a new scale, not only was the radical improvement of farm animals and plants accelerated, but processes having little to do with agriculture helped to increase its effectiveness. Of these, the most important was transportation, for if food can be shipped in promptly from unstricken areas or central storehouses—or, in the present day, from the United States, Canada, or Australia—a shortage need not spread from its original locality. Beginning in the late nineteenth century, transocean shipping carried guano from deposits off the coast of Peru and later the artificial fertilizers first manufactured by German chemical firms. Long-distance transportation of food was facilitated by such subsidiary processes as canning, refrigerating, dehydrating, and freezing.

If production, processing, and distribution of food have improved prodigiously, and if the population that depends on it has grown apace, what of the balance between them? Are we relatively well off, or are we on the brink of disaster? The endless debate is encouraged by the fact that we do not know how much food is produced, what the population of the world is, or certainly how the relation between them will change over the next decades. For sizable portions of the world—including the most populous nation, Communist China—no records of food production are available; and some of the data that do exist about other countries must be taken as very rough estimates. In most less developed countries much of the food is grown on small family plots, whose produce seldom finds its way into statistics; the figures compiled, mainly from market transactions, are thus often considerably lower than what is grown and consumed.

Each year the Food and Agriculture Organization compiles the national statistics, such as they are, on food production. During the decade following 1945, according to this source, the world's agricultural production rose sufficiently both to repair the war damage and to make up for the increment to population. During the second postwar decade, food production rose by about 6 percent, or slightly faster than the population. According to the latest statistics available at the time of writing, food production per capita rose during 1962–72 by 0.8 percent overall, or by 0.3 percent in less developed countries, compared with 1.1 and 0.7 percent, respectively, during 1952–62.[21] Note that since the figures pertain to food production per capita, agricultural produce not used to feed humans and international shipments of food are excluded, and increases in population are included. According to the FAO's barometer, not only were the world's food supplies more than keeping up with people but they would continue to do so, assuming a population growth at the same rate, at least until 1985. Most significantly, the earlier search for new land, called the "Achilles' heel" of agricultural planning,[22] was to be largely supplanted by a more efficient use of land already in cultivation. Thus, the recommendation was to increase the land permanently under crops in all less developed countries from 210 million hectares in 1962 to only 223 million in 1985![23] For a considerable period no shortage of land would arise, since growing populations would require roughly the same acreage, or sometimes a little less as marginal land was retired from agricultural use.

The reason for this relatively favorable record of food production is, of course, no mystery: it derived in large part from the new varieties of grains developed over the past decade or two. Where these so-called superplants were successful, they overwhelmed the most optimistic anticipations. In West Pakistan, as a prime instance, a new race of wheat doubled the yield on a small experimental plot in 1964–65; five years later it was growing on 6.5 million acres.[24] The superplants that made this vastly greater efficiency possible had been produced by a long and tedious process, transferring the pollen of one species to the pistil of another. When such induced interbreeding was successful, it was still a matter of chance whether, as hypothesized, two desired characteristics would be combined in the new strain; and when this happened, the cross was typically sterile (like the mule, an analogous vertebrate). It may be that these shortcomings will soon be overcome. Research biologists have successfully produced a hybrid by extracting cells from sterilized leaves of two tobacco species and, in a suitable medium, inducing them to combine and develop into a new one. Since it starts with all the genes of naturally reproduced organisms, such a plant will probably be completely fertile, producing its own seeds generation after generation.[25] In other words, the remarkable improvement in food plants achieved over the past decade or two may be only the beginning of the transformation of agriculture that seemingly is in prospect.

The advance in the techniques of food production does not mean, however, that the problem of shortages is on the point of being solved, or even mitigated. The high-yield plants demand large amounts of fertilizer and water, and productivity is greatest on farms big enough to warrant mechanization. Thus (as during the enclosure movement in eighteenth-century England) those peasants in India or Pakistan who had been relatively well off were best able to adopt the new techniques, and it was they who personally profited from them. In five widely separated districts of India, one effect of the superplants was to sharpen class hostility. The "green revolution," a catchword modeled after the "industrial revolution," describes a process almost as complex; and it has become an all too apt designation of the social-political changes that the new agriculture is helping to effect.[26] The problem, in other words, is not that the population is increasing faster than food, but that the effective demand for nutriments is rising faster than the supply. Efforts to raise production to the level that the world's peasantry now wants are impeded by population growth, it is true, but only as one among several significant factors. Even so, the data do not suggest the mammoth disaster that many commentators have been predicting. In spite of the rapid increase of people in many less developed countries, the rise in the production of food has been slightly faster.

Malthus did not foresee, I repeat for emphasis, this amazing development of agriculture. His concentration on food and secondarily on space, though at the center of Malthusian arguments for the past generation or two, are perhaps the weakest element in his whole thesis. It should be noted also, however, that in contrast to today's simple-minded analysts Malthus stressed the social-political setting of food shortages. From the first to the seventh edition of the *Essay,* as I have noted in several contexts, its author moved from an ecological to a sociological perspective, thus from a narrow focus on biological needs to an appreciation of the cultural-social-economic complexities that these needs connote, and—most remarkably —from a deep pessimism to a cautious optimism. Malthus did not distinguish clearly between the end points of this change in his thought, probably because he did not see the matter clearly, but also because, here as elsewhere, he tried to argue both that like other living creatures man is subject to biological imperatives and that man is a cultural being whose expectations and techniques can affect his behavior greatly.

MALTHUS ON THE CORN LAWS

In England the word *corn* ordinarily means, of course, what Americans call "grain"; but in the context of the Corn Laws it included such staples as peas during the earlier period and, during Malthus's lifetime, it referred almost entirely to wheat. In the seventeenth century the laws included regulations of trade within Britain; later they were either bounties on exports or tariffs on imports. Most commentaries reduce the complexity of the issue by picturing the sides as representing rigidly delineated class interests. In a standard work on the debates, thus, we are informed that before 1660 the laws were administered in the interest of consumers, then in the joint

interest of producers and consumers, and following 1814 in
the interest of producers.[27] More generally, the issue is represented as between landowners and the rising industrialists,
with (once again) Malthus and Ricardo as their respective
spokesmen.[28] One reason that this kind of schematic history is
so attractive is that without such pigeonholes we barely know
how to classify the events. The many laws, repeatedly amended,
were composites, obviously the results of shifting compro-
mises; and the allegation by all disputants that they were
arguing in the *national* interest was not necessarily mere
hypocrisy.

The decade during which, by the conventional chronology,
England launched its industrial revolution was also the one
in which it began, though as yet intermittently, to depend on
a foreign supply of wheat. Imports increased from 104,000
quarter-tons in 1765 to 560,000 ten years later. The response
to this stupendous rise was the Corn Law of 1773, the most
important for more than a century, supplemented by new
acts in 1791 and 1804. According to the price of wheat, its export was prohibited or encouraged by a sliding bounty, and
its import was similarly regulated by a sliding tariff, with the
benefit and penalty both stipulated differently in the three
laws. The purpose remained the same—to prevent the price
from rising so high that the poor could not buy food and from
falling so low that the farmer could not profit from growing
grain. What had changed was not policy but the circumstances
in which it was applied, especially the dangerous dependence
on France, with which Britain was either at war or on the
brink of it. The new laws, however, were virtually inoperative;
the price of wheat rose and fell with little relation to the
attempt to regulate it.

With the final defeat of Napoleon, the average price of
wheat fell from 74*s*. 4*d*. in 1814 to 52*s*. 10*d*. in 1815, with a
consequent distress to agriculture. The new law of 1815, in
Fay's interpretation, was "defiantly protective," intended "to
fasten on a country at peace the protection furnished by a
generation of war." The debate was sharpened with the organization of the Anti-Corn Law League, through which Cob-
den and his associates hit on Corn Laws as an almost accidental
symbol of their developing effort to assist "the poor": "How
far, if at all, [the Corn Laws] raised the prices it is impossible,
even approximately, to determine. Several of the witnesses

before the Import Duties Committee of 1840—whose report is nothing more than a manifesto in favor of Free Trade—attempted the task, but arrived at their conclusions by making assumptions which were unwarranted."[29] The main success of the league was to convince Sir Robert Peel, who as head of a Tory government engineered the repeal of the tariff in 1846. With the stupendous growth of industry and the increase in population, it was impossible in his opinion for agriculture to keep up. At first he favored treaties setting the terms by which manufactured goods would be exchanged for food, but eventually he concluded that Britain needed protection in neither industry nor agriculture.

The prediction of the free-traders that their program would bring cheaper food proved to be false; after good harvests and bad, the price of wheat rose. "It is one of the ironies of history that during the half-century in which British agriculturists lived in terror of a bogey the bogey did not exist. British farming surmounted the repeal of the corn laws on a scale of ascending prices . . . In the 1870s, [however,] the bogey descended. Its feet were ships of steel, its arms railroads stretching over the prairies, and its belly was Chicago wheat."[30] In other words, one of the most sharply debated issues of the first half of the nineteenth century, generating a dispute in which every prominent political economist and statesman took part, turned out to be almost an irrelevance. The matter was decided not by free trade or tariffs, but by the McCormick reaper, the transcontinental railroad, and the ocean steamer.

Malthus wrote two pamplets on the matter, *Observations on the Effects of the Corn Laws* (1814) and *Grounds of an Opinion on the Policy of Restricting the Importation of Foreign Corn* (1815). In the year between the two publications, he moved from an impartial consideration of both sides to a conclusion in favor of protection.

In retrospect, *Observations* is the more interesting of the two, perhaps the only nonpartisan statement on the subject in the mass of print. As typically with any subject, Malthus began by reviewing the doctrine in *The Wealth of Nations*, which he found flawed because (as I have remarked) Smith had used labor to measure value, and corn to measure labor. "Few things seem less probable," Malthus thought, "than that Great Britain should naturally grow an independent supply of corn," given its developing concentration on manufacturing and the increasing number to be fed. A home-grown stock of food would continue to be available, then, only if it was provided artificially. Were the manifest advantages of free trade sufficient in this case to counterbalance its disadvantages?

Many of the questions both in morals and politics seem to be the nature of the problems *de maximis* and *minimis* in fluxions [Newton's term for the rate at which variables change], in which there is always a point where a certain effect is the greatest, while on either side of this point it gradually diminishes . . .

In whichever way it is settled, some sacrifices must be submitted to. Those who contend for the unrestrained admission of foreign corn must not imagine that the cheapness will be an unmixed good . . . On the other hand, those who contend for a continuance and increase of restrictions upon importation must not imagine that the present state of agriculture and its present rate of eminence can be maintained without injuring other branches of the national industry.

As in his search for what we term a population optimum, so here Malthus was fumbling after something like a cost-benefit measure of policy. In both instances he was clear about the fundamental point, that the decision was not between good and bad, or between industry and agriculture, but between a relative plus and a relative minus.

A year later, in *Grounds of an Opinion,* Malthus moved to the advocacy he had held in abeyance. The reasons, he said, were the details of evidence given to Parliament on the trend in wheat prices, the concomitant fall in the price of bullion, and the law just passed in France encouraging the export of wheat from that country. In any case, he argued, food was not merely one commodity out of others.

Let us suppose, for instance, that the inhabitants of the Lowlands of Scotland were to say to the Highlanders, "We will exchange our corn for your cattle whenever we have a superfluity; but if our crops in any degree fail, you must not expect to have a single grain" . . . Would it not be perfectly senseless in the Highlanders to think only of those general principles which direct them to employ the soil in the way that is best suited to it? If supplies of corn could not be obtained with some degree of steadiness and certainty from other quarters, would it not be absolutely necessary for them to grow it themselves, however ill adapted to it might be their soil and climate?

In short, Malthus decided in favor of some degree of protection not only because of the contingent factors that he spelled out in this second pamphlet but also because, as throughout his analysis of population, food was for him the prime need of humans, and its lack the chief of the positive checks.

WAR

Long before Malthus wrote his *Essay*, population growth had been linked to war in various ways. When Thomas More wrote in *Utopia* that "every man has by the law of nature a right to such a waste portion of the earth as is necessary for his subsistence," when Machiavelli asserted in his *History of Florence* that the barbarians of northern Europe, "living in a healthful and prolific climate, often increase[d] in such numbers that some of them [were] obliged to abandon their paternal lands and to seek new countries for their habitation," thus eventually destroying the Roman Empire, both were exemplifying a pattern that had become a commonplace of European thought. Walter Raleigh wrote a more specific work, *Discourse of War in General* (1650), in which he noted that the growth of population induced the "daily wars which afflict the whole earth," for "the want of room upon the earth, which pincheth the whole nation, begets the remediless [or "necessary"] war."[31] If for such mercantilist theorists war was justified, those of the same period who saw it as evil, such as Hobbes and Petty, also ascribed it partly to overpopulation.

Though these notions were incorporated into Malthus's book, they were far less prominent than one might suppose from later expositions of Malthusian thought. He divided the positive checks into two types—misery, "those which appear to arise unavoidably from the laws of nature," and vice resulting in misery, "those which we obviously bring upon ourselves, such as wars, excesses, and many others which it would be in our power to avoid." Did he mean that wars were evitable merely by the exercise of moral restraint and the consequent avoidance of overpopulation? Seemingly not, for the preventive check inhibits also the growth of the misery that "appears to arise" from the laws of nature. The only point in making the distinction, it would seem, is to state that man can prevent such "excesses" as war also by other means than controlling his numbers. But it is not a passage from which the writer's intent can be discerned easily.

What of the specific instances through the *Essay* by which this general thesis is exemplified? Among American Indians, Malthus wrote, "the very act of increasing in one tribe must be an act of aggression on its neighbors, as a larger range of territory will be necessary to support its increased numbers." "Their object in battle is not conquest but destruction," for "the life of the victor depends on the death of his enemy." Here, then, the relation is clear: among hunters with no more than a primitive agriculture, the inevitable competition for food is likely to result in incessant warfare. Wars of the ancient Greek states, similarly, "were not only almost constant, but extremely bloody." This was less so among the ancient Romans, for "wars do not depopulate much while industry continues in vigor." And in the Europe of Malthus's day war had "certainly abated, even including the late unhappy revolutionary contests . . . The ambition of princes would want instruments of destruction if the distresses of the lower classes of people did not drive them under their standards. A recruiting sergeant always prays for a bad harvest and a want of employment, or in other words a redundant population."

In a future society in which all would practice moral restraint, finally, the prevention of a redundant population "would remove one of the principal encouragements to offensive war . . . Indisposed to a war of offense, in a war of defense such a society would be strong as a rock of adamant . . . Every heart and hand will be united to repel an invader when each individual felt the value of the solid advantages which he enjoyed, and a prospect of change presented only a prospect of being deprived of them." In this passage Malthus had come full circle. Having begun in the First Essay with a sharp critique of the utopian blathering of Godwin and Condorcet, he ended the development of the Second Essay with a picture of the future that, though effected by a different means, in its essentials reflected some of the extravagant optimism of his age.

Rather few modern anthropologists have discussed the warfare of primitive people at all, not to say its relation to population pressure. A review of ethnographic writings on the subject denotes warfare "a hitherto unrecognized critical variable." When those who have studied the question offer an ecological perspective on primitive warfare, such an interpretation is likely to be questioned by others conversant with the particular peoples.[32] Most of today's anthropologists see the earlier efforts to derive general conditions of life from a primitive economy as old-fashioned. Analysts who transcend a single culture are likely to stress the wide range of differences in social form and cultural practice to be found among food gatherers. Malthus's characterization of American Indians, for example, was reasonably accurate of some tribes, but those in California were entirely pacific. To the degree that there is a consensus in the discipline, no one-to-one relation is seen to exist between a food-gathering economy and a proclivity to violence. For a more satisfactory explanation, one must include more than the two factors and try to establish multivariate correlations—for which neither the data nor the techniques were available to Malthus.

Malthus's thesis that the propensity to go to war declined with the rise of European civilization was remarkably accurate —for a period. The spread of industrialism from England to the Continent coincided with a phenomenon unheard of in the annals of the West—a century of peace in Europe. From 1815, the end of the Napoleonic wars, to 1914, the beginning of World War I, "apart from the Crimean war—a more or less colonial event—England, France, Prussia, Austria, Italy, and Russia were engaged in war among each other for all together only eighteen months. A computation of comparable figures for the two preceding centuries gives an average of sixty to seventy years of major wars in each."[33] To equate industrialism or capitalism or even nationalism with belligerence is inadequate. Even in the middle of the war of 1914–18, it was still possible to believe that this exceptional period would endure. "Just as an unexpected opposition to the free activities of the original Malthusian positive checks was found in moral restraint, so a relief from an inevitable belligerency among the nations of the world may be found in an enlightened attitude toward international relations."[34] But World War I not only marked the end of the Hundred Years' Peace; it ushered in the present era of totalitarian wars.

Of three main determinants of military deaths, the most important is the ability of the quartermaster corps to maintain supplies for both military and supporting civilian forces, and of the medical corps to impede infections of wounds; here the improvement has been phenomenal. The second most important is whether belligerant countries observe certain conventions even in fighting an all-out war. The third variable, the development of weapons of devastating power, is potentially the most important, but whether hydrogen bombs will ever be used also depends on politics more than technology. With the rise of totalitarianism during the twentieth century, the trend has been toward the obliteration of all limits to killing. Military conflicts have been more devastating since 1914 principally because the international structure of the nineteenth century broke down. In the two world wars, regulations of various kinds were successively abrogated—concerning places (for example, open cities), concerning weapons (tanks, poison gas, atomic bombs), concerning forms (declaration of war, treatment of prisoners), and concerning values (setting limits to the spoliation of property or of persons).

Malthus, obviously, could not foretell developments that would start several generations after his death. In the twentieth century what can be termed a Malthusian analysis of how population pressure affects expansionist tendencies has usually been an excuse for imperial ambitions. One source of the new discipline of geopolitics was the German geographer Friedrich Ratzel (1844–1904), who held that man's biological environment is a dominant influence on his way of life. In his *Political Geography* he used an organistic analogy to depict the "natural" processes of human societies' growth, decay, and inevitable death.[35] From Ratzel, trained as a biologist and writing at a time when Darwinian theories were important in all social disciplines, this was perhaps to be expected. A more specifically political interpretation of global configurations came from Mackinder's identification of the "heartland" of Eurasia as "the geographical pivot of history," the notion for which—though he later modified it considerably—he is best remembered.[36] These ideas were taken up by Karl Haushofer, a general become geographer who as director of the Institute for Geopolitics in Munich furnished the Nazis with a pseudo-scientific basis for their renewed *Drang nach Osten*. Not only would a nation squeezed into a "living space" too small for its numbers be forced to expand but, by the clear implication of the concept of lebensraum, that expansion would be legitimate, just, "natural." The fact that Germany was "a people without youth,"[37] that the state tried in every conceivable way to increase the country's fertility, might seem to reduce the relevance of this argument; but the success of propagandistic slogans is seldom set by logic.

The changes in Malthus's doctrine that started with the addition of preventive checks in the second edition of the *Essay* and continued throughout his life pertained, of course, mainly to fertility. What he had to say concerning mortality was hardly revised from the First Essay's dogmatic assertions, which were exemplified in chapters of the expanding book but not essentially modified. In retrospect, then, the analysis of mortality is far weaker than the portion of his theory that he worked on during his mature years.

That food-gathering peoples depend on a precarious supply of food was certainly not a false generalization, particularly if we keep in mind how little was known about them at the beginning of the nineteenth century. Malthus did note, moreover, what a modern anthropologist might suggest as the most important emendation—that tribes living on fish typically have a more secure subsistence than those that hunt animals. It is certainly also true that the growth in numbers associated with the rise of early civilizations was based fundamentally on the readier food supply that agriculture made available and, more broadly, that the increase of population over the whole of man's existence has depended on more effective techniques of food production. Malthus was certainly aware of the momentous improvements in every element of England's agrarian economy. That he did not extrapolate this upward trend to the much higher productivity technically possible today one can ascribe, perhaps, to his usual avoidance of a projection to any future utopia. Like all his contemporaries Malthus saw industry and agriculture as competing elements of the economy; but soon after his death the yet faster development of agriculture began to depend on prior developments in science and industry. Present food production is limited far less by the finite amount of arable land and other natural components than by social-political-cultural factors—which Malthus did discuss in passing, but only as supplements to what he deemed to be essential.

Even today most analysts find it difficult to put their specialty in a perspective as broad as world history, and Fourastié's references to the several famines per lifetime in early modern France would hardly be challenged by any historian of the period. It is only from a study of China or India that one could reach the judgment that Europe's food shortages were relatively minor aberrations in a far healthier balance between people and subsistence than in the other preindustrial civilizations. Though one can hardly fault Malthus for not seeing what is barely visible even now, it is curious, even so, that a man living in a country where virtually no one died of starvation paid relatively little attention to the diseases that caused most deaths. Again, one should not forget how recent our knowledge of infections is; when some fifty years after Malthus's death Semmelweis, Pasteur, and others propounded the notion that microscopic organisms could kill beings millions of times larger, experts thought them a bit eccentric, if not actually mad. Until it was possible to combat infections, it was largely correct, as Malthus wrote, that "while some [diseases] appear to yield to the efforts of human care and skill, others seem to become in proportion more malignant and fatal." Quoting Dr. William Heberden (one of George III's physicians), Malthus noted that the gradual shifts in causes of disease discernible from the bills of mortality were no more than alterations in the shape of the channel "through which the great stream of mortality is constantly flowing."

Up to roughly World War II, reductions in any country's mortality depended in large measure on the life-saving efforts that were available from its own social and economic development. In that period, thus, there was typically a high correlation between such social measures as the proportion literate of the population, say, and the average expectation of life at birth or the infant mortality rate. In the third quarter of this century, it became increasingly possible to cut drastically the deaths from diseases like malaria without going through the institutional structure of the societies affected. Powerful insecticides such as DDT were sprayed on mosquito-breeding areas first from airplanes and then, more effectively, from portable tanks. Largely by the virtual elimination of malaria as a cause of death, Ceylon's expectation of life at birth increased from 43 years in 1946 to 52 in 1947—a gain that had taken half a century in most Western countries. Throughout the world, thus, old age has become one of the main causes of death. The death rates of less developed countries, where the proportion of aged is very small, are therefore often lower than those of economically advanced countries with the most efficient health systems, where the proportion of aged is far larger. Taiwan, with an age structure favorable to survival combined with an efficient medical system, has the lowest death rate in the world.

This capsule summary of today's population explosion is worth recounting because it points up the fact that the growth of numbers in less developed countries—the reason for the revival of interest in Malthusian thought—was due to a factor that he left unanalyzed. We hear much more of attempts to reduce fertility, for fertility is the current problem, and of food shortages, which are potentially a greater problem; but in fact the dynamic element in the population-subsistence balance has been the use of Western technology, personnel, and money to bring mortality under mass control without initially affecting anything else except the rate of population growth.

9

Fertility

THAT PREINDUSTRIAL EUROPE, as compared with such other civilizations as classical India or China, was far less susceptible to famine was not due to Europe's superior agriculture. Though the evidence is not firm, one can reasonably argue that, on the contrary, the Chinese peasant was a far better husbandman than his Western counterpart. The principal reason for the contrast was that in Western Europe the institutional control of fertility had become a strong and general tradition, which was breaking down during Malthus's lifetime. It is only against this almost forgotten slice of social history that his policy recommendations can be understood; his suggestion that everyone exercise moral restraint, which to the denizens of our permissive age sounds wildly extravagant, was in fact an effort to bolster a system becoming moribund but far from dead. The trend in modern society has been to square the circle, to enjoy sexual relations and yet avoid conception through what are termed "Malthusian" or "neo-Malthusian" practices. Most accounts of the birth-control movement hardly do justice to Malthus; the short summary here is intended only to set the record straight in that one respect. For the enormous emphasis given to the means by which conception is controlled invites us to ignore the complexity of potential parents' decisions whether or not to have another child—and on this crucial point Malthus was a far better analyst than most "Malthusians," including those active today.

THE EUROPEAN MARRIAGE PATTERN

In what has become a famous paper, John Hajnal described what he called "the European marriage pattern," which combined a high age at marriage with a large proportion who never married. As late as 1900, the percentages of Western European males still single at ages 45–49 ranged from 9 in Denmark and Germany to 16 in Belgium and Switzerland and 20 in Ireland, and of females from 10 in Germany to 20 in Portugal and 29 in Iceland. Even after the spread of modern contraception was well under way, in other words, throughout Western Europe one person in seven or eight remained single during the whole of his or her fecund years. The deviations from the pattern were in such countries as Spain, which also in other respects fitted only partly into Western European culture, and Germany, with its substantial Slav population in the eastern region. The brake that prevented many from ever marrying, moreover, inhibited others from marrying early. Also in 1900, almost 90 percent of males and some 70 percent of females were single at ages 20–24, and well over half of the males and something under half of the females still at ages 25–29. As against cultures in which virtually everyone marries and most girls at or very shortly after puberty, the Western European system represented an enormous check on the potential increase of population.[1]

Starting from the relatively complete and accurate statistics on the beginning of the twentieth century, Hajnal worked his way back through several centuries seeking with less and less complete data to discover how and when the European marriage pattern arose. "That some change in marriage habits took place between the fourteenth century and the eighteenth seems scarcely in doubt. In the Middle Ages the betrothal of children and the marriage of very young adolescents were apparently widespread . . . These practices had almost entirely disappeared by the eighteenth century." One strand of evidence is etymological. The word *husband* derives from two words meaning "house" and "dwell," and its original meaning (still preserved in *husbandman* and *husbandry*) was a householder, a man who had a home. The Middle English word for an unmarried man was *anilepiman*. These two terms, one referring to the management of property and the other to marital status, gradually became associated as opposites, *anilepiman* coming to mean a man who had no living and therefore could not marry, and *husband,* a man who was able to care for a family and therefore could get (or, eventually, was) married.[2]

Another clue pertains to the institution that was developed in order to prevent the partition and repartition of family plots. In the "stem family," the entire property went to a single heir, and his siblings either moved away or remained as unmarried members of the family. The typical unit, thus, consisted of a peasant, his wife and minor children, his unmarried brothers and sisters, and perhaps his aged father and mother, plus a number of farmhands who often slept in the same house and ate with the rest of the household. For the much smaller proportion of the population living in towns, similar inhibitions were imposed by guilds, which generally prohibited marriage until a young man had advanced a good distance toward becoming a master craftsman. In both the rural and the urban sectors, then, most younger people were assured a place in life with, judged by the standards of the times, good security and reasonable comfort; but for this many had to pay what we might regard an onerous price, forgoing a home and family of their own for many years past their puberty or, for a significant proportion, permanently.

When Hajnal wrote his paper he could refer to the stem family as an accepted datum, but since then the social history of Europe has developed considerably. The term (in French, *famille souche*) derives from Frédéric LePlay (1806–82), who believed that it supplanted an older patriarchal type of family, but that the change had no ill effects on the society or nation. (This was not true, in his view, of the third type, "the unstable family" characteristic of the modern working class, which resulted in national decay.) In various places in his voluminous writings LePlay described the stem family as it supposedly existed in particular areas, and his generalizations from these instances—as is typically true of historical demography—comprised an extrapolation from these few pockets of European peasantry. As he conceived the stem family, it combined what Peter Laslett terms a "patriline," or a succession of male heads of household directly descended from each other; a legal arrangement to make the family's property inalienable; and the domestic group of "two married couples with their children, the head of the second being the child of the first," which Laslett renamed "multiple family household, disposed downward." The point of Laslett's critique was not to introduce this more cumbersome jargon but to challenge the usual prior assumption that the stem family, in any of the alternative meanings given the term, was the dominant form in early modern Europe.[3] According to Laslett, England's mean household size "remained fairly constant at 4.75 or a little under from the earliest point for which we have found figures until as late as 1901."[4] How much faith to put in the figure one does not know, for (as Laslett scrupulously points out) the definition of *household* was never very precise; with a number of servants, lodgers, unmarried relatives, and so on included with the nuclear or multiple family, the significance of the data, if we accept them as accurate and representative, is still somewhat in doubt.

The challenge that Laslett posed to LePlay touches on Hajnal's reconstruction of the European marriage system, but not crucially, for the inhibition of marriage, and especially of early marriage, did not depend necessarily on the prevalence of the stem family. According to Laslett, the average age of Elizabethan and Jacobean brides was something like 24, and that of bridegrooms nearly 28.

> Marriage was an act of profound importance to the social structure . . . It gave the man full membership of the community, and added a cell to village society. It is understandable, therefore, that marriage could not come about unless a slot was vacant, so to speak, and the aspiring couple was fit to fill it up— . . . a cottage which had fallen empty, . . . a plot of land which had to be taken up, . . . a bakery, or a joinery, or a loom which had to be manned anew. This meant that all young people ordinarily had to wait before they were permitted to marry.[5]

Because of such impediments, a considerable proportion of the population never married. And of those who were widowed, many at ages well below the lapse of fecundity, only a tenth to a third remarried, according to a compilation of records from various countries for the sixteenth to the eighteenth centuries.[6]

An 1824 report on the English Poor Law discussed the "old system" in the countryside by which men "did not marry until they were perhaps 30 years of age, and until they had got a little money and a few goods about them."[7] This was the historical context of Malthus's observations on fertility. The moral restraint that he proposed, thus, was based on a fully institutionalized tradition that had developed over several centuries and would persist, though with weakening force, for two or three generations after his death. Moral restraint, a part of what we would term "responsible parenthood," was one of the more significant checks on fertility.

When Malthus wrote in the second chapter of the *Essay* that "population invariably increases where the means of subsistence increase, unless prevented by some very powerful and obvious checks," many read him as asserting the first portion of the sentence without the limiting clause. On a time scale, the powerful and obvious checks were embedded in two types of institutions—both in the "old system" that Hajnal analyzed and in the new pattern of family life that he noted in Western European countries. There were thus three family types, which succeeded each other in sequence while also overlapping during several generations. The traditional family is the one that Hajnal described. As the checks to early marriage became unenforceable, this merged into the proletarian family, with a considerably larger number of children and a frequent indifference to their legitimacy. And when family responsibilities were cut in order to move up the social ladder, the result was the bourgeois family, whose smaller size was realized first by a postponement of marriage and later by the use of contraceptives.

THE TRANSITION IN FAMILY TYPE

There is no single statement on the fertility of Malthus's period comparable to the relatively authoritative view of someone like McKeown on mortality. The data of the period are no worse for births than for deaths, but the difficulties in interpreting them are on a different scale altogether. Britain's mortality definitely declined during Malthus's lifetime; but whether fertility remained constant or rose slightly has not been settled to the satisfaction of present-day analysts. We can reasonably assume that everyone wanted a longer and a healthier life; but one of the issues in the analysis of family size is how and when the desire for fewer children arose. We know a good bit about the development of the principal means of death control and enough about their dissemination to speculate plausibly on their probable effect; but the practice of such a contraceptive means as coitus interruptus may have ranged, for all we know or can ever find out, from nil to the entire adult population. The trend in fertility, even if it could be traced with full accuracy, would combine the procreative effects of the several patterns of reproduction, which could be distinguished numerically only with far fuller data than will ever be available. It is because of such difficulties that I must resort to the explication of the three ideal types.

The traditional family type imposed constraints so onerous that they could be maintained only so long as the institutional framework persisted in which they were embedded. Young men and women were induced to remain single because the social pressure from the villagers among whom they lived was effective, and because those who accepted the norm and postponed or forwent marriage received as a quid pro quo the assurance of lifetime security. With the transformation of agriculture that the enclosure movement signaled, the sizable migration to cities and new industrial areas, and the lack of family—or, indeed, any—control over many of these migrants, the supports of the traditional pattern eroded.

A crucial sign of this disorganization was that a far larger proportion of children were born out of wedlock. The percentage of all births listed as illegitimate is not as satisfactory a measure as the number of illegitimate births per thousand unmarried or widowed women in the fecund range, since the former (called the illegitimacy ratio) can vary also with the number of women who might give birth to bastards. Data are seldom available, however, to mark the trend by the second measure (called the illegitimacy rate). But the rise was too sharp to be a consequence merely of poor data or the use of a less than fully satisfactory index. "The years 1790–1860 were, in virtually every [European] society or community we know about, the peak period of illegitimacy."[8] So wrote Edward Shorter in an interesting survey, which Laslett criticized only to reach the same conclusion: from the 1650s to 1842, England's illegitimacy ratio rose from slightly less than 1 to over 7 percent.[9] No single factor suffices to explain this shift in bastardy from a minor aberration to an alternative social pattern, but several contributed to the transformation.

In all Germanic countries (though apparently less in England than on the Continent), there was a tradition of what is sometimes called "bundling" but better "window wooing," a literal translation of the Dutch *venstervrijen*. By this folk norm premarital intercourse was usual, and marriage did not take place until after the bride was pregnant; but with respect to both timing and the mate chosen, these were typically planned conceptions arranged in order to avoid the disaster of a sterile marriage.[10] In the Netherlands, strangely, the custom endured longest in the strictest Calvinist circles, which were also the most traditional. In the fundamentalist village of Staphorst, for example, the typical one-family house has a window built low in the brick wall so that a young man can conveniently step out of his wooden shoes on to the bed of the family's unmarried daughter. In the 1920s several ministers fulminated from their pulpits against such young people who spent Saturday night in sin and then went to church on Sunday morning; and finally this effort succeeded—in changing the traditional night for window wooing from Saturday to Friday. In the mid-1930s still, well over a third of the first births in Staphorst were within seven months of the wedding ceremony; and according to a government survey just before World War II, "forced marriages" in all of the Netherlands ranged from just over 13 percent in large towns to 16 percent in villages.[11] So long as local controls were in effect, window wooing hardly ever resulted in an illegitimate birth; but once these controls were lessened the custom invited dalliance.

Under the old system the peasant household often included, as I have noted, relatives and servants who were virtually members of the family. With the shift to larger and more commercial farms, the relation between the master of the house and female servants became less family-like, with far greater possibilities of sexual exploitation. According to Shorter's survey, the occupational grouping most subject to illegitimacy was domestic servants, whether rural or urban. The number of female factory workers grew more slowly, but among them one finds "staggering" illegitimacy ratios, ranging up to more than half in Vienna of the 1860s. Whether those in a position to exploit employees fathered most of the bastards we do not know; certainly some maidservants and factory girls were made pregnant by young men of their own social class, who were also freed from old-style village constraints.

In short, one effect of the industrial revolution was to swell greatly the number of casual workers, ousted from relative comfort at the lower level of the village and unable to find a similarly secure place in a new society in formation. People in such circumstances, then as now, often do not marry before bearing children, let alone exercise control over their number. Those whose lives were disrupted by profound economic changes generally could maintain family norms only if they were embedded in lower-class churches that imposed controls almost absurdly strict by middle-class standards—Methodism or the Salvation Army or, in the United States, the fundamentalist sects of the South among both Negro and white poor.

In one of Lee Rainwater's surveys, he found that "some respondents are quite passive and fatalistic about family planning; they do nothing because they do not think anything will help, or they go through the motions of using a method in which they have little confidence (and therefore do not use it very consistently) ."[12] In his urban American sample, some 14 percent of the middle-class Catholics responded with this hapless passivity, and some 24 percent of the unskilled workers. But among the casual workers and the unemployed, whether white or black, almost two out of every three did not believe enough in any future to plan anything, including their families. It is virtually impossible to devise an ameliorative program that will affect such persons, who consider neither the costs nor the benefits of their acts. They are not "rational" as this word is used in the social disciplines; that is, they do not consciously choose among known alternatives on the basis of their probable effect—the type of behavior that Max Weber called *Zweckrationalität* and modern economists have incorporated in their concept of utility.

But is so emotional a process as procreation ever really rational, and has the degree of foresight involved in family formation changed with modernization? One way to answer such questions is to assume that all who have children are well aware of what they are doing and to discuss how their rational behavior differs under specified conditions. According to one recent review of fertility theory, thus, where wealth flows from the young to the old it is economically desirable to have the physiologically maximum number of children; where it flows from the old to the young the economic criterion sets no children at all as the optimum. In other words,

parents who expect their children to work to support them in
their old age will beget prodigiously; those who expect to have
to pay for their children's college education will be more
circumspect. One can admit the reasonableness of the distinction while retaining a good deal of curiosity about the "social"
factors that, in both family systems, inhibit parents from
following the economic injunctions to the limit.[13] Or, in Gary
Becker's similar application of the concept of utility specifically to modern American society:

> A family must determine not only how many children it has but
> also the amount spent on them—whether it should provide sepa-
> rate bedrooms, send them to nursery school and private colleges,
> give them dance or music lessons, and so forth . . . If more is
> voluntarily spent on one child than on another, it is because the
> parents obtain additional utility from the additional expenditure,
> and it is this additional utility which we call higher "quality"
> . . . Economic theory . . . suggests that a rise in income would
> increase both the quality and quantity of children desired.[14]

This thesis was called "a generalization and development" of
Malthus, but the assertion that "an increase in income would
lead to a relatively large increase in family size" derived, in
fact, only from the First Essay. In all Western countries
throughout the modern period, the typical correlation between
income and fertility has been *negative*—a fact that Malthus
tried to explain in the later development of his theory. In
Becker's model this prevalent deviation was assigned to an
unanalyzed factor: "the relative preference for children—or,
in other words, 'tastes'— . . . permits, although it does not
predict, fertility differences that are unrelated to 'economic'
factors." In short, those who generalize from some decisions
of some parents to the thesis that family building is ordinarily
a rational process must fall back on "social" factors or "tastes"
to adjust their theories to reality.

A more common belief, virtually axiomatic among family
sociologists, is that with modernization there has been a shift
toward greater rationality in decisions concerning marriage
and childbearing. Indeed, the norm summed up in the adage
ascribed to Luther—that "God makes children and He will
also nourish them"—is hardly to be found in the Western world.
More generally, it is held that the family used to be a de-

pository of traditional values, impervious to the calculating manipulations that characterized other enclaves of human society. But the sizable store in medical history of amulets, spells, medicaments, and whatever to combat childlessness hardly indicates—however ineffective most of them were—a reluctance to "interfere" in a "natural" process. And the inhibitions to large families that we have noted—Europe's family system, various types of contraception or abortion, and widespread infanticide—suggest that rationality was applied in an antinatalist as well as a pronatalist sense. In preindustrial societies the designation of persons deemed suitable to wed was also by a careful calculation: adult members of two kin groups arranged a marriage between adolescents in order to provide the optimum setting for the rearing of the next generation. In modern Western countries, on the contrary, the two young people select each other on the basis of their mutual attraction, and usually their parents accede to any choice that does not do outrage to their hopes. In this respect, in other words, the trend has been from more to less rational.

According to the conventional timing, in the West the ideology of romantic love was developed by troubadours at medieval courts, but in that early version it was a sentiment appropriate only between a man and a woman not linked by the tedium of a family bond. As the basis of a marriage defined as desirable, romantic love came much later. Its first important proponent was Samuel Richardson (1689–1761), whose creative work, he declared, was intended "to cultivate the principles of virtue and religion in the minds of the youth of both sexes." Pamela, the heroine of his first novel, was a servant in the house of a nobleman who, after trying in every way to seduce her, ended after a series of failures by offering marriage. The symbolic contest between the libertine nobility and the virtuous lower and middle classes is close to the surface, and Richardson's enormous popularity was perhaps due more to his message than to the literary quality of his works. The influence of *Clarissa* on Diderot's *La Religieuse* is apparent, and when his mentor . died Diderot wrote: "O Richardson, Richardson, a man unique in my eyes, you will be my teacher for all time. Forced by pressing needs I shall sell my books, but you will stay with me on the same shelf as Moses, . Homer, Eurypides, and Sophocles." Nor was this extravagant praise idiosyncratic. Rousseau reacted similarly to the French translations; after reading the German translations, Goethe asserted that Richardson had "made the citizen world attentive to a more delicate morality."[15]

The bourgeois family started, then, from the mutual attraction of the couple, and the self-imposed postponement that Malthus prescribed seemingly would become a less and less realistic policy as the decision when to marry moved from the older to the younger generation. But the full effect of this significant shift was not evident until the twentieth century, and even today our ethical norms and laws contain some residue of the notion that a marriage implies new responsibilities, which presumably can be met best by persons well beyond puberty. During the nineteenth century, the members of the rising middle class generally had the smallest families. This paradox—that persons financially better able to care for offspring typically had fewer—was at first explained as a symptom of biological degeneration: the physiological ability of women to bear children was being impaired by their new way of life. Indeed, without the clinical evidence that accumulated only later, how could one be sure that it was not, say, the unhealthful riding of bicycles that caused ladies who owned them to have fewer babies? And when this nineteenth-century theory disappeared, it was partly supplanted by others hardly less fanciful—for instance, that the decline in the average size of the Western family was due to factors like "the widespread habit of excessive washing."[16] Recurrently the idea that modern life damages man's (and especially woman's) ability to reproduce has been associated with diet. This supposed relation was given its first book-length exposition in Doubleday's *True Law of Population*. Whenever a species or genus is endangered, he wrote, nature "invariably" arranges to increase its fecundity, especially when the danger arises from inadequate nutrition. In human societies, the same principle applies to the social classes:

> There is in all societies a constant increase going on amongst that portion which is the worst supplied with food—in short, among the poorest. Among those . . . well supplied with food and luxuries, a constant decrease goes on . . . In a nation highly and generally affluent and luxurious, population will decrease and decay. In poor and ill fed communities, population will increase in the ratio of the poverty.[17]

A similar formulation, that the high-protein diet of well-to-do classes and nations was responsible for their generally smaller families, was propounded as late as the 1950s in a best-selling book.[18] But most demographers today would agree that cleanliness and good food, together with all other conditions conducive to good health, increase reproductive capacity to the degree that they affect it at all, but that these physical factors have often been negated in industrial societies by the higher social valuation put on small families.

Not malnutrition but the best possibility of moving to a higher social rung induced the middle classes to adopt the norm of small families.

> Any man tends . . . to climb unceasingly, as oil rises in a lamp wick . . . For one who starts at the bottom to arrive at the top, it is necessary to run fast and not to be encumbered with baggage. Thus, while an ambitious man can be served by a good marriage, because of either the wealth or the contacts it brings him, his own children, particularly if they are numerous, almost inevitably slow him down.[19]

This process, which Dumont labeled "social capillarity," he regarded as disastrous for France, for the inverse correlation between status and family size meant that most of each generation were being born at the bottom socially, and possibly also genetically. A far superior analysis of the process is the book by J. A. Banks entitled *Prosperity and Parenthood: A Study of Family Planning among the Victorian Upper Classes*. As Britain's industrialization began to open up lucrative positions (which the established upper class did not deign to accept), it was possible for many to rise into the new middle class; but to compete successfully aspirants had to establish and maintain an appropriate respectability. The paraphernalia of gentility included a growing number of servants at a better and better address, an ever larger and more expensive carriage, sons who attended boarding school and, toward the end of the century, also university. Among such family expenditures, the one item that could be cut was the number of offspring, and this saving was effected first by a postponement of marriage. Among the clergymen, doctors, lawyers, members of the aristocracy, merchants, bankers, manufacturers, and others of the gentleman class who married between 1840 and

1870, the average age was a shade under 30 years. "Anthony Trollope's advice to a young lady, 'Fall in love, marry the man, have two children, and live happily ever afterwards,' seems neatly to sum up the outlook of the later period," when the at first surreptitious use of contraceptives spread among the middle class and permitted the same end by a less painful means.[20] The movement to disseminate this birth control was named, as everyone knows, after Malthus.

MALTHUS AND NEO-MALTHUSIANISM

The opposition to contraception and abortion that Malthus shared with respectable society of his time may have been strengthened by his Christian faith and ecclesiastic position, but the main reason that he himself gave for his stance derived rather from his hope of bettering our lot on earth. The tension between population and subsistence, which in his schema is the major cause of misery and vice, can also have a beneficial effect. For a man who postpones marriage until he is able to support his family is driven by his sexual urge to work hard. The use of contraceptives permits sexual gratification free, as it were, and therefore it does not generate the same ambition and perseverance as would either a chaste postponement of marriage or children to care for. If a misunderstanding of Malthus's meaning was possible in the First Essay, this possibility should have been removed by a very specific denunciation of birth control that he made in an appendix to the 1817 edition. Referring to James Grahame, a Scottish advocate who wrote a book on population[21] as well as pamphlets on canals and usury (not, of course, the better known Scottish poet of the same name), Malthus asserted,

> I should always particularly reprobate any artificial or unnatural modes of checking population, both on account of their immorality and their tendency to remove a necessary stimulus to industry. If it were possible for each married couple to limit by a wish the number of their children, there is certainly reason to fear that the indolence of the human race would be very greatly increased, and that neither the population of individual countries nor of the whole earth would ever reach its natural and proper extent. But the restraints which I have recommended are quite of a different character. They are not only pointed out by reason and sanctioned by religion, but tend in the most marked manner to stimulate industry.[22]

Even on a topic usually argued in terms of religious precepts, "Rev." Malthus took his stand largely on secular grounds.

The first important figure to amend Malthus's population doctrine by advocating contraception was Francis Place (1771–1854). Like Samuel Pepys or Samuel Johnson, Place was a Londoner through and through, but one whose fascination with the city focused on its lower classes, which he observed with sympathy and knowledge. Apprenticed at 14 to a master in the leather trade, he several years later led an unsuccessful strike of journeymen and was proscribed by all in the trade. Eventually he became a well-to-do tailor and then a full-time reformer, active in the movement to repeal the combination laws prohibiting trade unions, the campaign to establish London University, the reform bill to extend suffrage, the Anti-Corn Law League, and the Chartists. In him and the group of like-minded men who met regularly in his library there were combined all the reformist attitudes of the early nineteenth century—the utilitarian theory of Jeremy Bentham, working-class militancy, constitutional reform, and the self-help of the middle class. Perhaps the most attractive of the birth-control advocates, Place shared many of the movement's defects. His literary style was so wooden and repetitive that efforts to publish his autobiography failed until 1972. Like most birth controllers, he was an atheist, thus linking a sensitive social reform to a then unpopular view of the cosmos.[23]

When he was 19, Place married a girl of 17, and the couple had a total of fifteen children. Neither in practice nor in doctrine was he a proponent of moral restraint. His *Illustrations and Proofs of the Principle of Population* was published in 1822, only two years after Godwin's attack on Malthus in *Of Population;* and Place's work was intended, as its subtitle informed the reader, to be "an examination of the proposed remedies of Mr. Malthus and a reply to the objections of Mr. Godwin and others." He wrote:

If . . . it were once clearly understood that it was not disreputable for married persons to avail themselves of such precautionary means as would, without being injurious to health or destructive of female delicacy, prevent conception, a sufficient check might at once be given to the increase in population beyond the means of subsistence . . . The course recommended will, I am fully persuaded, at some period be pursued by the people, even if left to themselves . . .

> The most effectual mode of diminishing promiscuous inter-
> course is marriage . . . If means were adopted to prevent the
> breeding of a larger number of children than a married couple
> might desire to have, and if the laboring part of the population
> could thus be kept below the demand for labor, wages would rise
> so as to afford the means of comfortable subsistence for all, and
> all might marry.[24]

Place noted that Malthus seemed "to shrink from discussing
the propriety of preventing conception," possibly from fear
of "encountering the prejudices of others." It is indeed remarkable, particularly in retrospect from the subsequent
linkage of his name with the birth-control movement, that
Malthus had so little to say about it. He did make the dis-
approving comment I have quoted, but he never responded to
the extremely friendly Francis Place, who—unlike Richard
Carlile, for instance[25]—did not publish his book anonymously.

As it developed from this initial impetus, neo-Malthusianism was no less an invention of the nineteenth century than,
say, the vulcanization of rubber, which made possible the
manufacture of more efficacious contraceptive devices. As one
would expect, most accounts have been written by persons
sympathetic to the international movement, whose leaders
have generally been pictured less as sectarians than as larger-
than-life heroes.[26] Why was it that, during the very decades
when Malthus's population doctrine was gaining almost automatic acceptance as part of the influential discipline of
economics, the related doctrine of neo-Malthusianism was
propagated by an embattled minority? One answer is that the
use of contraceptives was opposed by the prurient leaders of
Victorian society—or if not the use, then the open advocacy
of the use. But another and often more important reason for
the isolation of neo-Malthusians was that they were in the
main the type of people who expounded unpopular opinions
of all kinds.

Though such important Englishmen as Bentham and John
Stuart Mill believed in its principles, the leaders of the Malthusian League were far lesser figures. "With the exception of
Marie Stopes (who never quite reconciled herself to the fact),
all the leading pioneers of birth control were convinced free-
thinkers. Most of their writings on the subject were issued by
secularist publications."[27] Charles Bradlaugh, for instance,
published an essay titled *Jesus, Shelley, and Malthus* in which

he linked the espousal of birth control as the most important step to eliminate poverty to such deliberate affronts to religious persons as his assertion that "the Bible blasphemes humanity."[28] Though he was in some respects rather conventional in his attitudes toward sex and marriage (he did not believe, for instance, that remarriage was appropriate for a divorced person), Bradlaugh gave the impression of supporting free love by his praise of George Drysdale's *Elements of Social Science*—a stance that, according to Annie Besant, "was the origin of his worst difficulties."[29] Drysdale's work, a book of some 600 finely printed pages, was the most important statement of the movement, appearing in thirty-five English editions and translated into at least ten other languages. By his extensive and sympathetic exposition of classical economic theory, Drysdale bound the advocacy of contraception to a kind of simplified Ricardianism (thus, *not* Malthus's economic theory) ; and by his attacks on the family in "an exposition of the true cause and only cure of the three primary social evils: poverty, prostitution, and celibacy," he bound it to free love. More generally, the advocacy of birth control often overlapped with the support of other sectarian views: pacifism, temperance, vegetarianism, and sometimes—but not necessarily—feminism. Annie Besant opened her autobiography with her horoscope, for "that there is a real science of astrology I have no doubt." Eventually she joined the Theosophical Society; "I heard a Voice that was later to become to me the holiest sound on earth."[30]

In the United States the first book on birth control, *Moral Physiology* (1830), had been written by Robert Dale Owen, the oldest son of Robert Owen. It was followed shortly by Charles Knowlton's *Fruits of Philosophy* (1832), which is remembered chiefly as the subject of a notorious trial in England. After circulating for decades with a modest sale of about a thousand copies a year, Knowlton's little book was suddenly banned. Its proscription may have been due to the illustrations included in a new edition (though no copies of this are extant) or to a more censorious mood indicated by the organization of a Society for the Suppression of Vice, which may have initiated the trial of Bradlaugh and Besant for distributing the work. These reformers were less interested in its content than in the principles of a free press; they organized a Freethought Publishing Company and challenged the censorship with a new edition, of which copies were promptly delivered to the magistrate, the London police, and the city solicitor. At their trial the two defendants used the witness stand to air their views, which were reported at length even in provincial newspapers. So it was that after decades of obscurity the neo-Malthusian movement was suddenly given more publicity than it could ever have generated itself. *Fruits of Philosophy,* which argued that many children destroy family life, did not touch on what the defendants saw as the main problem, the effect of overpopulation on society. In 1877, the year of their trial, Annie Besant published her own pamphlet, *The Law of Population,* to state the neo-Malthusian doctrine that the working classes must raise themselves up from their poverty by limiting their procreation.[31] Several decades later the American movement was helped by a similar episode, when Margaret Sanger challenged the legality of the Comstock Act, in which "the prevention of conception" was defined as "obscene" and thus was proscribed from the mails.[32]

The recurrent association of neo-Malthusianism with every heterodox or crackpot idea was aggravated in England by nepotism. Charles Robert Drysdale (1829–1907), president of the Malthusian League from its founding in 1877, was the brother of George R. Drysdale (1825–1904), author of *The Elements of Social Science.* Charles Robert wrote much of the contents of the league's monthly *The Malthusian,* of which he was editor, as well as many of its pamphlets.[33] He edited two works, *Medical Opinions on the Population Question* (1901) and *Clerical Opinions on the Population Question* (1904), noting members of those two professions who were willing to support the practice of contraception publicly. George also wrote pamphlets,[34] with the author identified on the title pages as either "G. R." or "A Doctor of Medicine, Author of *The Elements of Social Science.*" Then there was Alice Vickery (1844–1929), wife of Charles Robert, who acted as the league's expert on feminism, writing such brochures (undated) as *A Programme of Women's Emancipation* and *A Women's Malthusian League.* Charles Vickery Drysdale (1874–1961), their son, and his wife, Bessie Drysdale (1871–1950), waged the attack of Malthusians against socialists in, for example, her pamphlet *Labour Troubles and Birth Control* (1920).

The literary style of this mass of print, admonishing the

faithful to the practice of a new creed, can be illustrated by a Victorian imitation of *Lysistrata* entitled *The Strike of a Sex: A Novel:*

> "Excuse me, sir," I cried, "but I beg you to tell me what horrible misfortune has befallen this place . . . Has some fearful plague devastated it? For Heaven's sake, tell me, where are the women?" . . .
>
> "Is it possible that you are not aware of the Great Women's Strike which has now been in progress here for more than three months? The women of this country have combined as a sex to utterly refuse to perform any longer those duties and functions which have hitherto been magnanimously marked out for them by man as the sole tasks predestined for them by the Creator" . . .
>
> "Where have the women gone, and their innocent children?" . . .
>
> "The women have simply wholly withdrawn from their habitations with men. They have taken possession of the commodious buildings of a large institute on the hill overlooking the town . . . Woman's abandonment of man has been complete, and," he added with a shudder, "*final,* unless the guarantee they ask is given them" . . .
>
> "But what is this freedom that woman seeks?"
>
> "It is . . . the right to the perfect ownership of her own person . . . In short, they demand, as a final, inalienable right, that man shall give them an irrevocable, perpetual guarantee that no woman from this time forth and forever shall be subjected to the woes of maternity without her free and specific consent in all cases" . . .
>
> It seemed as though my heart must burst at beholding the mighty spectacle of man and woman thus forever reconciled and united as they never had been since they were driven from the Garden of Eden . . . I was sobbing with convulsive joy.[35]

It is difficult for an outsider, particularly one from another era, to judge the effect of exhortatory writings; but this inept effort, atypical only in its pretentiousness, must strike anyone of the modern age initially as funny, very soon as boring Was the response from the Victorian and Edwardian public entirely different; or were the members of the sect, like sectarians of any type, addressing mainly themselves, the faithful adjuring the faithful to keep the faith?

One of the greatest weaknesses of neo-Malthusianism was the hostility between it and socialism, two competitors in utopian wares. To my knowledge Marx himself never commented on the birth-control movement that was so prominent in England from the Bradlaugh-Besant trial to his death six years later, but this abstention did not carry over to Marxist or other socialist organizations. According to C. V. Drysdale, neo-Malthusianism was "the especial *bête noire* of the Socialists, land reformers, and other advocates of redistribution and democratic control" and was thus "disliked by the laboring classes which it was especially intended to help."[36] The reason, in the view of Marie Stopes, was that "the intense antisocialism of the Malthusian League antagonized the great mass of the working people."[37] To lay the blame exclusively on either side is hardly adequate. The dispute derived in part from Malthus's distaste for the French Revolution and in part from Marx's virulent attacks on Malthus. Socialists not only followed Marx in these denunciations, not only welcomed a rapid growth of population as a sign of social health; many opposed contraception as intrinsically immoral, and some were indifferent to the travail that repeated births impose on mothers.[38] After all, woman is, in Proudhon's notorious view, physically, intellectually, and morally inferior to man, existing somewhere between his plane and that of animals.

The most significant socialist movement in the half-century before 1914 was not in England or France but in Germany, whose party was both the direct inheritor of the Marxist tradition and the largest and most influential unit of the Socialist International. According to a thorough survey made in 1922, German socialists were still opposed to family planning "almost without exception."[39] Party leaders like the elder Liebknecht, Lassalle, and Bebel, together with dozens of lesser figures, both repeated Marx's arguments against Malthus and applied them against neo-Malthusians. The most widely distributed version of the party's view was Bebel's *Woman*, which can be taken as the main example of German Social Democratic orthodoxy. Only in a capitalist society, Bebel wrote, does population tend to grow faster than the food available to it. "Socialism is better able to preserve the equilibrium between population and means of subsistence than any other form of community," for under socialism man will for the first time "consciously direct his entire development in accordance with natural laws." Controlling population growth was not an urgent problem, for the world had "a superabundance of land capable of cultivation, awaiting the labor of fresh hundreds of millions." When a reduction in family size did become necessary, this would not be realized by any means so distasteful as the use of contraceptives. "It is not impossible that the increase of population may depend materially on the kind of nourishment eaten. If this were once ascertained with certainty, the number of inhabitants might be more or less exclusively regulated by the manner of eating."[40]

Karl Kautsky's book on the subject, *The Influence of Population Increase on Social Progress* (1880), is interesting for its unusual attempt to find a compromise between Marx and Malthus. In the view of the young Kautsky, Malthus was wrong in his main thesis, that population *always* tends to increase faster than the supply of food on which it must subsist. But he was right in his assertion that every improvement in the state of the lower classes is accompanied by an increase in their numbers, an increase that has no automatic check to its indefinite continuation. (This is, of course, almost precisely the opposite of the actual thesis of the Second Essay.) Improved methods of production can merely postpone the danger of overpopulation, and the practical issue is to find an acceptable means of reducing the number of births, with contraception "the least of the evils among which we must choose."

> The question can no longer be *whether* birth control should be used, but only *when* it should be used, and which type of such control we should choose . . . The sterile rejection of population theory, at least on the part of socialism, is definitely out of place, for the two are not in principle incompatible . . . Only a transformation of society can extirpate the misery and vice that damn nine-tenths of the world to a lamentable existence; but only a regulation of population growth . . . can forestall the recurrence of this evil.[41]

Forty years later, when Kautsky wrote another work on the same subject, he noted in the preface that "as a callow young fellow who understood nothing of Marxism, I saw it as my most important task to revise it." In this mature, more orthodox exposition of Marx's views on how population growth functions in a capitalist economy, there is nothing very new. The most interesting chapters are on population and socialism. In spite of the fact that farm hands are "veritable fanatics" in their craving for small plots of their own, the socialist state would succeeed in absorbing them into its much more efficient collectivized agriculture, which would enable the society to expand food production "much faster than any possible population growth . . . for at least a century." True, mortality would fall "enormously," but fertility would also decline as the new woman took an interest in "the possibility of enjoyment and creativity in nature, art, and science." In short, socialist society would be perfect, as defined; for whenever population growth varies from the optimum, "public opinion and the conscience of individuals will make women's duties clear."[42]

The opposition to birth control, one should remember, was not merely a doctrinal stance of the party's intellectuals. For example, in 1913 the whole membership participated in mass meetings "against the birth strike." Especially in Germany, where the Social Democratic party was both large and deeply embedded in the personal lives of its adherents, hostility to planned parenthood was probably a factor of considerable importance in determining the fertility of working men. Class differences in family size, ordinarily explained by the greater religious or cultural traditionalism of the lower strata, may have derived also from the fact that their main antitraditionalist ideology included an almost passionate ban on the use of birth control. With the often significant Marxist component in political analysis and policy formation in less developed countries today, the intellectual elite has sometimes also been reluctant to recognize how serious an impediment rapid population growth can be to modernization.[43]

The position on Malthus and neo-Malthusians was carried over almost intact from democratic to totalitarian types of socialism. A book called *The Position of National Socialism on the Population Theory of Malthus and His Disciples* is remarkable mainly for its unusual accuracy: Malthus is identified as a professor, and the analysis of his population theory is based on the exposition in six editions of the *Essay* and relevant portions of the *Principles*. If one passes over the obsession with race, which permeated Nazi writings on whatever subject, the work might have been written by almost any of the socialist theorists. Marriage is not an "egoisme à deux," as with neo-Malthusians, but an extrapolation to a higher and more worthy stage of human life; and it is the policy of the state to support the family and encourage population growth. Any seeming excess of people can be countered by one of three measures: "inner colonization," that is, the transfer of workers to areas with a demand for labor; the acquisition of new territory and its colonization; and the support of industry and commerce.[44]

Communist doctrine under Stalin was more rabid on this point. In Soviet publications of the early 1950s birth control was identified as "the man-hating ideology of imperialists," "a bestial imperialist policy of aggressive wars and extermination." "Lackeys of American monopolies openly advocate cannibalism and try to justify the demoniacal plans for the mass extermination of peoples."[45] Opposition to any kind or degree of birth control was associated, moreover, with Marxist theory in the most extravagant form conceivable. In 1947 the Soviet delegate to the United Nations Population Commission, speaking at its first meeting, stated the orthodox dogma with breathtaking abandon: "I would consider it barbaric for the Commission to contemplate a limitation of marriages or of legitimate births, and this for any country whatsoever, at any period whatsoever. With an adequate social organization it is possible to face any increase in population."[46]

The most important element in the neo-Malthusian message was not the social theory in which the recommendations were enveloped, even less the literary style of the movement's writings. Most important was the contraceptive means that the practitioners proposed. In spite of the widely held belief to the contrary, birth control was not invented in the nineteenth century. Coitus interruptus, which Norman Himes judged to be "the most popular, widely diffused method of contraception," was by his guess "probably nearly as old as the group life of man."[47] It is only one of the ways that, so far as we know, contemporary primitives control their fertility; according to an early survey, without exception *every* primitive people had some means to restrict the increase of population: abstention from marriage, delayed marriage, periodic abstention from intercourse, coitus interruptus, prolonged lactation, other types of contraception, abortion, infanticide.[48] Of twenty-two medical writers of ancient Greece and Rome (all whose works are extant and not on irrelevant topics), eleven discussed contraceptive methods, and fifteen discussed ways of inducing abortion, apart from the texts in which the two were confused.[49] Of course, many of these methods were hardly effective; even Soranus, whose work has been depicted as "the most brilliant and original account of contraceptive techniques written prior to the nineteenth century,"[50] passed on the standard combination of superstition and effective practice. On the one hand, he suggested that the woman hold her breath during the sexual act or sneeze and drink something cold immediately after it; on the other hand, he recommended spermicides that physicians were still prescribing in the 1930s. As I have noted, historians have recently argued that infanticide was common in Western Europe until some time in the nineteenth century, and it was certainly much more so in such other civilizations as classical India, China, and Japan. Condoms made of the dried gut of a sheep were available in eighteenth-century London; Casanova had called them "English overcoats," and Boswell complained that they reduced the pleasure of the sexual act.[51]

How much of this contraceptive knowledge was preserved and, in Malthus's day, transmitted by word of mouth we do not know. Historians depend on written records, but to publish specific instructions on the control of births subjected the author and the printer or publisher to the risk of prosecution. Neither the work by James Grahame to which Malthus referred in his comment on birth control nor Francis Place's *Illustrations and Proofs* gives any hint of how, apart from the moral restraint that Malthus advocated, the limitation of family size was to be effected. The first printed information was in a series of handbills written either by Robert Owen or, more probably, by Place, perhaps with the advice of his friend Thomas Wakley, the medical reformer who founded and for a period edited *The Lancet*. The first of these, addressed "To the Married of Both Sexes," recommended that "a piece of sponge about an inch square be placed in the vagina previous to coition and afterwards withdrawn by means of a double twisted thread or bobbin attached to it . . . The sponge should, as a matter of preference, be used rather damp and when convenient a little warm." Alternatively, "the husband [should] withdraw previous to emission so that none of the semen may enter the vagina of his wife." In a second handbill, addressed "To the Married of Both Sexes in Genteel Life," there was substituted for the twisted thread "a very narrow ribbon," and coitus interruptus was omitted. And in the third version, "To the Married of Both Sexes of the Working People," it was stressed more that the sponge should be washed between one occasion and the next, and coitus interruptus was again omitted. A fourth version with no important additions exists in manuscript but was never printed.[52] An investigation of these "diabolical handbills," which focused on J. E. Taylor of the *Manchester Guardian* and then on Richard Carlile, had the same effect as the Bradlaugh-Besant trial two generations later, serving mainly to make the propaganda known. Though Place was denounced as "the mainspring that moves the whole infernal machine," he was not prosecuted.[53] How much information these first English publications brought to their readers we cannot know. The use of sponges and tampons as contraceptive devices goes back to before the Christian era, and the method was noted earlier in French publications; Himes speculates on whether the handbills represented a diffusion from France or an independent discovery.

In *The Elements of Social Science,* Drysdale noted five methods of contraception: the "natural" or what we would term the rhythm method, with intercourse limited to that portion of the menstrual cycle when, it so happens, conception would be *most* likely; coitus interruptus, an "unnatural" method that is "physically injurious, . . . apt to produce nervous disorder and sexual enfeeblement and congestion from the sudden interruption it gives to the venereal act, whose pleasure moreover it interferes with"; the sheath, which "dulls the enjoyment and frequently produces impotence in the man and disgust in both parties"; the sponge, "by far the best of these mechanical means"; and "the injection of tepid water into the vagina immediately after intercourse, . . . also a very effectual means of preventing impregnation." This is a strange compendium from the bible of the Malthusian League. The arbitrary distinction between "natural" and "unnatural" means of limiting procreation was in later decades combated even in the columns of *The Malthusian.*[54] And the notion that withdrawal causes nervous disorders, or that the use of a condom causes impotence, ranks among the favorite superstitions of the movement's more rabid opponents. Essentially Drysdale repeated the recommendation offered in the diabolical handbills; his second method, a douche of tepid water, represented a retrogression from Knowlton, who had proposed that one should "add something to the water that should not hurt the woman but yet kill the tender animalcules or, in other words, destroy the fecundating property of the semen."

In 1913 the Malthusian League issued a new pamphlet, *Hygienic Methods of Family Limitation,* which recommended withdrawal, a douche, or the condom. This was a step up from Drysdale but still not the most effective methods known at the time. As Marie Stopes wrote, "Had the Malthusian League's leaflet not been so very brief as regards useful methods and so indiscriminate in its recommendation of various rather harmful ones, I should never have written *Wise Parenthood,*" her own manual on family limitation. In a revised edition of the league's pamphlet, published in 1922, the "natural" method of Drysdale was ruled out altogether and the condom and pessary, especially the latter, were recommended.[55] As early as the 1850s all the basic processes of rubber manufacturing had been worked out and the manufacture of "questionable rubber goods" was booming at least in the United States.[56] Condoms were not necessarily without flaws, and pessaries had to be carefully fitted to be effective; but these were still better than the methods recommended by the official birth controllers of Britain until the third decade of this century.

To sum up: Little can be said concerning people's knowledge of contraceptive methods, but it is reasonable to assume that the simpler ones—coitus interruptus, a douche, a sponge—were part of popular lore well before any notice was taken of them in print. Advocacy of birth control, even by physicians, was not usually in advance of general knowledge; Knowlton's feelings were hurt when another physician testified at his trial, probably correctly, that there was nothing new in his recommendation of an astringent douche. This does not mean, of course, that folk methods were—or are—necessarily effective. According to a recent survey of mothers of six or more children in Leeds, one reasonably effective method still was what was variously termed "pulling out," "being careful," "being sensible," or "getting off at Hillgate," the bus stop before the one for home. Folk methods of inducing a menstrual flow included such a drink as milk stout boiled with two or three teaspoons of nutmeg, a solution of Tide or Epsom salts, quinine, or various "female pills" obtainable from a druggist or herbalist. Not surprisingly in view of such alternatives, almost half of the sample preferred female sterilization to any type of contraception or abortion.[57] That one finds the inhabitants of an English city still so ignorant in the 1970s suggests how little impact the neo-Malthusian movement has had on some women in the lower classes.

This is not to say, one should emphasize, that the reduction of family size was not a momentous social change. It was induced most fundamentally, however, by the prior decline in mortality and the consequent rise in the number of living children in each family, and in social-economic terms by the new ambitions that capitalist industrialism stimulated. Whether the birth-control movement also effected some decline in the birth rate, and if so how much, cannot be determined with certainty; but its contribution, if any, was surely smaller than it has ordinarily been adjudged.

FERTILITY IN TWO REPUBLICS

In the abstract it might be possible to test the efficacy of neo-Malthusian movements in various Western countries by relating the organizations' apparent strength to the rate of fertility decline. But particularly the first factor, and for the early part of the modern period also the second, would be very difficult to specify precisely. We can approach such a broader analysis, however, by noting the reactions to both Malthus and the birth-control movement in the two countries where family size fell first and most rapidly—the United States and France.

Benjamin Franklin, whose short work on population influenced the content of the Second Essay, was only one of a number of colonial Americans who expounded, more or less clearly, some of the main points in Malthus's theory.[58] This was hardly surprising in view of the fact that it was from this population that Malthus derived his generalization that under the most favorable conditions humans can double their number in every generation; and during the first years of the new nation both Federalists and Republicans generally endorsed Malthus. But some of the most important political issues during the nineteenth century were related to the determinants of population growth, and those on either side tended to divide also in their attitude toward what was taken to be Malthus's theory. The most complete historical review of population doctrines in the United States, thus, is in two more or less equal parts, "anti-Malthusians" and "Malthusians."[59]

The first of these divisive issues was slavery, and the doctrine that population tends to press on the means of subsistence and thus to lower wages was introduced into the debate as early as the constitutional convention of 1787, eleven years before the date of the First Essay. In the following decades some version of Malthus's principle was used to support both sides of the sharpening dispute. According to George Tucker of Virginia, "the great law of human destiny so ably developed by Malthus" would spell the doom of slavery, which he deemed to be incompatible with the "most advanced stages of society." Long before population density reached its maximum, he averred, "the price of labor will have so fallen that the value of a slave will not repay the cost of rearing him, in which case slavery, no longer profitable to the master, will naturally expire." He even set the date when this would take place—between 1903 and 1923 or, in a revised estimate after the annexation of Texas, before 1943.[60] The more usual argument, however, was a defense of slavery based on the principle of population, and commentators hostile to Malthus have been delighted to stress this association.[61] Malthus was appalled by such a conclusion from his work, "exactly the opposite" of what he had said. In later editions of the *Essay*, he devoted a portion of the appendix to reinforcing his stand that "a consideration of the laws which govern the increase and decrease of the human species tends to strengthen in the most powerful manner all the arguments in favor of abolition." For slave populations (as well as those of Africa from which slaves were drawn) are subjected to such "unusual" and "excessive" checks that their growth is typically very slow. Yet "by the eve of the Civil War Malthus's doctrines had been woven and integrated into a perfect theoretical defense of slavery."[62]

In the latter decades of the century, somewhat similarly, the *Essay* was used, particularly by Francis A. Walker, the period's most prolific and probably most influential writer on population, to argue for the restriction of immigration. In an article published in 1873, he gently derided the notion that, because the number of Americans had increased by about a third during each of the two decades following the 1790 census, this extraordinary growth might be expected to continue. The decline in fertility, he declared, came "later than it had been reasonable to expect," brought about by industrialization and urbanization but "covered from the common sight by a flood of immigration unprecedented in history." Twenty years later, when the source of immigrants was shifting from Northwestern to Southern and Eastern Europe, Walker found that the influx, "instead of constituting a net reinforcement to the population, simply resulted in a replacement of native by foreign elements." He proved this by referring to the same projection that earlier he had dismissed, but now he used it in the contrary sense. A threefold increase in the number of immigrants, he asserted, had merely caused the native birth rate to decline proportionately; the American "was unwilling himself to engage in the lowest kind of day labor with these new elements of the population . . . [and] even more unwilling to bring sons and daughters into the world to enter into that competition." For him, the public issue was how to protect "the quality of American citizenship from degradation through the tumultuous access of vast throngs of ignorant and brutalized peasantry."[63] Like the defense of slavery, this opposition to immigration on frankly racist grounds was based on a seemingly plausible interpretation of Malthus's theory. In the United States even more than in England, in other words, the principle of population was entangled in polemics and used in a manner hardly in accord with the author's intent.

The decline of fertility that Walker noted had been in process for perhaps a century, starting long before the immigration that he opposed. There is sparse written evidence that the colonial population had used prolonged nursing and especially coitus interruptus to inhibit conception; and in the 1830s, as I have noted, Robert Dale Owen and Charles Knowlton published works advocating birth control and, in the latter case, recommending an astringent douche. The circulation of such works was considerable, even enormous. In 1858 about a fourth of the advertising in one New England newspaper pertained to medicines and treatments for "secret diseases," abortion, and contraception. Frederick Hollick's *The Marriage Guide*, first published in 1850, went through over three hundred printings, with a total sale of almost a million copies. The range of birth-control methods described more or less accurately, whether to advocate or to condemn, was wide: abstinence or infrequent intercourse, a rhythm method based on an inaccurate timing of ovulation, intercourse without ejaculation, coitus interruptus, condoms, "womb veils" (that is, cervical caps), sponges, douches, abortion. In 1864 a New Hampshire physician complained that the 123 types of pessary he knew of were converting the vagina into "a Chinese toy shop." Also recommended were such chemicals and extracts as ergot, cotton root, aloes, savin, tansy, opium, iodine, lemon juice, vinegar, prussic or sulfuric acid, and Lysol! If a woman could avoid an orgasm, according to some authorities, she would not become pregnant. Electric devices were said to render the semen sterile. The more startling items in this listing, it is true, were in the inventory of quacks, but one should keep in mind that even in the best medical circles knowledge of the physiology of reproduction was slight and often faulty.[64]

This dissemination of contraceptive propaganda was driven underground in 1873, when the Comstock Law was passed; and until the decade after the First World War, when Margaret Sanger's efforts culminated in the institution of a birth-control movement, the record is much more difficult to document. This had little or no effect on the country's fertility. Most of the decline in family size from perhaps seven children in the colonial period to the present more modest dimensions took place before a neo-Malthusian movement of any sort came into being. The link between organized ideology and behavior that is assumed in most accounts is certainly not validated in the American case.

Nor is it in the French one. One should recall that the translator of the *Essay* was a Swiss professor at the University of Geneva and that he found it expedient to write a fifty-page introduction designed to dispel the antipathy assumed to exist in a francophone audience. France's birth rate had started its secular decline around the middle of the eighteenth century, so that by the time the *Essay* appeared its doctrine opposed not only the utopianism it attacked but also a pronatalist sentiment that over the following decades would become general. In his standard work on the history of population theory, Gonnard gave a full and accurate account of Malthus's thought, largely favorable but ending with two sharply worded criticisms. Malthus, he held, underestimated the destructive force of "civilization"; the unhealthful conditions associated with industrialism and urbanism, "as we have seen," generated positive as well as preventive checks. Second, in spite of the pessimism for which he had been reproached, on one point Malthus was too optimistic: "With the 'improvement' that he anticipated, Malthus neglected to ask whether it might not become excessive, . . . above all, whether for many men the barrier between moral restraint and restraint through vice is not terribly fragile—in a word, whether civilized beings, in avoiding the perhaps illusory Charybdis of overpopulation, have not risked a more dangerous reef, the Scylla of depopulation."[65] According to Gonnard, though initially the *Essay* met with strong opposition in England, "by 1830, the general trend among English economists was Malthusian." This was hardly the case in France, as he showed with citations not only from such socialists as Fourier and Louis Blanc but from such "bourgeois" economists as Bastiat, Leroy-Beaulieu, Villey, Charles Gide, and others. Some of Malthus's contemporaries— for example, Say and Joseph Garnier[66]—thoroughly approved of his ideas, but later in the nineteenth century he came under attack from all sides. The *Essay*, according to such critics, was not a work of science but a polemical effort, doctrinal and dogmatic, and in spite of the elaboration in later editions based less on factual evidence than on its a priori thesis.[67] Louis Salleron, whose appraisal was more nearly balanced, was also mainly negative: "Historic developments here [in France] have completely denied the validity of Malthus's expectations . . . Simple reasoning suffices to convince one of his error . . . Why was Malthus so blind to these manifest realities? Because he was obsessed with the problems of his own time—that is, with the great misery that reigned among the poor classes of his country."[68] In other words, whatever worth Malthus's work had was specific to the Britain of his lifetime, for allegedly he failed to note the diversity of population characteristics in the rest of the world. Only the exceptional person among recent French commentators has offered a less parochial judgment: "Can one say that Malthus's theory, perhaps valuable in 1798, is today completely outdated? . . . We do not think so, . . . [for] the present situation in Western Europe is not that of the entire world, and it seems to be almost impossible to consider the future without evoking the menacing shadow of the English clergyman."[69]

For those whose understanding of the principle of population was rudimentary, the trend in French fertility was enough to invalidate it. As early as 1851, the rate of natural increase (that is, of the excess of births over deaths) was only 2.4 per thousand population, and by 1891–1900 it had fallen to 0.6— in each case, lower than that of any other Western European country. Neo-Malthusianism in such a context was generally regarded as irrelevant or vicious. The editor of a collection of writings on the subject classified them into five categories: liberal economists, pronatalists, socialists and Communists, Catholics, and "theorists of the optimum and of freedom of choice." Under each of these headings, the dominant position was opposition to contraception or, at least, to the organized advocacy of birth control.[70] On the one hand, Malthus was accused of propounding a theological doctrine; on the other hand, only true religion could counteract the trends he tried to analyze.[71] A book on misery and numbers was subtitled with a forthrightness that summed up the French opinion of both the man and the movement, "The Malthusian Bugbear."[72]

Negatively, then, the United States and France had in common a widespread misunderstanding of the *Essay;* a hostility to Malthus's ideas, stronger in France but prominent in both countries; a weak birth-control movement, in the United States organized only in the twentieth century, and in France under continuous and effective attack. The other common characteristic was that, compared to the rest of the Western world, family size fell very early to levels that, in France, were exciting alarm even during Malthus's lifetime. The means of effecting this lower fertility were simply folk methods, only sometimes efficacious, often dangerous; knowledge of them spread by word of mouth, along commercial routes, or often through the denunciations of those opposed to their use. In neither country was a birth-control movement at all a significant factor in bringing about the reduction in natality.

What, then, did the two nations share that might have produced this common effect? It requires no great cogitation to arrive at the answer that it was in these countries that ideas of personal liberty and freedom of choice first circulated widely. The doctrines of the two revolutions, though derived from principles enunciated earlier in England and France, were so strongly and repeatedly emphasized that their proponents began to apply them not only to narrowly political issues but also to such seemingly extraneous questions as how to choose between a numerous progeny and alternative ways of spending one's time, money, and effort. As I have remarked, such a pronatalist analyst as Arsène Dumont believed that it was the love of luxury that led to a desire for smaller families. Though Dumont borrowed this concept of social capillarity from Malthus, there was an important difference: what Dumont denounced as the product of a selfish and effete society was for Malthus the means of evading the horrors of the positive checks.

MALTHUS's THEORY OF FERTILITY

According to Charles Robert Drysdale, "the phrase, 'improper arts,' is the only point on which the so-styled Neo-Malthusians differ from Malthus."[73] This dogma of the movement has become doctrine for all, but it is seriously misleading. However great the opposition to Malthus, he did not aggravate it by linking his policy recommendations to every aberrant cause from atheism to free love, from astrology to vegetarianism. Without the ceaseless activity of the Drysdales, contraception might well have acquired its present respectability decades earlier in spite of Malthus's almost incidental opposition to this means of achieving a lower fertility. Moreover, the neo-Malthusian propaganda had the effect of concentrating policy narrowly on the *method* of contraception, a false lead that is still followed in current efforts to control births.

Family-planning programs in less developed countries, set up usually with some American financing and often under the partial direction of American researchers, have typically been based on several postulates that have proved to be more or less invalid. In a country that as a whole is overpopulated, it has been assumed that it is in the interest of every individual to have fewer children. Supposedly a problem arises, then, only because not everyone behaves in accord with his self-interest. Perhaps family-building habits continue after the sharp decline in infant mortality has made them inappropriate; perhaps various traditional beliefs (typically denigrated as superstitions) inhibit the diffusion of contraception; perhaps—and this has usually been denoted the main factor—too few contraceptive means are available at a price the lower classes can afford. The "solution," thus, is to furnish at cost, or even gratis, intra-uterine devices, vasectomies, or whatever, and to combat any reluctance to the idea of small family size by an intensive propaganda campaign.

Programs based on this rationale have not been remarkably successful. On Taiwan, often taken to be the showpiece of antinatalist campaigns, the substantial decline in fertility started before the birth-control program was initiated and thereafter proceeded independent of it.[74] The comparable decline in other similarly small and well managed states (such as Hong Kong, Thailand, Puerto Rico, Costa Rica), many of them also islands, was generally due at least in part to the stimulus of a growing economy; these were developing rather than merely less developed areas. The large, heterogeneous, often poorly governed states that have suffered most from the effects of rapid population growth (such as India, Pakistan, Bangladesh, most Arab countries, most of Central America) have statistics too poor to determine whether fertility has fallen, not to say whether a presumed decline resulted from family-planning programs. One can definitely assert, however, that the effect of these programs has been stupendously less than their sponsors originally anticipated.

The neo-Marxist view opposed to this current neo-Malthusianism denies the conjunction between the welfare of the community and that of the individuals that comprise it, the fundament of liberal political theory. The whole is not equal to the sum of its parts. Among two of the largest social classes of India, by Mamdani's analysis, it is in the economic interest of each person to have many children, even though the overall consequence of this breeding is disastrous. The smallholder operates with too tight a budget to hire even one farmhand and must therefore depend on family labor; and if a son or two find work in a city and send back some of their earnings, the peasant's circumstances can become a bit less straitened. The landless farm laborer, similarly, earns his pittance during peak seasons from piece rates paid to a family team, in which even a small child can add more to the pot than he takes from it.[75] The "solution" requires a fundamental change in property relations, rather than mere appeals to self-interest; and it is typical to end such a diagnosis by contrasting India (which is an open enough society for its ills to be apparent to all) with Communist China (where the government itself does not know even the population size, not to say the rate of its growth). In such socialist countries as the Soviet Union

212

and China, the collectivization of agriculture was imposed with a brutality exceptional even by totalitarian standards, with two contrary effects on the population-resources ratio. On the one hand, the millions killed off in each of the countries both reduced what was deemed to be a surplus in rural areas and facilitated the task of keeping those who survived under state control. On the other hand, the damage at least to Soviet agriculture has been permanent; it manages to stay afloat only by the state's reluctant, "temporary" acquiescence in private plots, whose produce is periodically supplemented by massive imports of food grains from capitalist countries.

This dispute between present-day neo-Malthusians and neo-Marxists, so prominent in the discussion of birth-control programs particularly of less developed countries, is a strange commentary on Malthus's actual theory. Though both of the current ideologies have of course developed their own theses and rationalizations, to some degree both derive from Malthus. Neo-Malthusianism inherited the overemphasis on contraceptive means from the nineteenth-century movement, and if one restores to this truncated version the portion of Malthus's theory that the Drysdales and others dropped, it is akin to what is now called neo-Marxism. Both elements were associated with utilitarian theory.

Utilitarianism is one variant of what is now termed the theory of social choice, which relates rational decisions of individuals to the trend in the whole society. According to Bentham, not only does each person behave in order to maximize his "pleasures" and minimize his "pains" (as measured by their intensity, duration, relative certainty, propinquity, and other characteristics), but the best society is that in which the sum of pleasures is greatest and that of pains is least.[76] The basic notions of utilitarianism go back as far as Helvetius, whom Bentham cited, and were subsequently developed through the emendations particularly of Pigou into a theory of social welfare, which in a loose way still dominates the usual evaluation of policies in democratic societies. But Kenneth Arrow, who had proved that the calculus of utilitarianism or social welfare is logically impossible, was not excessively optimistic about analyses subsequent to his critique:

The main results of the theory so far have been negative. That is, if we impose some reasonable-sounding conditions on the process of forming social choices from individual preference, it can be demonstrated that there are no processes which will always satisfy those conditions . . . Although there is no thoroughly satisfactory resolution, and there probably can never be a truly all-embracing one, some of the recent contributions are illuminating and very likely hopeful.[77]

Though as a utilitarian Malthus implicitly accepted the theses that all men are rational and that their combined social choices add up to the best of possible societies, in his own analysis he did not follow either of the Benthamite postulates. The structure of the *Essay* emphasizes his division between eras or places with a high mortality and those with a low fertility. Book I is on checks "in the less civilized parts of the world and in past times," Book II on those "in the different states of modern Europe." After a mainly economic miscellany in Book III, the final chapters of the work deal with "future prospects," which he judged with a degree of optimism. However, when he spelled it out, the optimism pertained only to Western Europe, particularly to England, Scotland, Norway, and Switzerland, where marriages "are the latest or the least frequent." Like today's analysts, Malthus divided the world between what we term developed and less developed countries, in which fertility is and is not under adequate control. To speak of "Malthusian pressure" in present-day India or Egypt or Central America implies that Malthus was half right; in fact, he was correct also about the trend in Western Europe and its overseas extensions.

A classification by national populations can be only very rough, for in every country the various sectors generally differ significantly in the attitudes and behavior patterns relevant to population growth. Not only was Malthus aware of the then barely discernible inverse correlation between social class and family size, but he came to regard this as the main clue to correct social policy. Many in the upper classes saw this class division as fixed, a chasm between Disraeli's "two nations," between the civilized and the mass of animalic poor. For Malthus, however, the proletariat represented a social problem that could be solved by progressive improvement of their condition. Everyone who believed himself trapped at the bottom of society, he thought, should be encouraged and helped to rise, and in doing so to acquire the self-confidence and self-reliance that he lacked. Family planning, like any other type of planning, depends on faith in the future, and no one is likely to consider what he will do tomorrow unless he feels himself a free agent, living in a country with both civil and political liberty. In short, the spread of moral restraint from the middle classes in which it was generally practiced would be, he hoped, through the embourgeoisement of the lower classes: as they acquired a higher standard of life, they would also adopt the small-family system.

In Malthus's theory, wages are determined by the amount of money available for that purpose and by the level of demand workers set, and generally these two factors change together. For "when the funds for the maintenance of labor are rapidly increasing and the laborer commands a large portion of necessaries, it is to be expected, if he has the opportunity of exchanging his superfluous food for conveniences and comforts, he will acquire a taste for these conveniences, and his habits will be formed accordingly."[78] That is to say, workers who moved into the middle-class income range would come to aspire to a middle-class style of life. This rise in workers' standards of living could be greatly facilitated by an appropriate political setting:

> Of all the causes which tend to generate prudential habits among the lower classes of society, the most essential is unquestionably civil liberty. No people can be much accustomed to form plans for the future who do not feel assured that their industrious exertions . . . will be allowed free scope . . . [Moreover,] civil liberty cannot be permanently secured without political liberty, . . . [which] teach[es] the lower classes of society to respect themselves by obliging the higher classes to respect them.[79]

In line with these ideas, Malthus advocated a system of universal free education.

> In most countries, among the lower classes of people, there appears to be something like a standard of wretchedness, a point below which they will not continue to marry and propagate their species . . . The principal circumstances which contribute to raise [this standard] are liberty, security of property, the diffusion of knowledge, and a taste for the comforts of life. Those which contribute principally to lower it are despotism and ignorance.[80]

How little these ideas penetrated even to those close to Malthus can be illustrated from the lectures of Richard Jones, who succeeded him as professor of political economy at the East India College. Malthus's enumeration of the checks to population he found "both defective and unhappy," for "vice, misery, and moral restraint do not comprise all the checks to population, unless we extend in an unjustifiable manner the meaning of these terms." His principal emendation was to substitute for "moral restraint" the phrase "voluntary restraint"—hardly a momentous revision.

> [Malthus's] error will be eliminated from our views, if instead of assuming that mankind are always pressing on to the limits of the food that can be produced, we assume, what is true, that the power of increase is always exerted till it brings all ranks of men up to the limits of the subsistence each class requires in order to satisfy its cravings, not merely for food, but likewise for the commodities necessary to supply all the wants and gratifications which are essential to maintain them in comfort and contentment.[81]

Like a number of other instances that I have noted, this was less a refutation of Malthus than a paraphrase of his amended theory.

Malthus certainly believed firmly that each person is responsible for his own fate, and he continually exhorted everyone to follow his injunctions to practice moral restraint. "The happiness of the whole is to be the result of the happiness of individuals, and to begin with the first of them . . . He who performs his duty faithfully will reap the full fruits of it, whatever may be the number of others who fail."[82] This perfect expression of the classical liberal model applied to the problem of fertility hardly represented the whole of Malthus's thought on the subject. He did not believe that those who procreated too abundantly should be merely exhorted to desist. Decisions of potential parents whether to have a (or another) child are typically based, he held, on their circumstances, which differ systematically between the social class with generally small families and that with too high a fertility for the good of either the parents or society. Good social policy, then, begins by reducing this gap, bringing the social conditions of those that reproduce to excess and those that do not closer together. This program, paradoxically, cut off Malthus from another source of possible support.

216

If anyone had polled the English population in 1798 on the number of children they desired, presumably a substantial proportion would still have replied, "It is up to God." Malthus was attacked by conventional Christians because, in effect, he asserted, "No, it is up to you!" And, on the other hand, Malthus is attacked by modern liberals because when they hold that it is up to the state to care for its subjects, he would have countered, "No, it is up to the people themselves!" To hold every person responsible for his behavior, denying him the escape of blaming either Providence or Society, is a moral rather than an empirical stance—a moral stance that fits in with neither of the ideologies that overlapped during the first decades of the nineteenth century.

10

The Malthusian Heritage

ALTHUS'S WAS NOT a simple mind, whatever its faults and lacks. He was a pious Anglican who saw man not merely as a spiritual being but as a member of Homo sapiens, ultimately no more independent of biological instincts and needs than any other species. He was a Whig and a country gentleman, a firm opponent of revolution who worked for fundamental reform, a meliorist intensely suspicious of every facile utopianism. As professor and scholar, he was a determined empiricist deeply embedded in theoretical abstraction. For him these were not contradictions but complexities; a man of his quality was able to see the several sides of the questions he dealt with.

For almost a century and a half the terrible simplifiers have been at work on Malthus's thought, breaking down into the discrete dualities his effort to resolve oppositional forces and assigning to him, on the basis of this or that partial quotation, only one of Janus's two faces. In the attempt in this chapter to sum up his thought and interpret its significance for us in the last decades of the twentieth century, it is convenient to proceed with a series of such dualities. Of these, the most basic, the one whose import ranges over the whole of Malthus's life and thought, is that between nature and nurture, between man as animal and as cultural being, between physiological and sociological determinants of human behavior.

MALTHUS TO DARWIN AND WALLACE

That Darwin and Wallace hit upon the theory of evolution at the same time and, in a rare spirit of scientific cooperation, agreed to share the consequent honor is a well known instance of the simultaneous discovery of one of our civilization's fundamentals. Fewer persons may be aware that for both men Malthus's principle of population was the crucial catalyst that brought their vast data into meaningful order.

Fifteen months after I had begun my systematic enquiry [Darwin wrote in his *Autobiography*], I happened to read for amusement Malthus on *Population,* and being well prepared to appreciate the struggle for existence which everywhere goes on from long-continued observation of the habits of animals and plants, it at once struck me that under these circumstances favorable variations would tend to be preserved and unfavorable ones be destroyed. The result of this would be a new species. Here, then, I had at last got a theory by which to work.[1]

When as a young man Wallace was visiting the Leicester library, he perused Malthus's *Essay,* "the first work I had yet read treating of any of the problems of philosophical biology," which he "greatly admired for its masterly summary of facts and logical induction to conclusions." Some twelve years later, when on a field trip in tropical Asia he was suffering from a bout of fever, Wallace recalled what he had absorbed.

Every day during the cold and succeeding hot fits I had to lie down for several hours, during which time I had nothing to do but to think over any subjects then particularly interesting me. One day something brought to my recollection Malthus's *Principles,* . . . [and] I thought of his clear exposition of "the positive checks to increase" . . . As animals usually breed much more rapidly than does mankind, the destruction every year from these causes must be enormous in order to keep down the numbers of each species . . . It occurred to me to ask the question, Why do some die and some live. And the answer was clearly, that on the whole the best fitted live . . . Then it suddenly flashed upon me that this self-acting process would necessarily *improve the race,* because in every generation the inferior would inevitably be killed off and the superior would remain—that is, *the fittest would survive* . . . I became convinced that I had at length found the long-sought-for law of nature that solved the problem of the origin of species.[2]

On the Origin of Species, Darwin's statement of this joint theory, was one of the most influential works of our age. It is difficult to think of a broad area of science, the social disciplines, or moral philosophy that was not affected by it. Over the rest of his life Darwin was subjected to abuse that paralleled or even exceeded that poured over Malthus, and occasionally the link between them was pointed up, as in a famous paper by Samuel Haughton (1821–97), a physiologist and professor of geology at Dublin University. "What has Haughton done," Darwin wrote to his friend Joseph Hooker, director of Kew Gardens, "that he feels so immeasurably superior to all us wretched naturalists, and to all political economists, including that great philosopher Malthus?"[3] On the other hand, those who would praise Darwin but denigrate Malthus found it needful to remind us that if Darwin had not read the *Essay* probably little would have changed; "for he had plenty of examples of what happens to an animal population when it outgrows its normal means of subsistence."[4]

Though Darwin anticipated the criticism he received from theologians and the lay public, he was surprised by some scientists' charge that one cannot reach certainty by mere induction from no matter how great an accumulation of evidence. As Wallace remarked, over the three and a half years prior to his creative bout of fever he had collected 8,540 species of insects, and "I might have spent the best years of my life in this comparatively profitless work." But in fact Darwin was not merely the Tycho Brahe of biology; he was also the Newton. In a defense of Darwin's deductive method titled "Creation by Law," Wallace spelled out the logical sequence of the propositions contained in *Origin,* but there embellished with so much illustrative detail that the reader could lose the path from one rigorous conclusion to the next.

From "the law of multiplication in geometrical progression" (the fact that all species have the power to increase their number up to as much as a thousandfold per year) and "the law of limited population" (the fact that the number of living individuals of each species typically remains almost stationary), one deduces that there is a *struggle for existence.*

From the struggle for existence and "the law of variation"

(the fact that though offspring generally resemble their parents, each one differs from them), one deduces that there is a *survival of the fittest* or a "harmony of nature": "when a species is well adapted to the conditions which environ it, it flourishes; when imperfectly adapted, it decays; when ill adapted, it becomes extinct."

From the survival of the fittest and the universal, unceasing change in the environment, one deduces that there is a continuous change in organic forms, which eventually differentiate enough to become new species.[5]

This is "the doctrine of Malthus applied with manifold force to the whole animal and vegetable kingdoms, for in this case there can be no artificial increase of food and no prudential restraint from marriage." "It is therefore perhaps not surprising," Antony Flew continued from Darwin's comment, "that the logical skeleton of theory which provided the organizing and supporting framework for all Malthus's inquiries and recommendations about population resembles in almost every respect . . . the theoretical framework of *The Origin of Species,*" though with certain relatively minor differences that Flew then considered.[6] In a talk some fifty years after Darwin's classic first apeared, Wallace reviewed again the flow from Malthus to the theory of evolution. "What influenced me was not any special passage or passages," he declared, "but the cumulative effect of Chapters 3 to 12 of the first volume . . . In these chapters are comprised very detailed accounts from all available sources of the various causes which keep down the population of savage and barbarous nations." Then, in order to give an idea of the kind of facts Malthus adduced, Wallace reviewed in detail that portion of the *Essay.*[7]

In short, whether we ask the two men who developed the theory of evolution or some of the better commentators of our own time, the principle of population was more than a mere clue to the most revolutionary thesis ever advanced in biology. It was the scaffolding on which Darwin and Wallace hung their data, the base from which they advanced to new theoretical insights. The notion of struggle.is common in Western thought; the novel element in Malthus that made him important for Darwin and Wallace was his thesis about intraspecific rather than interspecific competition.

The distinction between man and all other living beings was

not absolute with either Malthus or Darwin. At the very beginning of the *Essay*, the reader will recall, Malthus noted "the
constant tendency in all animated life to increase beyond the
nourishment prepared for it," adding that the effects of this
tendency are "more complicated" in man than in "plants
and irrational animals." Indeed, in the view of many critics
the chief fault of the principle of population was precisely
that it brought man fully into nature, basically on a par with
animals that require food and are driven to reproduce. With a
part of his mind, Darwin wanted to avoid aggravating the attacks on him; five years after the first edition of *Origin*, he
offered Wallace the notes he had collected on human beings,
for he doubted that he would ever use them. Once past this
period of ill health and consequent depression, Darwin wrote a
"Chapter on Man," which subsequently grew into *The Descent of Man*. After working on it for three years, he had not,
as he wrote to Hooker, "the remote idea whether the book is
worth publishing." He promised to send the Harvard botanist
Asa Gray a copy, warning him, however, that parts would undoubtedly offend him, and "if I hear from you, I shall probably receive a few stabs from your polished stiletto of a pen."
In fact, the reception given *Descent* was less hostile than Darwin had anticipated. Its argument had been implicit in
Origin, and the attacks on that work, that "mixture of ignorance and insolence" as T. H. Huxley termed it, had somewhat
subsided in the dozen years since 1859, the dawn of the new
biological era.[8] Even so, as late as the 1890s "Darwinism" (as
contrasted with "Lamarckism") was in considerable disrepute
among biologists.

Homo sapiens differs from plants and animals in the possession of "culture," however one defines that large and vague
term; and the ideological war that the *Origin* set off was
brought to a seemingly permanent cease-fire by emphasizing
that residual distinction. But one of the most interesting trends
in biology during the past several decades has been the rise of
ethology, whose practitioners ascribe at least to higher animals
some of the characteristics once assigned only to man. In his
essay on Malthus, Boulding set off "plump" creatures (oysters,
robins, domestic cats), whose populations are not limited
merely by food, from "skinny" ones (coyotes, deer, alley cats),
for which the supply of food is as crucial as it should be by
the Malthusian principle.[9] In the exposition of this almost

playful suggestion by such a zoologist as Wynne-Edwards, the Darwinian model does not apply completely to many animals. When the populations of some species of fish and birds, some other classes of vertebrates, and some insects and crustaceans reach what might be termed an optimum level, their fertility temporarily declines.

> Population density must at all costs be prevented from rising to the level where food shortage begins to take a toll of the numbers, . . . [for such an effect] would be bound to result in chronic overexploitation and a spiral of diminishing returns. Food may be the *ultimate* factor, but it cannot be invoked as the *proximate* agent in chopping the numbers, without disastrous consequences. By analogy with human experience we should therefore look to see whether there is not some natural counterpart of the limitation agreements that provide man with his only known remedy against overfishing [for example]—some kind of density-dependent convention, it would have to be, based on the quantity of food available but "artificially" preventing the intensity of exploitation from rising above the optimum level.[10]

The "conventions" by which particular species reduce their rate of growth include reduced fecundity, the abandonment or killing of offspring, prolonged immaturity, and so on—thus, both physiological adaptations and changes in behavior patterns. Though some zoologists regard this as an extreme statement of the thesis, it had the value of stimulating other biologists to examine more closely the issues thus raised. And though, in Edward Wilson's view, "one after another of Wynne-Edwards's propositions about specific 'conventions' and epideictic displays were knocked down on evidential grounds or at least matched with competing hypotheses of equal plausibility," his fundamental points remained at issue.[11]

Indeed, Wilson's own masterful exposition of "sociobiology, the new synthesis," includes in its very language large slices of what some years ago would have been put down as rank anthropomorphism—not only "culture" and "society" but "role," "tradition," "altruism," and so on through both the basic concepts and many particular ones of the social disciplines. It is manifest, moreover, that he does not use such terms metaphorically; he is not merely employing a human analogy to assist in the analysis of other creatures. At least some animals

223

have "the rudiments of culture," and though its wider range in man has not been specified genetically, this "underprescription does not mean that culture has been freed from the genes. What has evolved is the capacity for culture, indeed the overwhelming tendency to develop one culture or another."[12] Not surprisingly, reviews by sociologists have expressed a certain lack of enthusiasm for the proposition that they are studying mere epiphenomena, whose fundamental features are understandable only to a biologist.

DARWIN TO SOCIAL DARWINISM

The idea that some animal species shared some characteristics once thought to be exclusively human, however repugnant to some critics, fitted in with the modern temper: it might be regarded as a salutary upward mobility to raise simians to a manlike status. In the long run, thus, the greater opposition has focused on the converse proposition that man behaves in some ways like an animal. This has been an affront not merely to traditional Christians but to the liberals and utopians who in the later decades of the twentieth century have largely taken over the task of setting society's ethical norms.

"Social Darwinism," which might reasonably have been defined as the application of Darwin's theory to social phenomena, has usually been interpreted merely negatively, as "a short-lived theory of social evolution, . . . which rationalized and justified the harsh facts of social stratification in an attempt to reconcile them with the prevalent ideology of equalitarianism."[13] In this narrower sense, the theory derived mainly from Spencer and, in the United States, Sumner.

Herbert Spencer (1820–1903), a truly extraordinary polymath, was largely self-educated. At 17, he took a job in railway construction and over some three years developed his learning in mathematics into a competence in civil engineering. As a young man he wrote a series of letters for *The Nonconformist*, an organ of advanced Dissenters, arguing for the total extension of the suffrage, the separation of church and state, and the limitation of state power; against Corn Laws and slavery. Then for five years he worked as a junior editor of *The Economist*, thus earning enough to support himself while he began his serious writing and, in the process, meeting many eminent and influential men. *Social Statics*, his first larger opus, argued in the broadest terms for freedom of speech, of property, of behavior: "every man has the freedom to do all that he wills provided he infringes not the equal freedom of any other man." His subsequent works, most in several volumes, dealt with the principles of psychology, the elements of metaphysics and epistemology, the principles of biology, the place of sociology in the hierarchy of disciplines and its proper methodology, the principles of sociology, and, in a reversion to his first theme, *Man versus the State*.

Running through this corpus was a consistent theme of philosophical anarchism, strongly reminiscent of Godwin's *Political Justice*. The link was not fortuitous; Godwin's book was much read and admired in the radical circle of Derby that Spencer frequented as a young man. Probably because his knowledge grew from private reading rather than from university courses, Spencer was outside the main stream of Victorian social thought; he derived directly from Adam Smith and the other Scottish moralists, from Priestley and Paine.[14] But the same social analysts who might revere the anarchism of Godwin condemned the laissez-faire of Spencer; after its redefinition, liberalism had come to signify not a break with mercantilist restrictions but rather the reimposition of state controls on economic and social processes. It was mainly because his politics was out of joint with the twentieth century that Spencer's general reputation waned so rapidly after his death.

To say that Spencer was first and foremost an evolutionist is not to say that his thought derived from Darwin's theory. As defined by Spencer,

Evolution is a change from a less coherent state to a more coherent state, . . . from the uniform to the multiform . . . While the more or less distinct parts into which the aggregate divides and subdivides are also severally concentrating, these parts are simultaneously becoming unlike—unlike in size, or in form, or in texture, or in composition, or in several or all of these . . . [In short,] evolution is definable as a change from an incoherent homogeneity to a coherent heterogeneity, accompanying the dissipation of motion and integration of matter.[15]

This process differs from Darwin's biological evolution in far more than the range of the phenomena to which it applies. Spencer offered a preliminary version of his theory a decade before the publication of *Origin*. Not only was it he who coined the phrase "survival of the fittest" but it was he more than Darwin who popularized the word "evolution," which was used rather sparingly in the first editions of *Origin*.[16] For Spencer evolution was Lamarckian; still in the 1890s, when many or most biologists had accepted natural selection as the means of evolutionary change, Spencer held that acquired characteristics can be inherited. It would be more logical, almost, to dub Darwin a "biological Spencerian" than to repeat the typical reverse ascription. Even that link would be dubious: that Darwin got his "economy of nature" from Malthus (rather than an economic theory from Smith or Ricardo) may have led to a quite different understanding of evolutionary change.

Nor is the link between Malthus and Spencer as manifest as some have made it.[17] Malthus's First Essay was, of course, not only a response to Godwin's utopianism but also one font from which the gloomy science of nineteenth-century economics derived; and though Malthus tempered his pessimism greatly during the succeeding editions, he never approached universal euphoria. The reversal of Malthus's philosophical stance, implicit in some of Darwin's peripheral writings,[18] is blared forth in Spencer's clarion call to inescapable progress. The very population pressure that by Malthus's principle results in vice and misery is, in Spencer's transformation, the stimulus to evolutionary progress. At the end of a paper on "a theory of population," he speculated on what human characteristics would be enhanced; for "in conformity with the general law of adaptation, increase will take place only where it is demanded," namely, not in strength, probably not in swiftness or agility, to some degree only in mechanical skill or the better coordination of complex movements. The main change, because there is "ample demand for it," will be in greater intelligence and a better morality, meaning an improved power of self-regulation. In short, the "inevitable redundancy of numbers" stimulates an improvement in the production of food and other necessities and thus "involves an increasing demand for skill, intelligence, and self-control," a constant exercise of these qualities, and therefore a gradual growth in them.[19] It is a delightful paradox that the very mechanism that Malthus used to refute Godwin's utopianism was turned on him to prove the inevitability of indefinite progress.

In *The Principles of Sociology* Spencer traced the progress of mankind to his time through successive stages reminiscent of the schemata of a dozen earlier thinkers. That Engels had happened to use Lewis Henry Morgan's evolutionary classification for his own account of how man rose from primitive to civilized status has raised Morgan to the level of a Founding Father, whom to this day Marxists treat with a sometimes absurd deference.[20] A more interesting example is Hobhouse, a considerable part of whose vast and learned corpus—*Morals in Evolution* (1906), *Social Evolution and Political Theory* (1911), *The Material Culture and Social Institutions of the Simpler Peoples* (1915), *Social Development, Its Nature and Conditions* (1924) —was directly related to evolutionary theory. He tried, however, to distinguish himself from Spencer, whose theory he interpreted as a justification for economic exploitation. Insofar as evolution is a blind struggle for existence, "any sort of growth," it does not imply the upward tendency inherent in "progress," which Hobhouse defined rather as "the growth of social life in respect of those qualities to which human beings attach or can rationally attach value."[21] Similarly, T. H. Huxley had Spencer in mind when, in his famous essay "Evolution and Ethics," he declared that "the ethical progress of society depends, not on imitating the cosmic process, still less in running away from it, but in combating it."[22] But such strictures were less a repudiation of a peace-loving Lamarckian like Spencer than of a quite different application of Darwinian evolution to social phenomena. In Spencer's view, not only were war and aggression "natural" only to savage society, but any society in which warfare prevails must be described still as "savage."[23] This is in sharp contrast to the glorification of struggle in Marx and especially Engels,[24] not to say Napoleon or Lenin.

More generally, Spencer influenced many others whose political orientations were quite different from his own. He was so close to Beatrice Potter that he wanted her to be his literary executor, and even after Mrs. Webb (as she later became) changed radically, she wrote that his *First Principles* had had "a very great influence on my feelings and thoughts."[25] Veblen's concept of conspicuous consumption as a survival from a warlike past is pure Spencer. More notable is such an influential modern theorist as Talcott Parsons, who in his first major work pronounced Spencer's thought to be "dead"—even though the entire framework of Parsons's structural functionalism derived from the man whose work he dismissed. In Spencer's words, "There can be no true conception of a structure without a true conception of its function. To understand how an organization originated and developed, it is requisite to understand the need subserved at the outset and afterwards."[26] As Andreski put it with characteristic succinctness, "Spencer has been recently kept in oblivion largely because he said more clearly, as well as somewhat earlier, what some of the influential theorists of today claim as their discoveries."[27]

The influence of theories of biological evolution on the social disciplines was much broader than even the wide range of Spencer's writings might suggest.[28] If continual adaptations to the environment determine the path of evolutionary change, then the interaction between the organism and its habitat is a crucial factor in biological analysis, carried on most intensively in the separate discipline of ecology. As it developed at the University of Chicago, "human ecology" took over into the cultural context some of the key processes of plant and animal ecology—"competition," "succession," and so on. There is indeed a "struggle for existence," as Robert Park was fond of pointing out, and business firms do compete for desirable space, as Ernest Burgess was likely to rephrase the dictum—but such processes take place within a limiting normative framework that has no counterpart in lower forms of life. Like some other biological metaphors in social analysis, in the long run this one was less helpful than confusing—in this case because the fundamental distinction between physiological and cultural was systematically muddled.

The relation of Marxist theory to Darwinian evolution is somewhat similar. With only contempt for "utopians" who tried to bring about socialism by their own efforts, Marx distinguished his uniquely "scientific" socialism as a description of what must ensue independent of man's will—yet spent the whole of his mature life working to advance the inevitable culmination of capitalist development. In a graveside address to his fellow revolutionary, Engels drew a close parallel between the two theories: "Just as Darwin discovered the development of organic nature, so Marx discovered the law of development of human history: the simple fact, hitherto concealed by an overgrowth of ideology, that mankind must first of all eat, drink, have shelter and clothes, before it can pursue politics, science, art, religion, etc." This "overgrowth of ideology" had been pierced, of course, by Malthus, but Marx hardly appreciated the emphasis on biological imperatives in the principle of population. After Marx's death his association with evolutionary theory was reinforced by two letters ostensibly from Darwin, one acknowledging receipt of "your great work on Capital" and the other joining Marx in depreciating religion; but these were almost certainly forged by Edward Aveling, Marx's common-law son-in-law, a man whom even many socialists found to be despicable.[29]

An alternative hypothesis that "cultural details are for the most part adaptive in a Darwinian sense, even though some may operate indirectly through enhanced group survival," also has its difficulties. This is the conclusion that Wilson drew from his suggestion that ethics be removed from the hands of philosophers and "biologized."[30] Suppose one takes this rationale seriously and applies it to some of the awesome happenings of the twentieth century. Trotsky considered Stalin to be a deformed instrument for the necessary transformation of Soviet (and, eventually, world) society; and there was a sect of French Trotskyists (comprising, it so happened, mainly Jews) who held the same view of Hitler, who would consolidate the obsolete petty nationalisms of European states into one more efficient continent, which Berlin technicians would run as a single unit. Or consider, more specifically, the forced collectivization of Soviet agriculture, which by Stalin's own estimate cost something like 20 million lives to realize.

> With 50 (or 40, or 30) million more people in the villages after the [Second World] War, could the rate of extraction of agricultural "surplus" have been as high as it was? If not: Could recovery in urban living standards from the postwar low in 1946 have been as fast as it was? Could there have been as large an urban population, and hence as rapid a reconstruction and further economic growth, as there was in the late 1940s and the 1950s? . . .
>
> If both the total and the rural population of the USSR were now [in 1958], say, 50 million larger than they are, the urban population would comprise not about 45 percent of the total population as it does, but about 35 percent.[31]

One supposes that Professor Wilson, a civilized product of Western culture, would find some difficulty in describing the wanton murder of 20 million as biologically adaptive and therefore—to use an archaic word—good, or even in avoiding the issue by questioning whether in the long run Soviet society constitutes an improved adaptation to the environment.

At the opposite pole from Wilson's acceptance of evolution as ultimately beneficial is a direct intervention in man's genetic inheritance. The inverse correlation between education and fertility, and thus implicitly between innate intelligence and family size, was widely interpreted as the means by which the genetic quality of Western populations was being reduced. Such a sentiment is now often associated with reactionary fanatics, but it was shared, for instance, by such a well known socialist intellectual as Sidney Webb:

> It is the differential character of the decline in the birth rate, rather than the actual extent of the decline, which is of the gravest import . . . In Great Britain at this moment [1913], when half, or perhaps two-thirds, of all the married people are regulating their families, children are being freely born to the Irish Roman Catholics and the Polish, Russian, and German Jews, on the one hand, and to the thriftless and irresponsible, . . . on the other . . . This can hardly result in anything but national deterioration; or, as an alternative, in this country gradually falling to the Irish and the Jews.[32]

Nor should eugenics, "the guidance of human evolution" as Hermann Muller called it,[33] be judged only by the effusions of extremist proponents; Muller's political orientation is suggested by the fact that he worked at the Moscow Institute of Genetics until the reality of Soviet society appalled him; his professional competence is indicated by the Nobel prize in physiology and medicine he was awarded in 1946.

What, the reader may ask, has all this to do with Malthus? Very little, in fact; but in persistent myth, quite a bit. In 1977 so reputable a publishing firm as Alfred A. Knopf published a book entitled *The Legacy of Malthus: The Social Costs of the New Scientific Racism*. Allen Chase, the author, warned in the preface that he is "neither a scientist nor a professional historian," but simply "a writer." It would be no benefit to list the errors of fact and interpretation replete in this work. The reader who has reached this chapter will know that Malthus was no racist, was opposed vehemently to slavery, was motivated by a lifetime hope of benefiting mankind, and—in sharpest contrast to such trash—was a scrupulous scholar.

MALTHUS ON EDUCATION

The trend in literacy during Malthus's lifetime is not at all easy to establish, and the ideologies on both sides of the debate on whether to extend primary education are also murky. The measure of "literacy" that historians typically use is the signing of one's name to, say, a marriage registry; and even if one accepts the spotty data as representative of the general population, so modest an index hardly suggests the association with humane letters that the ability to read can connote. One modern commentator manages both to condemn the English upper classes for depriving the poor of schooling and to agree with Lévi-Strauss's preposterous assertion that "the primary function of writing as a means of communication is to facilitate the enslavement of other human beings."[34]

One important impetus to mass education had been the Reformation, for the Protestant doctrine that each believer should draw religious sustenance directly from the Bible implied a general ability to read it. A Society for the Promotion of Christian Knowledge was founded as early as 1698, and over the following decades parochial charity schools were set up in various parts of England and Wales, with a total enrollment of around 30,000 pupils in 1750. The explicit function of moral instruction persisted as public secular schooling became established.[35] Calvinism was particularly significant in this respect; the Protestant cantons of Switzerland were pioneers in compulsory education for everyone, and Rousseau's *Nouvelle Héloïse* and *Émile*, translated into English in the early 1760s, disseminated an enthusiasm for education per se.[36] In Britain, the best national system of mass education was to be found in Presbyterian Scotland, which generated also such manifestations of high culture as excellent universities and the *Edinburgh Review*.

Any tendency to exaggerate the progress made during the first decades of the nineteenth century is undercut by the several works of Joseph Kay (1821–78), who while still a student at Trinity College was appointed a traveling fellow of Cambridge University. He did research throughout Western Europe and compared data on the education of the poor in the various countries. From 1801 to 1841, he pointed out, the population of Yorkshire had almost doubled and that of Lancashire had grown by almost three times. The congregation of workers into these industrial districts had two dangers—"a low state of intellect, occasioning improvidence, and an absence of religious feeling, producing immorality and insubordination." In the 1840s children were required to attend school until the age of 8, but the schools "in very many cases [are] so poor that they do more *harm* than good." Europeans, he reported, were amazed that after three years of full prosperity England still had to spend almost £5 million annually in poor relief.[37]

In the middle of the nineteenth century, according to the statistics that Kay compiled, nearly eight million persons in England and Wales could not read or write, and more than half of the children between 5 and 14 were not attending school. Only basic reading, writing, and "Scripture history" were taught, with nothing of mathematics, geography, history, or science. Most schools had one room with a single teacher for all pupils; in the towns the instruction was often given in small and unventilated cellars or garrets. In the villages teachers were usually women, in the towns sometimes men; both were themselves miserably educated and poorly paid, willing to accept their posts only because they were not fit for any other employment. Proportionate to its population, England had only a quarter as many normal schools as any other country of Western Europe, where the teachers' training was for three years (rather than the year to eighteen months in England) at government expense (rather than by the ad hoc arrangements in England).[38] "England alone appears in this respect to have misunderstood the genius of Protestantism. With the wealthiest and most enlightened aristocracy, the richest and most influential church, and the most enterprising middle class, her lower orders are as a mass more ignorant and less civilized than those of any other large Protestant country in Europe."[39]

Adam Smith's advocacy of tax-supported public schooling, though it fitted in with some of the Scottish tradition, was a radical proposal for England. His rationale is in some respects amazingly modern. Every commentator has noted Smith's argument in favor of the division of labor, but few have remarked that he was aware of its effects on factory workers. "The man whose whole life is spent in performing a few simple operations . . . has no occasion to exert his understanding . . . He naturally loses, therefore, the habit of such exertion, and generally becomes as stupid and ignorant as it

is possible for a human creature to become."[40] The leaders of
the Scottish Enlightenment, more generally, anticipated some
of the negative consequences of the congregation of lower-
class masses in industrial cities, and thus the probable deterioration in both morals and literacy.[41] In the main, however,
Smith recommended state aid to education for its practical
effects—not "a little smattering of Latin" but geometry and
mechanics, which could be applied in virtually every craft.
"The improved dexterity of a workman may be considered in
the same light as a machine or instrument of trade, which
facilitates and abridges labor and which, though it costs a
certain expense, repays that expense with a profit." Religious
education might be useful, but its cost in Smith's opinion
should be "defrayed altogether by those who receive the immediate benefit of such education and instruction, or by the
voluntary contribution of those who think they have occasion
for either the one or the other."[42]

Smith's arguments in favor of universal primary education
were repeated by most economists of the classical school,[43] and
by none more enthusiastically and effectively than Malthus. He
stressed less than Smith or Ricardo the economic gains from
the dissemination of vocational skills, noting how ignorant the
educated part of the community generally was of geometry
and mechanics, and expressing some doubt whether these
could be usefully taught to the lower classes. For Malthus,
education was the main means of the embourgeoisement that
he advocated, and thus was tied in directly with his principle
of population. His belief that education was morally useful
should not be interpreted, however, as an implicit proposal
that the instruction be religious in content. "It is surely a great
national disgrace," he wrote, that lower-class education should
be left to a few Sunday schools, free to propagate "any kind
of bias which they please." The main political argument
against mass education, that the common people would be able
to read "such works as those of Paine," thus increasing the
tendency toward "a spirit of tumult and discontent," he regarded as plainly false. For "an instructed and well informed
people would be much less likely to be led away by inflam-
matory writings," since they could better judge the "false
declamation of ambitious demagogues." Indeed, Malthus's
declaration recalls the words of such American democrats as
Thomas Jefferson: "No government can approach to perfec-

tion that does not provide for the instruction of the people, . . . and as it is in the power of governments to confer these benefits, it is undoubtedly their duty to do it."[44]

Malthus's advocacy of each individual's moral restraint was only the lesser part of his program for population control; he also pushed—to repeat for emphasis—for the type of government under which this deterrent would best flourish. In his writings, the negative correlation between station in life and number of children was increasingly stressed as the clue to the population problem. In order to bring the lower classes up to the self-control and social responsibility exercised by those with more money and education, Malthus asserted, the poor should also be given more money and education.

The influence of the [*Essay*] will be better understood if a comparison be made between two speeches about the Poor Law made by . . . Whitbread, in 1796 and 1807. In 1796, he demanded [only] that the justices of the peace should be authorized to fix the wages of labor at every three months' session . . . Eleven years later, Whitbread, applauded by Malthus, proposed a bill whose principal features were a regularization and democratization of the right of suffrage in parochial assemblies, and a system of universal popular instruction. Between 1796 and 1807, the influence of Malthus had been felt by the Liberal party. It was a democratic influence. As concerns the education of the poor in particular, the radical theory of popular instruction is Malthusian in origin.[45]

MALTHUS A LIBERAL-CONSERVATIVE

The usual estimate of his overall political stance is that "Rev." Malthus was a reactionary, or "at best" a dyed-in-the-wool conservative. This is almost routine; judgments intended as vilifications have all but carried the day. If only for that reason, it may be worthwhile rounding out the quotations from Malthus's own works with two from authoritative commentators. The first is by Sidney and Beatrice Webb, who almost alone among socialist scholars had a correct appreciation of Malthus's social philosophy.

No argument could be founded on the "principle of population" against Trade Union efforts to improve the conditions of sanitation and safety, or to protect the Normal Day. And the economists quickly found reason to doubt whether there was any greater cogency in the argument with regard to wages . . . From the Malthusian point of view, the presumption was, as regards the artisans and factory operatives, always in favor of a rise in wages. For [as Malthus had written in the *Principles*] "in the vast majority of instances before a rise of wages can be counteracted by the increased number of laborers it may be supposed to be the means of bringing into the market, time is afforded for the formation of . . . new and improved tastes and habits . . . After the laborers have once acquired these tastes, population will advance in a slower ratio, as compared with capital, than formerly" . . . The ordinary middle-class view that the "principle of population" rendered nugatory all attempts to raise wages, otherwise than in the slow course of generations, was, in fact, based on sheer ignorance, not only of the facts of working-class life, but even of the opinions of the very economists from whom it was supposed to be derived.[46]

The second is a perceptive appraisal by the historian of ideas, Gertrude Himmelfarb:

The initiation [of the lower classes] into the middle classes was, in effect, the defeat of the principle of population. If Malthus had to abandon the latter (at least implicitly), he was more than recompensed by the former, for the embourgeoisement of the lower classes did prove to be, as he hoped, both their deliverance and society's salvation. In this, even more than his predictions about population, he was truly the prophet of our times . . .

Was it deliberate on Malthus's part, or unconscious poetic irony, that the final sentence of the last edition should have echoed, *but in reverse,* the opening sentence of the first? The fallacy of the age, the first edition had proclaimed, was to suppose that "the great and unlooked for discoveries" in scientific affairs were a portent of progress in social affairs. The hope of the age, he now concluded, was that these discoveries would, in some measure, be such a portent of progress: "Although we cannot expect that the virtue and happiness of mankind will keep pace with the brilliant career of physical discovery, yet, if we are not wanting to ourselves, we may confidently indulge the hope that, to no unimportant extent, they will be influenced by its progress and will partake in its success." The image of society as enthralled by nature, impervious to scientific or moral influence, yielded to the vision of society liberated from nature, enlightened and refined.[47]

In a stimulating essay on the philosophical content of conservative thought in the early nineteenth century, Karl Mannheim noted that one crucial factor was one's perception of time. "The progressive experiences the present as the beginning of the future, while the conservative regards it simply as the latest point reached by the past." But the whole thrust of Malthus's arithmetic and geometric progressions was to the future; and Marx (whom we may take as the polar opposite), though he hypothesized the extrapolation of current trends to a future utopia, concentrated his writing on connecting the capitalist system with its historical past. Or, in Mannheim's words, "The conservatives replaced Reason with concepts such as History, Life, the Nation." Malthus, on the contrary, extended the legitimate use of reason to the family, which conventional contemporaries regarded as the sanctum of traditionalist norms; while for Marx reason was indeed subsumed in an irrepressible History. Or: The conservative "starts from a concept of a whole which is not the mere sum of its parts . . . The conservative thinks in terms of 'We' when the liberal thinks in terms of 'I.' " Marxist analysis is wholly in terms of social classes, wholes greater than the sum of the individuals that make them up; and Malthus, like all who participated in developing the theory of market relations, began every analysis with the individual consumer or individual parent.[48] The paradoxes could be continued, but perhaps the point has been made that even so gifted an analyst as Mannheim is likely to define the past by criteria derived from his interpretation of the present.

To say that we see the past in terms of the present is not, of course, to cite a remediable fault. Everyone is a creature of his own age, and when he visits another historical period, it is with all of the inherent prejudices and misperceptions of any alien. But if this lack is not recognized as such—or, worse, is defined as a virtue—the result is what Herbert Butterfield called the whig interpretation of history. Of course, Catholics have written about the Reformation, and reactionaries about how the monarchy distintegrated, but "Clio herself is on the side of the whigs."

The whig historian stands on the summit of the twentieth century, and organizes his scheme of history from the point of view of his own day . . . Events must be judged by their ultimate issues, which, since we can trace them no farther, we must at least follow down to the present . . . It is only in relation to the twentieth century that one happening or another in the past has relevance or significance for us . . . The fallacy lies in the fact that if the historian working on the sixteenth century keeps the twentieth century in his mind, he makes direct reference across all the intervening period . . . This immediate juxtaposition of past and present, though it makes everything easy and makes some inferences perilously obvious, is bound to lead to an oversimplification of the relations between events and a complete misapprehension of the relations between past and present.[49]

If we extend the meaning of "whig" to include what in our day is more aptly labeled "progressive," interpretations of Malthus exemplify this critique all too often. Writers conventional to their core—that is, following twentieth-century conventions—condemn a man who died in 1834 for every difference from their own parochial views.

More generally, the persistent practice of attaching a political label to Malthus is rendered meaningless, or worse, by the all but total reversal in the significance of most designations in the hundred fifty years since Malthus's death. In the radical-liberal heyday, "left" meant toward increased personal freedom; then it acquired the additional meaning of toward increased state control over the economy and society. It is manifest, however, that these two goals do not always lie in the same direction. When Robert Nisbet spelled out the point in relation to the founding of sociology, he must have grated the sensibilities of many left-liberal or socialist colleagues. As he showed, sociology's fundamental postulates on the relation between society and man are also the premises of classical European conservatism—that society is not an aggregate of discrete particles but an entity with its own laws of development; that this entity is historically, logically, and ethically prior to any one of its elements; that the irreducible unit of social analysis or policy, therefore, is not the individual but a manifestation of the whole, a social relationship.[50] Indeed, the forwardest-looking progressive could give ready assent to these propositions. For the "magnificent episode" of classical liberalism, as Keynes termed it in one of his characteristically memorable phrases, was sandwiched between the autocratic monarchy (with its mercantilist economy and established church) and the social-welfare state (with its at least partly planned economy and its managed public relations). Looking forward or backward from the high point of the Benthamite era, many of the contrasts would be the same.

Malthus opposed the French revolutionaries, and for such ideologues as Shelley this alone defined him as a reactionary. Most revolutions are totalist; their leaders are against the whole of traditional society, without distinction, and destroy wantonly whatever comes within their grasp. As a consequence, the noble aims of the social upheaval are never achieved, and its original progenitors are killed off. Consider, in contrast, the "conservative revolution"—as Morison called it—that established the United States, in S. M. Lipset's phrase, the first of the new nations. Indeed, the declared purposes of the American revolution were radical or even utopian, but these characteristics did not constitute the whole phenomenon. In large part, the momentum was defensive—to maintain the traditional rights of freeborn Englishmen and to do this, in many cases reluctantly, even to the point of breaking with the home country. The men who conducted the revolution and set up the independent state were typically reasonable in their expectations and moderate in their actions.

The conservatives of the Revolution . . . believed in all the fundamental things of our Revolution—independence, the abolition of hereditary elements, starting with monarchy; and the rights of man . . .

The American Revolution differed from most of the other great revolutions because it stopped just about where those who started it wanted it to stop. In 1789 we had the same leaders as in 1775, except that some of the early agitators, like Tom Paine, had gone to France, and obscure Sons of Liberty in Boston and Philadelphia had disappeared. They were not, like the Girondins in France and the Mensheviks in Russia, destroyed by purges and terror; they merely slipped into oblivion because they had nothing constructive to offer.[51]

A more noteworthy instance is the Japanese revolution of 1868, known to history as the Meiji "Restoration." The Emperor was restored to the full of his earlier power; and such traditional institutions as the family and religion were reinforced rather than discarded. As a consequence, the most rapid social-economic development ever in world history was brought about with a minimum of disorganization. Starting from virtually zero (artificially maintained during the Tokugawa era by Japan's enforced isolation from alien influences), the country became a modern industrial society within decades, able to compete with Britain for her markets, powerful enough to defeat first China and then Russia. By the materialist measure that Marxists profess to use, *this* was the successful societal transformation of modern times.

In several contexts I have called Malthus a utilitarian, and whether this is a just appellation depends on how specifically one defines that rather loose designation. As Halévy used the word, virtually everyone interested in social issues during Malthus's lifetime approached them in a utilitarian framework, and that is not an unreasonable interpretation. Certainly no one was aware of the modern criticisms focused on the incalculable relation between individual preference and social choice, Malthus no more than Bentham himself. In the one important respect that set Malthus off from most of his contemporaries, he is less subject to present-day criticisms. Utilitarianism, it is charged, "makes integrity as a value more or less unintelligible," for the elaborate calculus relating pleasure to pain passes over the moral norm that each person is responsible for what he does.[52] Certainly Malthus could not have stressed more the fact that he believed in individual responsibility as the key to his ethical system; this norm alienated him from both conventional Christians and quasimercantilists.

To appraise the frequent judgment of Malthus as a political reactionary, in short, we must first of all consider the criteria that are being applied. Malthus was an active member of the Whig party, and the social reforms he advocated—in addition to the crucial one of universal schooling—included an extension of the suffrage, free medical care for the poor, state assistance to emigrants, and even direct relief to casual laborers or families with more than six children; similarly, he opposed child labor in factories and free trade when it benefited the traders but not the public.[53] Apart from such details, he was an honest and beneficent reformer, committed throughout his life to the goal that he shared with every liberal of his day— the betterment of society and of all the people in it.

Notes

1. His Times

1. Paley, 1786, pp. 241–245. Paley is placed in his context in Bland, 1973.
2. Quoted in Bee, 1955.
3. Bryson, 1945; Schneider, 1967.
4. J. B. Black, 1926, pp. 84–89. But see also Davie, 1973.
5. *Treatise of Human Nature,* part III, sec. III.
6. *Wealth of Nations,* Book I, chap. 2.
7. *Moral Sentiments,* part III, chap. 1.
8. Durkheim, *The Division of Labor in Society,* p. 399, quoted in Reisman, 1976, p. 69. See also Petrella, 1970.
9. Reisman, 1976, chap. 4.
10. Ibid., pp. 223–228; Stigler, 1971. Cf. Grampp, 1973.
11. Brazelton, 1977. See also Samuelson, 1977.
12. Rae, 1895, chap. 24.
13. Hart, 1968, chap. 5; 1970, chap. 5; McClatchey, 1960.
14. Chalmers, 1832, 1835.
15. Keir, 1807, p. 83.
16. Evans, 1929.
17. Beckwith, 1886, p. 3. Bready, 1926, p. 46. Biéler, 1963.
18. "A Clergyman," 1820. *Quarterly Review* 16 (1816) : 37–69. Sumner, 1818, II, 130. See also Sumner's review of the *Essay* in *Quarterly Review* 17 (1817) : 369–403.
19. Winstanley, 1935, p. 96.
20. Lloyd, 1837.
21. Tillyard, 1913, p. 112; cf. Mathieson, 1923.
22. Fetter, 1953. See also Clive, 1957.
23. Shepard, 1973.

24. Greer, 1935, chap. 2. See also Slavin, 1977.
25. Eversley, 1959, p. 301.

2. HIS LIFE AND WORK

1. Possibly following Payne, 1890, p. 101. A photograph of the tablet is reproduced in the *Economic Journal* 75 (1965) : 243.
2. Patricia James, 1966, p. 1.
3. Bagehot, 1915, p. 212.
4. Halkett and Laing, 1929, II, 192; IV, 314; V, 332. Otter, 1836, p. xxii.
5. Mowat, 1938; Guéhenno, 1966; Cranston, 1962.
6. *Capital,* I, 675–676.
7. Fogarty, 1958, p. vi.
8. Arthur Gray, 1926, p. 263. Cf. Gunning, 1854; Brittain, 1940.
9. Frend, 1793b.
10. Anon., 1841; Knight, 1971.
11. Anon., 1841.
12. Frend is quoted in Knight, 1971, p. 303. For "Richard Malthus," see ibid., p. 52.
13. Quoted in Otter, 1836, p. xxvii.
14. Patricia James, 1966, p. 7.
15. Otter, 1836, p. xxiii. For Malthus's circle of friends at Jesus, see Arthur Gray and Brittain, 1960, chap. 9.
16. Philips, 1961, pp. 124–132. Woodruff, 1953, chap. 8.
17. Woodruff, 1953, pp. 280–286.
18. Rutherford, 1816.
19. Woodruff, 1953, p. 286.
20. Stokes, 1959, pp. 47–53.
21. Martineau, 1877, I, 327.
22. Patricia James, 1966, p. xvi.
23. *Quarterly Review* 17 (April 1817). Horner, 1843, I, 419, 436–437. See also Everett, 1826, p. viii; Martineau, 1877, I, 209. Grampp, 1974.
24. Quoted by Fetter, 1953.

3. THE PRINCIPLE OF POPULATION

1. Bonar (1934) dramatized the opposition between father and son by constructing a supposed discussion between them.
2. Heckscher, 1935, I, 158.
3. Rae, 1895, chap. 28.
4. *Wealth of Nations,* Book I, chap. 8. See also Spengler, 1970, 1976.
5. Fage, 1953; Allen, 1970.
6. Morellet, 1822, chap. 24. Note, however, that O. H. Prior (in the introduction to the 1970 edition of the *Esquisse,* p. xxiv) calls

the allegation that Condorcet committed suicide a "legend, vulgarized since 1795."

7. Paul, 1876, chap. 1. Cf. Petersen, 1971.

8. *Political Justice,* I, 311; II, 500–501.

9. *Enquirer,* p. 60.

10. *Political Justice,* II, 506–511.

11. Ibid., I, 70, 93.

12. Paul, 1876, I, 294.

13. *Political Justice,* II, 518–519.

14. Ibid., II, 528.

15. Paul, 1876, II, 331.

16. The paradox was sharper during the considerable period when the 1798 version was not available in any modern reprint. That gap, fortunately, has been repaired on both sides of the Atlantic; and all three of the reprints now to be had are useful for their discerning introductions: London: Macmillan for the Royal Economic Society, 1926, with notes by James Bonar; Ann Arbor: University of Michigan Press, 1959, with a foreword by Kenneth E. Boulding; and Harmondsworth, England: Penguin Books, 1970, with an excellent introduction and useful notes by Antony Flew.

17. Zinke, 1967, p. 1.

18. Paul, 1876, I, 321–325.

19. *Parr's Spital Sermon,* pp. 55–74.

20. Bonar, 1924, pp. 414–415.

21. Patricia James, 1966, pp. 89, 118.

22. Michael Drake, 1966. See also Ross, 1825, I, 344–345.

23. A rough idea of how the book grew can be had from the dimensions of the several editions: 1798, one volume of 396 octavo pages; 1803, "a new edition, very much enlarged," one volume of 610 quarto pages; 1806, two volumes of 505 + 559 octavo pages; 1807, two volumes of 580 + 584 octavo pages; 1817, "with important additions," three volumes of 496 + 507 + 500 octavo pages; 1826, the last published during Malthus's lifetime, two volumes of 535 + 528 octavo pages; 1872, posthumous, 551 very full octavo pages.

24. Quoted by Flew, 1970.

25. Cf. Zinke, 1942. Some of the diffusion in other languages can be noted from an international bibliography (Amano, 1957). *German:* 1807, translated by Fr. H. Hegewisch, Altona: Hammerich. 1879, translated by Franz Stöpel, editor of the *Merkur,* Berlin: R. L. Prager, as vol. 2 in the *Bibliothek der Volkswirtschaftslehre und Gesellschaftswissenschaft.* 1905 (with a new edition in 1924–25), translated by Valentine Dorn with an introduction by Heinrich Waentig, author of *Wirtschaft und Kunst,* Jena: Fisher, as vols. 6–7 in the *Sammlung Sozialwissenschaftlicher Meister. Italian:* 1868, Turin, as vols. 11–12 in the *Biblioteca dell'Economista. Polish:* 1925, an abridgement of 184 pp. *Russian:* 1895, *Preliminary Outline* (the

first edition?) *of a Principle of Population. Chinese:* translations, undated, of the first and a later edition. *Japanese:* 1876, an outline of the *Essay* in 142 pp. 1910 (with seven reprints), an abridgement based on "the Ashley edition." 1923–24, two separate translations of the first edition of the *Essay.* 1933, a translation of Bonar, *Malthus and His Work* (1924). 1935, translation of the 6th edition of the *Essay,* followed by ten new translations or editions up to the 1950s.

26. Spengler, 1945.

4. Minor Quibbles and Gross Misunderstandings

1. Flew, 1963.

2. For example, Köhler, 1913; Hutchinson, 1967, chap. 4.

3. Fage, 1953; cf. McCleary, 1953, pp. 86–88.

4. Spengler, 1942, p. 29 and chap. 4.

5. Robert S. Smith, 1954, 1969; Stillman Drake, 1967.

6. Franklin, 1761 (published originally in 1751). Cf. Zirkle, 1957.

7. Mill, *Principles of Political Economy,* 1909, p. 359, quoted in Flew, 1963; but see also Nicholson, 1902, I, 180. Cannan, 1928, chap. 3; Robertson, 1942, which is a good commentary on several of these cavils.

8. W. A. Lewis, quoted in Flew, 1963.

9. Knibbs, 1928, p. 49n.

10. Cf. Schumpeter, 1954, p. 581.

11. Godwin, *Of Population,* p. 20; see also Whately, 1855, p. 120. McAtee, 1936. Kenneth Smith, 1951, p. 234.

12. Senior, 1829, p. 36; for a good comparison of the two points of view, see Rickards, 1854, lecture 3. Mombert, 1935.

13. Arimoto, 1977.

14. Weyland, 1816, p. 21; cf. Ravenstone, 1821, pp. 187–189; Loudon, 1836. But note also the defense of Malthus's use of *tendency* by Gavin Young, 1832.

15. Hickson, 1849, p. 7.

16. Coale, 1970a.

17. David Booth, 1823.

18. Hickson, 1849, pp. 9, 72–73.

19. Ensor, 1818, pp. 79, 370–371.

20. Twiss, 1845, pp. 22–29, 92–95, 28, 24.

21. Jarrold, 1806, pp. 68–71, 34.

22. *Don Juan,* XV, 38; XII, 14; IX, 9; XII, 20.

23. Pulos, 1952, 1955.

24. Potter, 1936; Curry, 1939; *Westminster Review* 22 (1835).

25. Southey, 1832, I, essay 4.

26. Hazlitt, 1806, p. 15. Albrecht, 1955; see also Albrecht, 1950.

27. De Quincy, 1823.

28. Quoted in Cole, 1947, pp. 88–89, 412.

29. Quoted in Kegel, 1958.
30. Paul, 1876, II, 258–259.
31. *Of Population,* pp. 106–108, 14, 231, 161.
32. Malthus, 1821. Cf. Rosen, 1970.
33. For Marx, see Meek, 1953; Platter, 1877. Engels, 1844.
34. *Theorien über den Mehrwert,* quoted in Meek, 1953, p. 164.
35. *Critique of the Gotha Programme,* p. 40.
36. *Capital,* I, 693; see also Coontz, 1957.
37. *Capital,* I, 652, 692, 697, 693, 672. Cf. the discussion in Sweezy, 1942, p. 223.
38. Sweezy, 1942, p. 89. Cf. Daly, 1971.
39. Cannan, 1892.
40. For Leroux, see McLaren, 1976; cf. Puynode, 1849. Proudhon is quoted in Sauvy, 1963, p. 44; cf. Proudhon, 1886. The quotation about socialists is from Sauvy, 1963, p. 41; see also Sauvy, 1966, 1968.
41. See also Simon Gray, 1815, 1817.
42. Cf. Lux, 1968.

5. ECONOMIC THEORY

1. See Bonar, 1924, pp. 221–222.
2. Sowell, 1974, pp. 6–7. See also Catherwood, 1939, chap. 4.
3. Ricardo, *Notes,* p. xiv. Cf. Bonar, 1929.
4. Ricardo, *Notes,* p. xiii.
5. Malthus, *Principles,* p. 4.
6. Schumpeter, 1954, pp. 472–473. Cf. D. P. O'Brien, 1975, pp. 69–70.
7. See, e.g., Mann, 1976.
8. Schumpeter, 1954, p. 471. Schumpeter himself perceived the economic discipline as too narrow; "if I have a function," he said in a farewell address to his Bonn students, "it is not to close doors but to open them" (Mann, 1971).
9. D. P. O'Brien, 1975, p. 69.
10. Sowell, 1974, pp. 52–53. "Money was only a 'veil,' to the general glut theorists as well as to the supporters of Say's law. The lone apparent exception to this was Malthus, who *mentioned* money as a neglected element, but who did not explore monetary phenomena or incorporate it into his analysis any more than the others" (ibid., pp. 55–56).
11. D. P. O'Brien, 1975, pp. 149, 151; cf. Schumpeter, 1954, p. 482. See also Malthus's *Investigation of the High Price of Provisions* (1800) and the comment by Harry Johnson (1949).
12. Malthus, 1811a, pp. 401–402.
13. *Definitions in Political Economy,* p. 15. Once again, it is of interest to note that Schumpeter (1954, pp. 188–189) supported this criticism. "Smith flounders so badly," he wrote, "that his fundamentally simple idea was misunderstood even by Ricardo. Accord-

ingly, he was credited with a labor theory of value—or rather with three incompatible labor theories—whereas . . . he meant to *explain* commodity prices by cost of production, which . . . he divides up into wages, profit, and rent." See also Meek, 1974, for a defense of Ricardo's position.

14. Ricardo, *Notes,* p. xxii. Cf. V. E. Smith, 1956.

15. On Ricardo compare Blaug, 1958, pp. 33–37. Malthus, *Principles,* p. 60.

16. *Principles,* pp. 98–100.

17. Schumpeter, 1950, p. 23, n. 2. For two opposed views, see Schumpeter's chap. 3, "Marx the Economist," and Sowell, 1967.

18. On the last point, see de Marchi and Sturges, 1973.

19. Jean-Baptiste Say (1767–1832), according to Guillaumont (1969, pp. 9–10), represented "liberal industrial thought"; Jean-Charles Léonard Simonde de Sismondi (1773–1842) a "humanitarian reaction." Both were Calvinists; and Sismondi, "like Malthus" (!), was the son of a clergyman; both visited England; and both admired Smith. Malthus was in frequent touch with both men; there is a collection of Say's so-called letters to Malthus (1820), mostly on their differences over effective demand. Sowell's paper on Sismondi (1972a) is also a succinct analysis of the issues at stake on both sides of the Channel.

20. Sowell, 1972b (see also Sowell, 1963) ; Baumol, 1977.

21. *Principles,* pp. 321, 323. Though Malthus's most fundamental point was to challenge the thesis that human wants can expand without limit, a good half of his recent critics, as Rashid (1977) points out, do not even mention the issue of satiety. Cf. Semmel, 1965.

22. Keynes, *Essays in Biography,* p. 144.

23. Keynes, *General Theory,* p. 32. Those who have tried to challenge this contrast have managed only to confirm it; as against such established personages as Marshall, Edgeworth, and Pigou (whom Keynes cited as having ignored the principle of effective demand), commentators noted such men as Lauderdale (Paglin, 1961; Gordon and Jilek, 1965; Lambert, 1966; Skinner, 1969), Major General Sir William Sleeman, and Captain W. R. A. Pettman, R.N. (R. D. C. Black, 1967). However one judges the validity of their opinions, one can hardly place such men in the main stream of economic doctrine.

24. Keynes, *General Theory,* p. 371. On the Continent, where the most prominent counterpart was Sismondi, McCulloch's role of denigrating Malthus as an economist was carried out, for example, in Blanqui's *Histoire de l'économie politique en Europe* (cf. Würgler, 1957, pp. 178–200).

25. Lambert, 1962, 1956.

26. Blaug, 1958, p. 240. Cf. Corry, 1959; Dubey, 1962.

27. R. D. C. Black, 1967.

28. Hollander, 1969.
29. O'Leary, 1942, 1943.
30. *Principles,* pp. 6–7.
31. Cf. Hollander, 1962.
32. Schumpeter, 1954, p. 887, n. 2.
33. Leibenstein, 1976.
34. Schumpeter, 1954, p. 641, n. 38.
35. *Principles,* p. 315.
36. Ibid., pp. 406–408.
37. Ricardo, *Notes,* p. cx.
38. Marx, *Theorien über den Mehrwert,* II:1, 306–307.
39. Schumpeter, 1950, pp. 38–42; Sowell, 1972b, pp. 169–171.
40. Sweezy, 1942, p. 178. See also Dobb, 1937, pp. 118–121; 1947, chaps. 6–8.
41. *Definitions in Political Economy,* pp. 65–67.
42. *Essay,* 1st ed., p. 78.
43. Dow, 1977. Cf. Vatter, 1959.
44. *Principles,* pp. 409–410.
45. Friedman, 1977; cf. Lerner, 1977.
46. Robbins, 1967.

6. THE POOR LAW AND MIGRATION

1. A. J. Taylor, 1975.
2. Engels, 1845, chap. 1. See also Chaloner and Henderson, 1974.
3. Gide and Rist, 1948, p. 134. As is typical with accounts of this type, this caricature of Malthus's thought was combined with such details of his life as that he had "three sons and a daughter," and that he wrote a work entitled *A Series of Short Studies Dealing with the Corn Laws.* In any case, we are informed, "history certainly has not confirmed his fears. No single country has shown that it is suffering from overpopulation" (p. 145). See also, e.g., Haney, 1924, chap. 11, where Malthus is also subsumed under "Pessimistic Tendencies"; Poynter, 1969, pp. xv–xvi and passim; Manning, 1838, appendix.
4. Bagehot, 1915, p. 224. Contrast Levin, 1966.
5. Connell, 1950, p. 25.
6. Ibid., pp. 51, 151–156, 57–58.
7. George O'Brien, 1918, p. 29 and passim.
8. E. M. Johnston, 1963, pp. 127–128, 1.
9. Ibid., pp. 104–116.
10. Pakenham, 1970; E. H. S. Jones, 1950.
11. Bolton, 1966, chap. 6. Cf. McCaffrey, 1966.
12. Bolton, 1966, p. 218.
13. Machin, 1964, pp. 12, 191, and passim.
14. MacDonagh, 1977, chap. 2. See also Ó Tuathaigh, 1972, chap. 3.

15. *Edinburgh Review* 12 (1808) : 336–355; 14 (1809) : 151–170. Both are reprinted in Semmel, *Occasional Papers.*

16. This passage has been interpreted, with the exaggerated partisanship typical of single-tax advocates, as an early version of Henry George's panacea; see MacDowell, 1977.

17. MacArthur, 1957.

18. Ibid.

19. Kennedy, 1973, chap. 7.

20. Hutt, 1954. Dr. Turner Thackrah, a physician, was an important witness before Sadler's committee investigating the factory system.

21. Hobsbawm, 1957.

22. Ashton, 1954.

23. J. D. Marshall, 1968, p. 11.

24. Cowherd, 1960. Indeed, a century after the reform of 1834, the points raised in both the majority and the minority reports of still another royal commission remained more or less the same. See Woodroofe, 1977.

25. J. D. Marshall, 1968, p. 21; cf. Gash, 1974.

26. Rose, 1971, p. 76.

27. Redford, 1976, chap. 6.

28. Rose, 1971, p. 58.

29. Deane, 1965, pp. 6–7.

30. Geoffrey Taylor, 1969, pp. 8–9.

31. Rose, 1971, pp. 30–33, 40–41.

32. Geoffrey Taylor, 1969, p. 107.

33. Rose, 1971, pp. 116–118.

34. *Essay,* Book III, chaps. 5–7.

35. Ingram, 1808, p. 71. The author, Rector of Segrave in Leicestershire, also wrote, among other works, *The Necessity of Introducing Divinity into the Regular Course of Academical Studies Considered, A Syllabus on Political Philosophy,* and *The Causes of the Increases of Methodism and Dissension.*

36. Polanyi, 1944, p. 80.

37. Quoted by J. S. Taylor, 1969.

38. *Report on the Poor Laws,* 1834, quoted in Griffith, 1926, p. 263.

39. *Report on Labourers' Wages,* 1824, quoted in Redford, 1976, p. 83.

40. Select Committee Relating to the Employment or Relief of Able-Bodied Persons from the Poor Rates, *Report,* 1828, quoted in Huzel, 1969.

41. Krause, 1958; Blackmore and Mellonie, 1927–28; T. H. Marshall, 1965; Huzel, 1969.

42. Blaug, 1963; J. S. Taylor, 1969. Cf. Blaug, 1964.

43. Glass, 1940.

44. Kälvemark, 1976. Cf. Pendleton, 1978.
45. Stanton, 1977.
46. MacDonald, 1977; Barmack, 1977; Sexauer, 1977.
47. Whitney, 1968; Schorr, 1966, p. 83.
48. Vadakin, 1968, p. 96.
49. Fulford, 1967, p. vii.
50. See the notebooks that he kept during this period—Whitbread, 1971.
51. Whitbread, 1807. Cf. Monck, 1807; Weyland, 1807; Parkinson, 1807.
52. Fulford, 1967, p. 179.
53. Whitbread, 1807.
54. Malthus, 1807. See also Cowherd, 1977, chap. 2.
55. Platky, 1977. Moreover, according to a preliminary survey in 1978, various federal aid programs cost not only stupendously large amounts but an additional $12,000 million annually in fraud (New York *Times,* April 16, 1978).
56. Redford, 1976, chap. 1.
57. Ibid., chap. 6 and p. 34.
58. Heckscher, 1935, II, 300.
59. H. J. M. Johnston, 1972, chaps. 2–3.
60. His name is cited variously as Wilmot, Wilmot Horton, Wilmot-Horton, and Horton; he married an attractive girl (whom her cousin Lord Byron celebrated in "she walks in beauty like the night") and, in accordance with his father-in-law's will, changed the Wilmot he was born with to Horton, his wife's name.
61. Quoted by Ghosh, 1963.
62. MacDonagh, 1955.
63. P. A. M. Taylor, 1976, p. 60.
64. Bloomfield, 1961.
65. Ó Tuathaigh, 1972, p. 114.
66. *Rural Rides,* April 19, 1830; quoted in Bloomfield, 1961, p. 95.
67. H. J. M. Johnston, 1972, chap. 8. See also McCulloch, 1826.
68. Scrope, 1832. See also Thornton, 1846.
69. Erickson, 1976, p. 22.
70. Saville, 1957, pp. 20–30.
71. Petersen, 1955b.
72. *Essay,* Book III, chap. 4.
73. U.K. Select Committee on Emigration from the United Kingdom, "Evidence of T. R. Malthus, May 5, 1827."
74. Ghosh, 1963.

7. POPULATION GROWTH

1. Esmonin, 1964.
2. Glass, 1973, chap. 1.

3. Price, 1780, p. 36; Howlett, 1781.

4. Arthur Young, 1898. See also Mingay, 1975.

5. Arthur Young, 1774, pp. 61–64, 88–89.

6. Robert Wallace, 1761; Hume, 1752. See also Mossner, 1943, chap. 5.

7. Helleiner, 1965, 1967. Cf. Langer, 1963, for a historian's view.

8. Glass, 1976.

9. *Essay*, pp. 253–255.

10. Wells, 1975, chap. 1.

11. The figures were calculated on the assumption that the increment was added once a year. If one assumes a continuous increase throughout each year, the doubling times would be, respectively, 7.15 and 21.0 years.

12. Wells, 1975, chap. 7.

13. *Essay*, p. 253.

14. Robbins, 1927.

15. Keynes, *General Theory*, p. 307.

16. Hicks, 1936.

17. Reddaway, 1939; Hansen, 1939.

18. Bladen, 1941.

19. Keynes, 1937; cf. Petersen, 1955a.

20. Cf. Rubin, 1960.

21. *Essay*, pp. 209n–210n.

22. Ibid., p. 268.

23. Ibid., pp. 163–170. The work of Muret was *Mémoires sur l'état de la population dans le pays de Vaud* (1766). According to present-day analysts even Muret's statistics were incorrect; the area was not becoming depopulated. See also Perrenoud, 1974.

24. Tuan, 1958.

25. This letter, never before published, was given to me by Mrs. Patricia James, who obtained a copy and permission to publish it from Lord Lyell, the owner. I thank both for making it available. The text follows, with brackets indicating words that Malthus crossed out. His "able mathematical friend" was Edward Otter.

"Dear Sir

"As it would always be my wish to acknowledge an error as soon as it was known to me, I should esteem it a particular favour, if in your widely-circulating review you could find room for the following remarks.

"In the 4th chapter of the 2nd book of the Essay on the principle of population, I endeavoured to prove that the proportion of annual marriages to annual births instead of expressing the average prolifickness of marriages as it was usually supposed to do, expressed a different thing, namely, the proportion of the born which lives to be married. I was perhaps the more readily induced to adopt the train of reasoning which led to this conclusion, as it appeared to solve some difficulties in the registers of the births and marriages of some countries, which did not seem easily to admit of another solution. The suggestions of an able mathematical friend and my own further reflections on this subject, have convinced me that I was wrong, and that although the old theory is incorrect, that which I would have substituted is even more so.

"In a register, the births and marriages are of course contemporaneous; but the marriages in the register of any particular year cannot be contemporaneous with the births from which they resulted; nor are the births contemporaneous with the marriages from which they were produced; consequently the proportion of births to marriages in any register, supposing the population to be either increasing or decreasing, cannot represent either the number of births from which one marriage results, or the number of children to a marriage, but something between the two, though nearer to the latter than the former, on account of the distance of time being less between the marriages and [the full and complete count of all] the births which they produce in the course of their duration, than between the births and the marriages which result from them. In fact a note [respecting] of Dr. Price (Observ. Vol i p 270) respecting the inferences to be drawn from the different proportions of births and marriages, which I alluded to as erroneous, I am now convinced is [just] correct; and if he has erred on this subject it is rather in his general and practical conclusions than in the [premises] reasoning on which they are founded.

"The proportion of annual marriages to annual births in registers is affected both by the [number] proportion of the born which lives to be married, and by the prolifickness of marriages, and these two causes [affect] produce an opposite effect on the registers. The greater is the proportion of the born which lives to be married, the greater will be the proportion of annual marriages to annual births, and the greater is the prolifickness of marriages, the less will be the proportion of annual marriages to annual births. Consequently, if, within certain limits, the proportion of the born which lives to be married, and the prolifickness of marriages, increase at the same time, the proportion of annual marriages to annual births may still remain unchanged; and this is the reason why the registers of different countries, in respect to marriages and births, are often found the same under very different rates of increase of population. At the same time it is impossible to reconcile so rapid an increase of population as is known to take place in some of the Russian provinces with registers which express a proportion of marriages to births as 1 to 3 and 1 to 3.6: for in this case it would appear, even after making every allowance for second and third marriages (a correction which should always be attended to) that all or nearly all of the born lived to be married which is impossible; and therefore it is necessary to suppose, that in the Russian registers, and some others, the omissions in the births are considerably greater than in the marriages, a supposition which on other accounts does not seem improbable.

"I am, Sir, Yours &c:

"T. R. Malthus"

There was a correspondence on this point in the *Monthly Magazine,* September 1804 to March 1805, in which Price's point of view was upheld by "M. N." (conceivably William Morgan, Price's nephew) and Malthus's by "W. D." (possibly William Dealtry, a mathematician and evangelical clergyman who became Malthus's colleague at the East India College). Cf. Brentano, 1909, p. 577.

26. Boulding, 1955.
27. Quoted in Barnett and Morse, 1963, p. 76.
28. Wright, 1923.
29. Meadows et al., 1972.
30. Mesarovic and Pestel, 1974.
31. Beer, 1977.
32. Among specifications of this intent, a prime instance was the Water Quality Control Act of 1972. In undisputed testimony before a congressional committee, it was estimated that this bill's aim of achieving 100 percent clean water by 1985 would cost some $2.3 million million, or more than the annual gross national product of the entire world. Yet members of Congress were so fearful of being attacked as proponents of "dirty water" that the act passed unanimously in the Senate and against only fourteen nay votes in the House.
33. U.S. Council on Environmental Quality *and* Environmental Protection Agency, 1972.
34. Coale, 1970b.
35. Coale and Hoover, 1958.
36. Boserup, 1965, p. 11 and chap. 8. See also Cohen, 1977.
37. Simon, 1977, chap. 23.
38. Ibid., p. 5n.
39. Ibid., p. 27.
40. Ibid., p. 475.

8. MORTALITY

1. Fourastié, 1972.
2. *Essay,* Book II, chaps. 8–9.
3. Cf. Chadwick, 1888.
4. McKeown, 1976, chap. 6.
5. Helleiner, 1965.
6. McKeown and Brown, 1965.

7. For example, Griffith, 1926. See also Razzell, 1977.

8. McKeown, 1976, pp. 107, 108–109.

9. Langer, 1974. See also Kellum, 1974; Trexler, 1974.

10. Trevelyan, 1942, p. 376. Cf. Edmonds, 1828, p. 15; 1832, chap. 11.

11. Drummond and Wilbraham, 1957, p. 392.

12. Alison, 1847, pp. v–vi.

13. Mallory, 1926, p. 1.

14. Ho, 1959, pp. 228–229, 292–300, 231–232.

15. Ambirajan, 1976.

16. Burn, 1841, pp. 6–7.

17. National Resources Committee, 1938.

18. Parreaux, 1969, p. 195.

19. Stevenson, 1974.

20. Charles Tilly, 1975. Contrast, e.g., D. E. Williams, 1976; Alan Booth, 1977.

21. FAO, 1975, table 1.

22. Spengler, 1966. Cf. Spengler, 1949.

23. FAO, 1970, I, 51.

24. Saitō, 1971.

25. Carlson et al., 1972.

26. Frankel, 1971, chap. 7.

27. Barnes, 1930, pp. xiv–xv.

28. Cf. Hollander, 1977.

29. C. R. Fay, 1932, chap. 3; p. 109.

30. Ibid., pp. 119–120.

31. Quoted in Hutchinson, 1967, chap. 2.

32. Otterbein, 1977. Vayda, 1969, 1974; King, 1976.

33. Polanyi, 1944, p. 5.

34. Edwin James, 1916.

35. Ratzel, 1897.

36. Mackinder, 1904.

37. *Land ohne Bauern—Volk ohne Jugend* (1940) was a pronatalist booklet by Friedrich Burgdorfer, Nazi Germany's principal demographer.

9. FERTILITY

1. Hajnal, 1965. See also Leasure, 1963; Sklar, 1974.

2. Homans, 1941, pp. 136–137.

3. Laslett, 1972, introduction. But see also Berkner, 1972, 1973; Fine-Souriac, 1977.

4. Laslett, 1972, p. 126.

5. Laslett, 1971, pp. 85, 94.

6. Grigg, 1977.

7. Griffith, 1926, p. 109.

8. Shorter, ·1973. Cf. Lee, 1977; Shorter, 1978. Shorter's implicit

approval of illegitimacy, or at least of the greater freedom that stimulated its rise, is challenged in Louise Tilly et al., 1976.

9. Laslett, 1977, p. 113. Cf. Knodel, 1972.

10. Wikman, 1937.

11. Petersen, 1960.

12. Rainwater, 1965, p. 201. See also Chamberlain, 1976b.

13. Caldwell, 1976.

14. Becker, 1960.

15. Boas, 1937, chap. 2.

16. Charles, 1936, pp. 182–183.

17. Doubleday, 1842, chap. 1.

18. Castro, 1952.

19. Dumont, 1890, pp. 106, 110.

20. Banks, 1954, pp. 48, 166–168.

21. Grahame, 1816.

22. *Essay,* p. 512.

23. Place, 1972.

24. Place, 1882, chap. 6, sec. 3.

25. Carlisle, 1826.

26. For example, Bonner, 1908.

27. Fryer, 1965, p. 11. Fryer himself worked for the official Communist newspaper, *The Daily Worker,* but broke with the Communists over the Soviet invasion of Hungary; see Goodwin and Fryer, 1958.

28. Bradlaugh, 1883.

29. Arnstein, 1965, pp. 20–21.

30. Besant, 1893, chap. 1 and p. 340.

31. Ledbetter, 1976, chap. 2; Besant, 1877.

32. Reed, 1978, chaps. 6–10.

33. For example, *The Principle of Population,* Malthusian Tract no. 1 (1877?); *The Struggle for Enjoyable Existence,* Malthusian Tract no. 2 (1877?); *Prostitution Medically Considered, with some of its social effects* (1866); *The Population Question According to T. R. Malthus and J. S. Mill, giving the Malthusian theory of overpopulation* (1878); *The Life and Writings of Thomas R. Malthus* (1887).

34. For example, *Population Fallacies: A defence of the Malthusian or true theory of society* (1860); *The Irish Land Question* (1869); and *State Measures for the Abolition of Poverty, War, and Pestilence* (1886).

35. Miller, 1891.

36. C. V. Drysdale, 1917, p. 4.

37. Stopes, 1923, p. 28. Cf. Bradlaugh, 1884; Hyndman and Bradlaugh, 1884; Haynes, 1954; D'Arcy, 1977.

38. Petersen, 1964, pp. 90–102.

39. Lewinsohn, 1922. See also Soetbeer, 1886; Unshelm, 1924.

40. Bebel, 1897, pp. 160ff.
41. Kautsky, 1880. See also Quessel, 1911.
42. Kautsky, 1921, chaps. 15–16. See also Kautsky, 1911.
43. As two examples, Malik, 1957; Mattelart, 1969.
44. Oestreich, 1936; pp. 20ff.
45. Quoted by Petersen, 1957.
46. Quoted by Sauvy, 1952, I, 174; see also Sauvy, 1948.
47. Himes, 1936, pp. 183–184.
48. Carr-Saunders, 1922. Cf. Caldwell and Caldwell, 1977.
49. Hopkins, 1965.
50. Himes, 1936, pp. 88–92.
51. Fryer, 1965, pp. 27–30.
52. Himes, 1927.
53. Field, 1931, pp. 47–51, 95–108.
54. Cf. Ledbetter, 1976, pp. 15–17.
55. Ibid., pp. 209–211.
56. Reed, 1978, p. 15.
57. Chamberlain, 1976a. Cf. Bone, 1973; John Peel and Carr, 1975.
58. Spengler, 1935a.
59. Spengler, 1933. See also Cady, 1931.
60. Spengler, 1935b.
61. In particular, Cocks, 1967; see also Cocks, 1971.
62. Spengler, 1935b.
63. Petersen, 1964, pp. 198–200. See also Spengler, 1933, pp. 654–661.
64. Wells, 1978; Reed, 1978, chap. 1.
65. Gonnard, 1923, pp. 290–292. See also Lang, 1913; Leroy-Beaulieu, 1913; and, for a German example, Brentano, 1910.
66. Garnier, 1857.
67. Poursin and Dupuy, 1972, chap. 2.
68. Salleron, 1972, chap. 2. See also Lutfalla, 1969.
69. Stassart, 1957, p. 54.
70. Armengaud, 1975, pp. 79–140.
71. Mounier, 1873–74.
72. Fréville, 1956.
73. C. R. Drysdale, 1887, p. 100.
74. Li, 1973.
75. Mamdani, 1972.
76. For a well rounded discussion, see Halévy, 1928, chaps. 1–3.
77. Arrow, 1977.
78. *Principles,* pp. 224–225.
79. Ibid., pp. 226–227.
80. *Essay,* pp. 436–441.
81. Whewell, 1859, pp. 93–113.
82. *Essay,* p. 404.

10. THE MALTHUSIAN HERITAGE

1. Darwin, 1887, pp. 42–43. Cf. Vorzimmer, 1969.

2. Alfred Wallace, 1905, I, 232, 361–362. See also Clodd, 1897, pp. 123–129; Habakkuk, 1959.

3. Hull, 1973, p. 216.

4. Clark and Pirie, 1951, p. 16.

5. Alfred Wallace, 1870, pp. 264–302.

6. Flew, 1959. See also Ruse, 1973; Bowler, 1976.

7. Alfred Wallace, 1908.

8. Darwin, 1887, pp. 284–287. See also Cowles, 1936; W. M. S. Russell, 1976; Greta Jones, 1978.

9. Boulding, 1955.

10. Wynne-Edwards, 1967, p. 11.

11. Wilson, 1975, pp. 109–110.

12. Ibid., p. 559. See also Campbell, 1975; Starobin, 1976; Hirshleifer, 1977.

13. Tax and Krucoff, 1968.

14. J. D. Y. Peel, 1971, chap. 1; 1972.

15. *First Principles,* p. 291. Cf. Perrin, 1976.

16. Cf. Bowler, 1975.

17. For example, R. M. Young, 1969.

18. Rogers, 1972; Bowen, 1879.

19. Spencer, 1852.

20. For example, Makarius, 1977.

21. Cf. Ginsberg, 1931; Owen, 1974.

22. Huxley, 1893. Cf. Bibby, 1972, pp. 139–150.

23. J. D. Y. Peel, 1971, chap. 6.

24. Cf. Kitchen, 1977.

25. Carneiro, 1967, p. xi.

26. *Principles of Sociology,* III, 3, quoted in ibid., p. xxxii. Compare Parsons's subsequent view that Spencer was "very close to a position of modern 'functional' theory in sociology and related disciplines. Indeed, on the level of 'approach' all the essential ingredients are present" (Parsons, 1961, p. vii).

27. Andreski, 1971.

28. See Russett, 1976.

29. Feuer, 1975, 1976. Cf. Ureña, 1977; Margaret Fay, 1978; Kapp, 1978.

30. Wilson, 1975, pp. 560–562.

31. Grossman, 1958.

32. Sidney Webb, 1913.

33. Muller, 1960. On the politics of the eugenics movement more generally, see Loren Graham, 1977.

34. Stone, 1969.

35. Bartley, 1871, chap. 1.

36. Pons, 1919.
37. Kay, 1846, chap. 1. See also Duke, 1976.
38. Kay, 1850, II, chap. 14.
39. Kay, 1846, p. 141.
40. *Wealth of Nations,* p. 734. Cf. Reisman, 1976, chap. 6.
41. Cf. Sanderson, 1972.
42. *Wealth of Nations,* pp. 737, 768. Cf. Freeman, 1969.
43. Tu, 1969.
44. *Essay,* Book IV, chap. 9.
45. Halévy, 1928, p. 244.
46. Sidney and Beatrice Webb, 1919, pp. 632–635.
47. Himmelfarb, 1960. Cf. Himmelfarb, 1955.
48. Mannheim, 1953.
49. Butterfield, 1931, pp. 13–14.
50. Nisbet, 1968, chap. 4.
51. Morison, 1977, pp. 234–253.
52. Bernard Williams, 1973, p. 99 and passim.
53. Bonar, 1924, p. 343.

Works Cited

ALBRECHT, WILLIAM P. 1950. *William Hazlitt and the Malthusian Controversy.* Albuquerque: University of New Mexico Press.
—— 1955. "Godwin and Malthus." *Proceedings of the Modern Language Association* 70: 552–555.

ALISON, WILLIAM P. 1847. *Observations on the Famine of 1846–7 in the Highlands of Scotland and in Ireland, as illustrating the connection of the principle of population with the management of the poor.* Edinburgh: W. Blackwood & Sons.

ALLEN, WILLIAM R. 1970. "Modern Defenders of Mercantilist Theory." *History of Political Economy* 2: 381–397.

AMANO KEITARO. 1957. *Malthus Bibliography.* Osaka: Kansai University. Reprinted from *Keizai Ronshu* [Economic Review of Kansai University] 7, no. 6.

AMBIRAJAN, S. 1976. "Malthusian Population Theory and Indian Famine Policy in the Nineteenth Century." *Population Studies* 30: 5–14.

ANDRESKI, STANISLAV. 1971. "Sociology, Biology and Philosophy in Herbert Spencer." In *Herbert Spencer: Structure, Function and Evolution.* London: Michael Joseph.

ANON. 1841. "Obituary of William Frend." *The Athenaeum,* no. 751 (March 19).

ARIMOTO MASATAKE. 1977. "A Note on *Tendency.*" *Linguistic Inquiry* 8: 697–699.

ARMENGAUD, ANDRÉ. 1975. *Les Français et Malthus.* Paris: Presses Universitaires de France.

ARNSTEIN, WALTER L. 1965. *The Bradlaugh Case: A Study in Late Victorian Opinion and Politics.* Oxford: Clarendon Press.

ARROW, KENNETH J. 1977. "Current Developments in the Theory of Social Choice." *Social Research* 44: 607–622.

Works Cited

ASHTON, T. S. 1954. "The Standard of Life of the Workers in England, 1790–1830." In F. A. Hayek, ed., *Capitalism and the Historians*. Chicago: University of Chicago Press.

BAGEHOT, WALTER. 1915. "Malthus." In Mrs. Russell Barrington, ed., *The Works and Life of Walter Bagehot*, VII, 212–226. London: Longmans, Green.

BANKS, J. A. 1954. *Prosperity and Parenthood: A Study of Family Planning among the Victorian Middle Classes*. London: Routledge & Kegan Paul.

BARMACK, JUDITH A. 1977. "The Case against In-Kind Transfers: The Food Stamp Program." *Policy Analysis* 3: 509–530.

BARNES, DONALD GROVE. 1930 (1961). *A History of the English Corn Laws from 1660–1846*. New York: Kelley.

BARNETT, HAROLD J., and CHANDLER MORSE. 1963. *Scarcity and Growth: The Economics of Natural Resource Availability*. Baltimore: Johns Hopkins Press.

BARTLEY, GEORGE C. T. 1871. *The Schools for the People, containing the history, development, and present working of each description of English school for the industrial and poor classes*. London: Bell & Daldy.

BAUMOL, WILLIAM J. 1977. "Say's (at least) Eight Laws, or What Say and James Mill May Really Have Meant." *Economica* 44: 145–162.

BEBEL, AUGUST. 1897. *Woman in the Past, Present, and Future*. San Francisco: Benham.

BECKER, GARY S. 1960. "An Economic Analysis of Fertility." In National Bureau of Economic Research, *Demographic and Economic Change in Developed Countries*. Princeton, N.J.: Princeton University Press.

BECKWITH, T. 1886. *God or Malthus? Is Over-population the Cause of Poverty? An Exposure of Malthusianism*. Newcastle-on-Tyne: J. W. Swanston.

BEE, ALISON K. 1955. "Montesquieu, Voltaire and Rousseau in Eighteenth-Century Scotland: A Check-List of Editions and Translations of Their Works Published in Scotland before 1801." Mimeographed. University of London.

BEER, ANNE. 1977. "Environmental Impact Analysis." *Town Planning Review* 48: 389–396.

BERKNER, LUTZ K. 1972. "The Stem Family and the Developmental Cycle of the Peasant Household: An Eighteenth-Century Austrian Example." *American Historical Review* 77: 398–418.

———— 1973. "Recent Research on the History of the Family in Western Europe." *Journal of Marriage and the Family* 35: 395–405.

BESANT, ANNIE. [1877]. *The Law of Population: Its consequences, and its bearing upon human conduct and morals.* London: Free-thought Publishing Co.

———— 1893. *An Autobiography.* 2nd ed. London: T. Fisher Unwin.

BIBBY, CYRIL. 1972. *Scientist Extraordinary: The Life and Scientific Work of Thomas Henry Huxley, 1825–1895.* Oxford: Pergamon Press.

BIÉLER, ANDRÉ. 1963. "La faim et l'amour: Essai critique théologique du 'Principe de population' de Malthus." In *Mélanges d'Histoire Économique et Sociale en Hommage au Professeur Antony Babel* . . . , II, 111–130. Geneva: n.p.

BLACK, J. B. 1926. *The Art of History: A Study of Four Great Historians of the Eighteenth Century.* New York: Crofts.

BLACK, R. D. COLLISON. 1967. "Parson Malthus, the General and the Captain." *Economic Journal* 77: 59–74.

BLACKMORE, J. S., and F. C. MELLONIE. 1927–28. "Family Endowment and the Birth-Rate in the Early Nineteenth Century," I and II. *Economic History* (supplement to *Economic Journal*) 1: 205–213 and 412–418.

BLADEN, V. W. 1941. "Population Problems and Policies." In Chester Martin, ed., *Canada in Peace and War: Eight Studies in National Trends since 1914.* New York: Oxford University Press.

BLAND, D. E. 1973. "Population and Liberalism, 1770–1817." *Journal of the History of Ideas* 34: 113–120.

BLAUG, MARK. 1958. *Ricardian Economics: A Historical Study.* New Haven, Conn.: Yale University Press.

———— 1963. "The Myth of the Old Poor Law and the Making of the New." *Journal of Economic History* 23: 151–184.

———— 1964. "The Poor Law Report Reexamined." *Journal of Economic History* 24: 229–245.

BLOOMFIELD, PAUL. 1961. *Edward Gibbon Wakefield: Builder of the British Commonwealth.* London: Longmans.

BOAS, FREDERICK S. 1937. *From Richardson to Pinero: Some Innovators and Idealists.* New York: Columbia University Press.

BOLTON, G. C. 1966. *The Passing of the Irish Act of Union: A Study in Parliamentary Politics.* London: Oxford University Press.

BONAR, JAMES. 1924. *Malthus and His Work.* New York: Macmillan.

———— 1929. "Ricardo on Malthus." *Economic Journal* 39: 210–218.

———— 1934. "Daniel and Robert Malthus: A Dialogue." *Economic Journal* 44: 718–722.

BONE, MARGARET. 1973. *Family Planning Services in England and Wales: An enquiry carried out on behalf of ·the Department of Health and Social Security.* London: H.M. Stationery Office.

BONNER, HYPATIA BRADLAUGH. 1908. *Charles Bradlaugh: A Record of His Life and Work by His Daughter.* London: T. Fisher Unwin.

BOOTH, ALAN. 1977. "Food Riots in the North-west of England, 1790–1801." *Past and Present,* no. 77, 84–107.

Works Cited

BOOTH, DAVID. 1823. *A Letter to the Rev. T. R. Malthus, M.A., F.R.S., being an answer to the criticism on Mr. Godwin's work on population which was inserted in the LXXth number of the Edinburgh Review* . . . London: Longman, Hurst, Rees, Orme, and Brown.

BOSERUP, ESTER. 1965. *The Conditions of Agricultural Growth: The Economics of Agrarian Change under Population Pressure.* Chicago: Aldine.

BOULDING, KENNETH E. 1955. "The Malthusian Model as a General System." *Social and Economic Studies* 4: 195–205.

BOWEN, FRANCIS. 1879. "Malthusianism, Darwinism, and Pessimism." *North American Review* 129: 448–472.

BOWLER, PETER J. 1975. "The Changing Meaning of 'Evolution.'" *Journal of the History of Ideas* 36: 95–114 and 367.

——— 1976. "Malthus, Darwin, and the Concept of Struggle." *Journal of the History of Ideas* 37: 631–650.

BRADLAUGH, CHARLES. 1883. *Jesus, Shelley, and Malthus; or pious poverty and heterodox happiness.* London: Freethought Publishing Co.

——— 1884. *Some Objections to Socialism.* London: Freethought Publishing Co.

BRAZELTON, W. ROBERT. 1977. "Samuelson's Principles of Economics in 1948 and 1973." *Journal of Economic Education* 8: 115–117.

BREADY, J. WESLEY. 1926. *Lord Shaftesbury and Social-Industrial Progress.* London: Allen & Unwin.

BRENTANO, LUJO. 1909. *Die Malthussche Lehre und die Bevölkerungsbewegung der letzten Dezennien.* Munich: K. B. Akademie der Wissenschaften.

——— 1910. "The Doctrine of Malthus and the Increase of Population during the Last Decades." *Economic Journal* 20: 371–393.

BRITTAIN, FREDERICK. 1940. *A Short History of Jesus College, Cambridge.* Cambridge, England: Heffer.

BRYSON, GLADYS. 1945. *Man and Society: The Scottish Inquiry of the Eighteenth Century.* Princeton, N.J.: Princeton University Press.

BURN, JOHN ILDERTON. 1841. *Familiar Letters on Population, Emigration, &c., with introductory letters now added on labour and the advantages of the allotment system.* 2nd ed. London: John W. Parker.

BUTTERFIELD, HERBERT. 1931 (1965). *The Whig Interpretation of History.* New York: Norton.

BYRON, GEORGE GORDON. 1818–23 (1971). *Don Juan,* ed. Truman Guy Steffan and Willis W. Pratt. 2nd ed. Austin: University of Texas Press.

CADY, GEORGE J. 1931. "The Early American Reaction to the Theory of Malthus." *Journal of Political Economy* 39: 601–632.

CALDWELL, JOHN C. 1976. "Toward a Restatement of Demographic

Transition Theory." *Population and Development Review* 2: 321–366.

—— and PAT CALDWELL. 1977. "The Role of Marital Sexual Abstinence in Determining Fertility: A Study of the Yoruba in Nigeria." *Population Studies* 31: 193–217.

CAMPBELL, DONALD T. 1975. "On the Conflicts between Biological and Social Evolution and between Psychology and Moral Tradition." *American Psychologist* 30: 1103–1126.

CANNAN, EDWIN. 1892. "The Malthusian Anti-Socialist Argument." *Economic Review* 2: 72–87.

—— 1928. *Wealth: A Brief Explanation of the Causes of Economic Welfare.* 3rd ed. London: King.

[CARLILE, RICHARD]. 1826. *Every Woman's Book; or, What Is Love?* 4th ed. London: R. Carlile.

CARLSON, P. S., H. H. SMITH, and R. D. DEARING. 1972. "Parasexual Interspecific Plant Hybridization." *Proceedings of the National Academy of Sciences* 69: 2292–2294.

CARNEIRO, ROBERT L. 1967. "Introduction" to *The Evolution of Society: Selections from Herbert Spencer,* Principles of Sociology. Chicago: University of Chicago Press.

CARR-SAUNDERS, A. M. 1922. *The Population Problem: A Study in Human Evolution.* Oxford: Clarendon.

CASTRO, JOSUÉ DE. 1952. *Geography of Hunger.* London: Gollancz.

CATHERWOOD, B. F. 1939. *Basic Theories of Distribution.* London: King.

CHADWICK, EDWIN. 1888. *The Malthusian Theory.* Paper read at the Political Economy Club. Publisher not given.

CHALMERS, THOMAS. 1832. *On Political Economy, in connexion with the moral state and moral prospects of society.* Glasgow: William Collins.

—— 1835. *On the Power, Wisdom, and Goodness of God as manifested in the adaptation of external nature to the moral and intellectual constitution of man.* 2 vols. London: William Pickering.

CHALONER, W. H., and W. O. HENDERSON. 1974. "Friedrich Engels and the England of the 'Hungry Forties.'" In Norman Gash, ed., *The Long Debate on Poverty.* 2nd ed. London: Institute of Economic Affairs.

CHAMBERLAIN, AUDREY. 1976a. "Gin and Hot Baths." *New Society* (July 15) : 112–114.

—— 1976b. "Planning versus Fatalism." *Journal of Biosocial Science* 8: 1–16.

CHARLES, ENID. 1936. *The Menace of Under-Population: A Biological Study of the Decline of Population Growth.* London: Watts.

CLARK, F. LeGROS, and N. W. PIRIE, eds. 1951. *Four Thousand Million Mouths: Scientific Humanism and the Shadow of World Hunger.* London: Oxford University Press.

"A Clergyman of the Established Church." 1820. *Sermons Preached before Friendly and Charitable Societies in the Country: and written chiefly with the view of illustrating the principles delivered by Mr. Malthus in his Essay on Population; of showing their accordance with the precepts of Christianity; and of making them familiar to the understandings of the lower orders.* London: J. Hatchard and Son.

CLIVE, JOHN. 1957. *Scotch Reviewers:* The Edinburgh Review, *1802–1815.* London: Faber & Faber.

CLODD, EDWARD. 1897. *Pioneers of Evolution from Thales to Huxley, with an Intermediate Chapter on the Causes of Arrest of the Movement.* London: Grant Richards.

COALE, ANSLEY. 1970a. "The Decline of Fertility in Europe from the French Revolution to World War II." In S. J. Behrman et al., eds., *Fertility and Family Planning: A World View.* Ann Arbor: University of Michigan Press.

——— 1970b. "Man and His Environment." *Science* 170: 132–136.

——— and EDGAR M. HOOVER. 1959. *Population Growth and Economic Development in Low-Income Countries: A Case Study of India's Prospects.* Princeton, N.J.: Princeton University Press.

COCKS, EDMOND. 1967. "The Malthusian Theory in Pre-Civil War America: An Original Relation to the Universe." *Population Studies* 20: 343–363.

——— 1971. "Malthus on Population Quality." *Social Biology* 18: 84–87.

COHEN, MARK NATHAN. 1977. *The Food Crisis in Prehistory: Overpopulation and the Origins of Agriculture.* New Haven, Conn.: Yale University Press.

COLE, G. D. H. 1947. *The Life of William Cobbett.* London: Home & Van Thal.

CONDORCET. 1795 (1970). *Esquisse d'un tableau historique des progrès de l'esprit humain.* Paris: J. Vrin.

CONNELL, K. H. 1950. *The Population of Ireland, 1750–1845.* Oxford: Clarendon Press.

COONTZ, SYDNEY H. 1957. *Population Theories and the Economic Interpretation.* London: Routledge & Kegan Paul.

CORRY, B. A. 1959. "Malthus and Keynes—A Reconsideration." *Economic Journal* 69: 717–724.

COWHERD, RAYMOND G. 1960. "The Humanitarian Reform of the English Poor Laws from 1782 to 1815." *Proceedings of the American Philosophical Society* 104: 328–342.

——— 1977. *Political Economists and the English Poor Laws: A Historical Study of the Influence of Classical Economics on the Formation of Social Welfare Policy.* Athens: Ohio University Press.

COWLES, THOMAS. 1936. "Malthus, Darwin, and Bagehot: A Study in the Transference of a Concept." *Isis* 26: 341–348.

CRANSTON, MAURICE. 1962. "Rousseau's Visit to England, 1766–7." *Essays by Divers Hands, Transactions of the Royal Society of Literature* N.S. 31: 16–34.

CURRY, KENNETH. 1939. "A Note on Coleridge's Copy of Malthus." *Proceedings of the Modern Language Association* 54: 613–615.

DALY, HERMAN E. 1971. "A Marxian-Malthusian View of Poverty and Development." *Population Studies* 25: 25–37.

D'ARCY, F. 1977. "The Malthusian League and the Resistance to Birth Control Propaganda in Late Victorian Britain." *Population Studies* 31: 429–448.

DARWIN, CHARLES. 1887 (1958). *Autobiography and Selected Letters,* ed. Francis Darwin. New York: Dover.

DAVIE, GEORGE E. 1973. *The Social Significance of the Scottish Philosophy of Common Sense.* Edinburgh: Constable.

DEANE, PHYLLIS. 1965. *The First Industrial Revolution.* Cambridge, England: University Press.

DE MARCHI, N. B., and R. P. STURGES. 1973. "Malthus and Ricardo's Inductivist Critics: Four Letters to William Whewell." *Economica* 40: 379–393.

DEQUINCY, THOMAS. 1823 (1890). "Malthus on Population" and "Malthus on the Measure of Value." In David Masson, ed., *The Collected Writings of Thomas DeQuincy,* IX, 11–36. Edinburgh: Black.

DOBB, MAURICE. 1937. *Political Economy and Capitalism.* London: Routledge.

———— 1947. *Studies in the Development of Capitalism.* London: Routledge.

DOUBLEDAY, THOMAS. 1842. *The True Law of Population shewn to be connected with the food of the people.* London: Simpkin, Marshall.

DOW, LOUIS A. 1977. "Malthus on Sticky Wages, the Upper Turning Point, and General Glut." *History of Political Economy* 9: 303–321.

DRAKE, MICHAEL. 1966. "Malthus on Norway." *Population Studies* 20: 175–196.

DRAKE, STILLMAN. 1967. "A Seventeenth-Century Malthusian." *Isis* 58: 401–402.

DRUMMOND, J. C., and ANNE WILBRAHAM. 1957. *The Englishman's Food: A History of Five Centuries of English Diet.* Rev. ed. London: Cape.

DRYSDALE, BESSIE. 1920. *Labour Troubles and Birth Control.* London: Heinemann.

DRYSDALE, CHARLES ROBERT. 1866. *Prostitution Medically Considered. with some of its social aspects.* London: Hardwicke.

———— [1877?] *The Principle of Population.* Malthusian Tract no. 1. London: Malthusian League.

—— [1877?] *The Struggle for Enjoyable Existence*. Malthusian Tract no. 2. London: Malthusian League.

—— 1878. *The Population Question according to T. R. Malthus and J. S. Mill, giving the Malthusian theory of over-population*. London: Bell.

—— 1887. *The Life and Writings of Thomas R. Malthus*. London: Standring.

—— ed. 1901. *Medical Opinions on the Population Question*. London: Standring.

—— ed. 1904. *Clerical Opinions on the Population Question*. London: Standring.

DRYSDALE, CHARLES VICKERY. 1917. *The Malthusian Doctrine and Its Modern Aspects*. London: Malthusian League.

[DRYSDALE, GEORGE R.] A Graduate of Medicine, Author of *The Elements of Social Science*. 1860. *Population Fallacies: A defence of the Malthusian or true theory of society* . . . London: Truelove.

[——] G. R. 1869. *The Irish Land Question*. London: Truelove.

[——] A Doctor of Medicine, Author of *The Elements of Social Science*. 1886. *State Measures for the Abolition of Poverty, War, and Pestilence* . . . London: Truelove.

—— 1905. *The Elements of Social Science; or physical, sexual and natural religion. An exposition of the true cause and only cure of the three primary social evils: poverty, prostitution, and celibacy*. 35th ed. London: Standring.

DUBEY, VINOD. 1962. "The Dangers of Accumulation: A Second Look at Malthus' Critique of Ricardo." *Indian Economic Review* 6: 30–40.

DUKE, FRANCIS. 1976. "Pauper Education." In Derek Fraser, ed., *The New Poor Law in the Nineteenth Century*. London: Macmillan.

DUMONT, ARSÈNE. 1890. *Dépopulation et civilisation: Études démographiques*. Paris: Lecrosnier et Babé.

EDMONDS, THOMAS ROWE. 1828. *Practical Moral and Political Economy; or, The government, religion, and institutions most conducive to individual happiness and national power*. London: Effingham Wilson.

[——] 1832. *An Enquiry into the Principles of Population, exhibiting a system of regulations for the poor; designed immediately to lessen, and finally to remove, the evils which have hitherto pressed upon the labouring classes of society*. London: James Duncan.

[EMPSON, WILLIAM]. 1837 (1963). "Review of *Principles of Political Economy*, by Malthus." *Edinburgh Review*, no. 130, 469–506. Reprinted in Semmel, 1963.

ENGELS, FRIEDRICH. 1844. "Umrisse zu einer Kritik der National-ökonomie." *Deutsch-Französische Jahrbücher*, pp. 86–114. Paris.

———— 1845 (1971). *The Condition of the Working Class in England*, ed. W. O. Henderson and W. H. Chaloner. Oxford: Blackwell.

ENSOR, GEORGE. 1818. *An Inquiry Concerning the Population of Nations: containing a refutation of Mr. Malthus's Essay* on Population. London: Effingham Wilson.

ERICKSON, CHARLOTTE, ed. 1976. *Emigration from Europe, 1815–1914: Select Documents*. London: Black.

ESMONIN, EDMOND. 1964. *Études sur la France des XVIIᵉ et XVIIIᵉ siècles*. Paris: Presses Universitaires de France.

EVANS, DAVID OWEN. 1929. "Pierre Leroux and His Philosophy in Relation to Literature." *Publications of the Modern Language Association* 44: 274–287.

EVERETT, ALEXANDER H. 1826. *New Ideas on Population: with remarks on the theories of Malthus and Godwin*. 2nd ed. Boston: Cummings, Hilliard.

EVERSLEY, D. E. C. 1959. *Social Theories of Fertility and the Malthusian Debate*. Oxford: Clarendon.

FAGE, ANITA. 1953. "La révolution française et la population." *Population* 8: 311–338.

FAY, C. R. 1932. *The Corn Laws and Social England*. Cambridge, England: University Press.

FAY, MARGARET A. 1978. "Did Marx Offer to Dedicate *Capital* to Darwin? A Reassessment of the Evidence." *Journal of the History of Ideas* 39: 133–146.

FETTER, FRANK WHITSON. 1953. "The Authorship of Economic Articles in the *Edinburgh Review, 1802–47*." *Journal of Political Economy* 61: 232–259.

FEUER, LEWIS S. 1975. "Is the 'Darwin-Marx Correspondence' Authentic?" *Annals of Science* 32: 1–12.

———— 1976. "On the Darwin-Marx Correspondence," with comments by others. *Annals of Science* 33: 383–394.

FIELD, JAMES ALFRED. 1931 (1967). *Essays on Population and Other Papers*. Port Washington, N.Y.: Kennikat Press.

FINE-SOURIAC, AGNÈS. 1977 "La famille-souche pyrénéenne au XIXᵉ siècle: Quelques réflexions de méthode." *Annales* 32: 478–487.

FLEW, A. G. N. 1959. "The Structure of Darwinism." *New Biology*, no. 28, 25–44.

———— 1963. "The Structure of Malthus' Population Theory." In Bernard Baumrin, ed., *Philosophy of Science, The Delaware Seminar*. New York: Wiley.

———— 1970. "Introduction" to Malthus, *Essay on the Principle of Population* and *A Summary View of the Principle of Population*. Harmondsworth, England: Penguin Books.

FOGARTY, MICHAEL P. 1958. "Introduction" to Malthus, *Essay on the Principle of Population*. Everyman ed. London: Dent.

Food and Agriculture Organization. 1970. *Provisional Indicative World Plan for Agricultural Development.* Rome.

—— 1975. *Population, Food Supply and Agricultural Development.* Rome.

FOURASTIÉ, JEAN. 1972. "From the Traditional to the 'Tertiary' Life Cycle." In William Petersen, ed., *Readings in Population.* New York: Macmillan.

FRANKEL, FRANCINE R. 1971. *India's Green Revolution: Economic Gains and Political Costs.* Princeton, N.J.: Princeton University Press.

[FRANKLIN, BENJAMIN]. 1761. *The Interest of Great Britain Considered, with regard to her colonies, and the acquisitions of Canada and Guadaloupe. To which are added, Observations concerning the increase of mankind, peopling of countries, &c.* 2nd ed. London: Becket.

FREEMAN, R. D. 1969. "Adam Smith, Education and Laissez-Faire." *History of Political Economy* 1: 173–186.

FREND, WILLIAM. 1788. *Thoughts on Subscription to Religious Tests, particularly that required by the University of Cambridge of candidates for the degree of Bachelor of Arts* . . . St. Ives: Printed by T. Bloom.

—— 1789. *A Second Address to the Inhabitants of Cambridge and Its Neighbourhood* . . . St. Ives: Printed by T. Bloom.

—— 1793a. *Peace and Union Recommended to the Associated Bodies of Republicans and Anti-Republicans.* St. Ives: Printed for the Author.

—— 1793b. *An Account of the Proceedings in the University of Cambridge against William Frend, M.A., Fellow of Jesus College, Cambridge, for publishing a pamphlet intitled* Peace and Union . . . Cambridge: Printed by B. Flower.

—— 1796–99. *The Principles of Algebra.* 2 vols. London: Printed by J. Davis for G. G. and J. Robinson.

—— 1798. *A Letter to the Vice-Chancellor of the University of Cambridge.* Cambridge: Printed by B. Flower.

—— 1801. *The Effect of Paper Money on the Price of Provisions* . . . London: J. Ridgway.

—— 1804. *The Principles of Taxation: or contribution according to means* . . . London: J. Mawman.

—— [1815]. *Tables for Ordinary Assurances on Lives.* London: Rock Life Assurance Co.

—— 1817. *The National Debt in Its True Colours, with plans for its extinction by honest means.* London: J. Mawman.

[——] W. F. 1831. *On the Greatest Number That Can Be Expressed by Three Figures,* $9^{(9^9)}$. London: Printed by J. Moyes.

—— 1832. *A Plan of Universal Education.* London: B. Fellowes.

FRÉVILLE, JEAN. 1956. *La misère et le nombre: L'épouvantail malthusien.* Paris: Éditions Sociales.

FRIEDMAN, MILTON. 1977. "Nobel Lecture: Inflation and Unemployment." *Journal of Political Economy* 85: 451–472.

FRYER, PETER. 1965. *The Birth Controllers.* London: Secker & Warburg.

FULFORD, ROGER. 1967. *Samuel Whitbread, 1764–1815: A Study in Opposition.* London: Macmillan.

GARNIER, JOSEPH. 1857. *Du principe de population.* Paris: Garnier Frères; Guillaumin et Cie.

GASH, NORMAN, ed. 1974. *The Long Debate on Poverty.* 2nd ed. London: Institute of Economic Affairs.

GHOSH, R. N. 1963. "Malthus on Emigration and Colonization: Letters to Wilmot-Horton." *Economica* N.S. 30: 45–62.

GIDE, CHARLES, and CHARLES RIST. 1948. *A History of Economic Doctrines from the Time of the Physiocrats to the Present Day.* London: Harrap.

GINSBERG, MORRIS. 1931. "The Work of L. T. Hobhouse." In J. A. Hobson and Morris Ginsberg, eds., *L. T. Hobhouse: His Life and Work.* London: Allen & Unwin.

GLASS, D. V. 1940. *Population Policies and Movements in Europe.* Oxford: Clarendon.

——— ed. 1953. *Introduction to Malthus.* New York: Wiley.

——— 1965. "Two Papers on Gregory King." In Glass and Eversley, 1965.

——— 1973. *Numbering the People: The Eighteenth-Century Population Controversy and the Development of Census and Vital Statistics in Britain.* Farnborough, England: Saxon House.

——— 1976. "Population: The Census, Great Britain and Ireland, 1801–1891." In P. and G. Ford, eds., *Population and Emigration.* Dublin: Irish University Press.

——— and D. E. C. EVERSLEY, eds. 1965. *Population in History.* Chicago: Aldine.

GODWIN, WILLIAM. 1793 (1946). *Enquiry concerning Political Justice and Its Influence on Morals and Happiness.* 3 vols. Toronto: University of Toronto Press.

——— 1797. *The Enquirer: Reflections on education, manners and literature.* London: G. G. and J. Robinson.

——— 1801 (1968). *Thoughts Occasioned by the Perusal of Dr. Parr's Spital Sermon . . .,* reproduced in facsimile in Jack W. Marken and Burton R. Pollin, eds., *Uncollected Writings . . . by William Godwin.* Gainesville, Fla.: Scholars' Facsimiles & Reprints.

——— 1820. *Of Population: An enquiry concerning the power of increase in the numbers of mankind, being an answer to Mr. Mal-*

thus's Essay on that subject. London: Longman, Hurst, Rees, Orme, and Brown.

GONNARD, RENÉ. 1923. *Histoire des doctrines de la population.* Paris: Nouvelle Librairie Nationale.

GOODWIN, DENNIS, and PETER FRYER. 1958. *The Newsletter Conference and the Communist Party.* London: Newsletter Pamphlet.

GORDON, B. J., and T. S. JILEK. 1965. "Malthus, Keynes, et l'apport de Lauderdale." *Revue d'Économie Politique* 75: 110–121.

GRAHAM, LOREN R. 1977. "Science and Values: The Eugenics Movement in Germany and Russia in the 1920s." *American Historical Review* 82: 1134–1164.

GRAHAME, JAMES. 1816. *An Inquiry into the Principle of Population: including an exposition of the causes and the advantages of a tendency to exuberance of numbers in society, a defence of poorlaws, and a critical and historical view of the doctrines and projects of the most celebrated legislators and writers, relative to population, the poor, and charitable institutions.* Edinburgh: Constable.

GRAMPP, WILLIAM D. 1973. "Classical Economics and Its Moral Critics." *History of Political Economy* 5: 359–374.

—— 1974. "Malthus and His Contemporaries." *History of Political Economy* 6: 278–304.

GRAY, ARTHUR. 1926. *Cambridge University: An Episodical History.* Cambridge, England: Heffer.

—— and FREDERICK BRITTAIN. 1960. *A History of Jesus College, Cambridge.* London: Heinemann.

GRAY, SIMON. 1815. *The Happiness of States: or, An inquiry concerning population, the modes of subsisting and employing it, and the effects of all on human happiness.* London: J. Hatchard.

[——] GEORGE PURVES. 1817. *All Classes Productive of National Wealth; or The theories of M. Quesnai [sic], Dr. Adam Smith, and Mr. Gray. Concerning the various classes of men, as to the production of wealth to the community, analysed and examined.* London: Longman, Hurst, Rees, Orme, and Brown.

[——] GEORGE PURVES. 1818. *Gray versus Malthus, the principles of population and production . . .* London: Longman, Hurst, Rees, Orme, and Brown.

GREER, DONALD. 1935. *The Incidence of the Terror during the French Revolution: A Statistical Interpretation.* Cambridge, Mass.: Harvard University Press.

GRIFFITH, G. TALBOT. 1926. *Population Problems of the Age of Malthus.* Cambridge, England: University Press.

GRIGG, SUSAN. 1977. "Toward a Theory of Remarriage: A Case Study of Newburyport at the Beginning of the Nineteenth Century." *Journal of Interdisciplinary History* 8: 183–220.

GROSSMAN, GREGORY. 1958. "Thirty Years of Soviet Industrialization." *Soviet Survey*, no. 26, 15–21.

GUÉHENNO, JEAN. 1966. *Jean-Jacques Rousseau,* trans. John and Doreen Weightman. 2 vols. London: Routledge & Kegan Paul.

GUILLAUMONT, PATRICK. 1969. *La pensée démo-économique de Jean-Baptiste Say et de Sismondi.* Paris: Éditions Cujas.

GUNNING, HENRY. 1854. *Reminiscences of the University, Town, and County of Cambridge from the Year 1780.* 2 vols. London: Bell.

HABAKKUK, H. J. 1959. "Thomas Robert Malthus, F.R.S. (1766–1834)." *Notes and Records of the Royal Society of London* 14: 99–108.

HAJNAL, J. 1965. "European Marriage Patterns in Perspective." In Glass and Eversley, 1965.

HALÉVY, ÉLIE. 1928 (1966). *The Growth of Philosophic Radicalism.* Boston: Beacon Press.

HALKETT, SAMUEL, and JOHN LAING. 1929. *Dictionary of Anonymous and Pseudonymous English Literature.* Edinburgh: Oliver and Boyd.

HANEY, LEWIS H. 1924. *History of Economic Thought: A Critical Account of the Origin and Development of the Economic Theories of the Leading Thinkers in the Leading Nations.* New York: Macmillan.

HANSEN, ALVIN H. 1939. "Economic Progress and Declining Population Growth." *American Economic Review* 29, no. 1, part I, 1–15.

HART, A. TINDAL. 1968. *Church and Society, 1600–1800.* London: S.P.C.K. for the Church Historical Society.

——— 1970. *The Curate's Lot: The Story of the Unbeneficed English Clergy.* London: Pall Mall.

HAYNES, DAVID R. 1954. "Neo-Malthusianism and Marxism." *Political Affairs* 33: 41–57.

HAZLITT, WILLIAM. 1806 (1930–34). *A Reply to the Essay on Population by the Reverend T. R. Malthus.* In P. P. Howe, ed., *The Complete Works of William Hazlitt,* I, 177–364. London: Dent.

HECKSCHER, ELI F. 1935. *Mercantilism.* 2 vols. London: Allen & Unwin.

HELLEINER, K. F. 1965. "The Vital Revolution Reconsidered." In Glass and Eversley, 1965.

——— 1967. "The Population of Europe from the Black Death to the Eve of the Vital Revolution." In E. E. Rich and C. H. Wilson, eds., *Cambridge Economic History of Europe,* IV, chap. 1. Cambridge, England: University Press.

HICKS, J. R. 1936. "Mr. Keynes's Theory of Employment." *Economic Journal* 46: 238–253.

HICKSON, W. E. 1849. *Malthus: An Essay on the Principle of Population in Refutation of the Theory of the Rev. T. R. Malthus.* London: Taylor, Walton, and Maberly.

HIMES, NORMAN E. 1927. "The Birth Control Handbills of 1823." *Lancet* 213: 313–316.

—— 1936. *Medical History of Contraception*. Baltimore: Williams & Wilkins.

HIMMELFARB, GERTRUDE. 1955. "Malthus." *Encounter* (August) : 53–60.

—— 1960. "Introduction" to Malthus, *On Population*. New York: Modern Library.

HIRSHLEIFER, J. 1977. "Economics from a Biological Viewpoint." *Journal of Law and Economics* 20: 1–52.

Ho PING-TI. 1959. *Studies on the Population of China, 1368–1953*. Cambridge, Mass.: Harvard University Press.

HOBSBAWM, E. J. 1957. "The British Standard of Living, 1790–1850." *Economic History Review* 10: 46–61.

HOLLANDER, SAMUEL. 1962. "Malthus and Keynes: A Note." *Economic Journal* 72: 355–359.

—— 1969. "Malthus and the Post-Napoleonic Depression." *History of Political Economy* 1: 306–335.

—— 1977. "Ricardo and the Corn Laws: A Revision." *History of Political Economy* 9: 1–47.

HOMANS, GEORGE CASPAR. 1941. *English Villagers of the Thirteenth Century*. Cambridge, Mass.: Harvard University Press.

HOPKINS, KEITH. 1965. "Contraception in the Roman Empire." *Comparative Studies in Society and History* 8: 124–151.

HORNER, FRANCIS. 1843. *Memoirs and Correspondence*. 2 vols. London: Murray.

HOWLETT, JOHN. [1781]. *An Examination of Dr. Price's Essay on the Population of England and Wales; and the doctrine of an increased population established by facts*. London: Printed for the Author by J. Blake.

HULL, DAVID L. 1973. *Darwin and His Critics: The Reception of Darwin's Theory of Evolution by the Scientific Community*. Cambridge, Mass.: Harvard University Press.

HUME, DAVID. 1739–40 (1888). *A Treatise of Human Nature*. 3 vols. Oxford: Clarendon.

—— 1752 (1903). "Of the Populousness of Ancient Nations." In *Essays: Moral, Political and Literary*. London: Frowde.

HUTCHINSON, E. P. 1967. *The Population Debate: The Development of Conflicting Theories up to 1900*. Boston: Houghton Mifflin.

HUTT, W. H. 1954. "The Factory System of the Early Nineteenth Century." In F. A. Hayek, ed., *Capitalism and the Historians*. Chicago: University of Chicago Press.

HUXLEY, T. H. 1893 (1894). "Evolution and Ethics." In *Collected Essays*, IX, 46–116. New York: Appleton.

HUZEL, JAMES P. 1969. "Malthus, the Poor Law, and Population in Early Nineteenth-Century England." *Economic History Review* 2nd ser. 22: 430–452.

HYNDMAN, H. M., and CHARLES BRADLAUGH. 1884. *Will Socialism*

Benefit the English People? Verbatim Report of a Debate. London: Freethought Publishing Co.

INGRAM, ROBERT ACKLOM. 1808. *Disquisitions on Population; in which the principles of the* Essay on Population, *by the Rev. T. R. Malthus, are examined and refuted.* London: J. Hatchard.

JAMES, EDWIN W. 1916. "The Malthusian Doctrine and War." *Scientific Monthly* 2: 260–271.

JAMES, PATRICIA, ed. 1966. *The Travel Diaries of Thomas Robert Malthus.* New York: Cambridge University Press.

JARROLD, THOMAS. 1806. *Dissertations on Man, Philosophical, Physiological, and Political; in answer to Mr. Malthus's "Essay on the Principle of Population."* London: Caddell and Davis.

JOHNSON, HARRY G. 1949. "Malthus on the High Price of Provisions." *Canadian Journal of Economics and Political Science* 15: 190–192.

JOHNSTON, EDITH M. 1963. *Great Britain and Ireland, 1760–1800: A Study in Political Administration.* Edinburgh: Oliver and Boyd.

JOHNSTON, H. J. M. 1972. *British Emigration Policy, 1815–1830: 'Shoveling out Paupers.'* Oxford: Clarendon.

JONES, E. H. STUART. 1950. *An Invasion That Failed: The French Expedition to Ireland, 1796.* Oxford: Blackwell.

JONES, GRETA. 1978. "The Social History of Darwin's *Descent of Man.*" *Economy and Society* 7: 1–23.

KÄLVEMARK, ANN-SOFIE. 1976. "Swedish Marriage Loans a Means of Increasing Population? A Preliminary Report." Mimeographed. Uppsala: Department of History, University of Uppsala.

KAPP, ELEANOR. 1978. *Eleanor Marx.* 2 vols. New York: Pantheon.

KAUTSKY, KARL. 1880. *Der Einfluss der Volksvermehrung auf den Fortschritt der Gesellschaft.* Vienna: Bloch und Hasbach.

———— 1911. "Malthusianismus und Sozialismus." *Neue Zeit* 29, part 1:2, 620–627, 652–662, 684–697.

———— 1921. *Vermehrung in Natur und Gesellschaft.* 3rd ed. Stuttgart: Dietz.

KAY, JOSEPH. 1846. *The Education of the Poor in England and Europe.* London: Hatchard and Son.

———— 1850. *The Social Condition and Education of the People in England and Europe, shewing the results of the primary schools, and of the division of landed property, in foreign countries.* 2 vols. London: Longman, Brown, Green, and Longmans.

KEGEL, CHARLES H. 1958. "William Cobbett and Malthusianism." *Journal of the History of Ideas* 19: 348–362.

[KEIR, WILLIAM]. 1807. *A Summons of Wakening; or the evil tendency and danger of speculative philosophy, exemplified in Mr. Leslie's* Inquiry into the Nature of Heat *and Mr. Malthus's* Essay on Population . . . [London:] Hawick.

KELLUM, BARBARA A. 1974. "Infanticide in England in the Later Middle Ages." *History of Childhood Quarterly* 1: 367–388.

KENNEDY, ROBERT E., JR. 1973. *The Irish: Emigration, Marriage, and Fertility.* Berkeley: University of California Press.

KEYNES, JOHN MAYNARD. 1933. "Robert Malthus: The First of the Cambridge Economists." In *Essays in Biography.* New York: Harcourt, Brace.

—— 1935. *The General Theory of Employment, Interest and Money.* New York: Harcourt, Brace.

—— 1937. "Some Economic Consequences of a Declining Population." *Eugenics Review* 29: 13–17.

KING, VICTOR T. 1976. "Migration, Warfare, and Culture Contact in Borneo: A Critique of Ecological Analysis." *Oceania* 46: 306–327.

KITCHEN, MARTIN. 1977. "Friedrich Engels' Theory of War." *Military Affairs* 41: 119–124.

KNIBBS, GEORGE HANDLEY. 1928. *The Shadow of the World's Future: or, The earth's population possibilities and the consequences of the present rate of increase of the earth's inhabitants.* London: Benn.

KNIGHT, FRIDA. 1971. *University Rebel: The Life of William Frend (1757–1841).* London: Gollancz.

KNODEL, JOHN. 1972. "Malthus Amiss: Marriage Restriction in 19th-Century Germany." *Social Science* 47: 40–45.

KÖHLER, WALTHER. 1913. "Die sozialwissenschaftliche Grundlage und Struktur der Malthusianischen Bevölkerungslehre." *Schmollers Jahrbuch,* 37, no. 3, 19–79.

KRAUSE, J. T. 1958. "Changes in English Fertility and Mortality, 1781–1850." *Economic History Review* 11: 52–70.

LAMBERT, PAUL. 1956. "The Law of Markets prior to J. B. Say and the Say-Malthus Debate." *International Economic Papers,* no. 6, 7–22.

—— 1962. "Malthus et Keynes: Nouvel examen de la parenté profonde des deux oeuvres." *Revue d'Économie Politique* 72: 783–829.

—— 1966. "Lauderdale, Malthus et Keynes." *Revue d'Économie Politique* 76: 32–56.

LANG, LOUIS. 1913. "Malthus en France." *Revue de Hongrie* 12: 334–359 and 416–439.

LANGER, WILLIAM L. 1963. "Europe's Initial Population Explosion." *American Historical Review* 69: 1–17.

—— 1974. "Infanticide: A Historical Survey." *History of Childhood Quarterly* 1: 353–365.

LASLETT, PETER. 1971. *The World We Have Lost.* 2nd ed. New York: Scribner's.

—— ed. 1972. *Household and Family in Past Time.* Cambridge, England: University Press.

—— 1977. *Family Life and Illicit Love in Earlier Generations: Essays in Historical Sociology.* Cambridge, England: University Press.

LEASURE, J. WILLIAM. 1963. "Malthus, Marriage and Multiplication." *Milbank Memorial Fund Quarterly* 41: 419–435.

LEDBETTER, ROSANNA. 1976. *A History of the Malthusian League, 1877–1927.* Columbus: Ohio State University Press.

LEE, W. R. 1977. "Bastardy and the Socioeconomic Structure of South Germany." *Journal of Interdisciplinary History* 7: 403–425.

LEIBENSTEIN, HARVEY. 1976. *Beyond Economic Man: A New Foundation for Microeconomics.* Cambridge, Mass.: Harvard University Press.

LERNER, ABBA P. 1977. "From Pre-Keynes to Post-Keynes." *Social Research* 44: 388–415.

LEROY-BEAULIEU, PAUL. 1913. *La question de la population.* Paris: Félix Alcan.

LEVIN, SAMUEL M. 1966. "Malthus and the Idea of Progress." *Journal of the History of Ideas* 27: 92–108.

LEWINSOHN, RICHARD. 1922. "Die Stellung der deutschen Sozialdemokratie zur Bevölkerungsfrage." *Schmollers Jahrbuch* 46: 813–859 (191–237).

LI, WEN L. 1973. "Temporal and Spatial Analysis of Fertility Decline in Taiwan." *Population Studies* 27: 97–104.

LLOYD, W. F. 1837. *Lectures on Population, Value, Poor-Laws, and Rent.* London: Roake and Varty.

LOUDON, CHARLES. 1836. *The Equilibrium of Population and Sustenance Demonstrated; showing, on physiological and statistical grounds, the means of obviating the fears of the late Mr. Malthus and his followers.* London: Longman, Rees, Orme & Co.

LUTFALLA, MICHEL. 1969. "Autour du principe de la population: Études de démo-économie." *Revue d'Histoire Économique et Sociale* 47: 550–556.

LUX, ANDRÉ. 1968. "Évolution et contradictions dans la pensée de Malthus." *Population* 23: 1091–1106.

MACARTHUR, WILLIAM P. 1957. "Medical History of the Famine." In R. Dudley Edwards and T. Desmond Williams, eds., *The Great Famine: Studies in Irish History, 1845–52.* New York: New York University Press.

MACDONAGH, OLIVER. 1955. "Emigration and the State, 1833–55: An Essay in Administrative History." *Transactions of the Royal Historical Society* ser. 5, vol. 5, 133–159.

——— 1977. *Ireland: The Union and Its Aftermath.* London: Allen & Unwin.

MACDONALD, MAURICE. 1977. "Food Stamps: An Analytical History." *Social Service Review* 51: 642–658.

MACDOWELL, MICHAEL A. 1977. "Malthus and George on the Irish Question: The Single Tax, Empiricism and Other Positions Shared by the 19th Century Economists." *American Journal of Economics and Sociology* 36: 401–416.

MACHIN, G. I. T. 1964. *The Catholic Question in English Politics, 1820 to 1830.* Oxford: Clarendon.

MACKINDER, HALFORD. 1904. "The Geographical Pivot of History." *Geographical Journal* 23: 421–444.

MAKARIUS, RAOUL. 1977. "*Ancient Society* and Morgan's Kinship Theory 100 Years After." *Current Anthropology* 18: 709–729.

MALIK, M. M. 1957. "Malthus—A Reactionary; Expanding Population—An Asset." *Federal Economic Review* (Karachi) 4: 24–34.

MALLORY, WALTER H. 1926. *China: Land of Famine.* New York: American Geographical Society.

[MALTHUS, THOMAS ROBERT]. 1798 (1970). *An Essay on the Principle of Population, as it affects the future improvement of society. With remarks on the speculations of Mr. Godwin, M. Condorcet, and other writers.* 1st ed. Harmondsworth, England: Penguin Books.

———— 1800 (1970). *An Investigation of the Cause of the Present High Price of Provisions: containing an illustration of the nature and limits of fair price in time of scarcity; and its application to the particular circumstances of this country.* London: J. Johnson. Reprinted in *The Pamphlets of Thomas Robert Malthus.* New York: Kelley, 1970.

———— 1807 (1953). *A Letter to Samuel Whitbread, Esq., M.P., on His Proposed Bill for the Amendment of the Poor Laws.* London: J. Johnson and J. Hatchard. Reprinted in Glass, 1953.

[————] 1809 (1963). "Newenham on the State of Ireland." *Edinburgh Review* 14: 151–170. Reprinted in Semmel, 1963.

[————] 1811a (1963). "Depreciation of Paper Money." *Edinburgh Review* 17: 339–372. Reprinted in Semmel, 1963.

[————] 1811b (1963). "Pamphlets on the Bullion Question." *Edinburgh Review* 18: 448–470. Reprinted in Semmel, 1963.

———— 1813 (1970). *A Letter to the Rt. Hon. Lord Grenville, occasioned by some observations of His Lordship on the East India Company's establishment for the education of their civil servants.* London: J. Johnson. Reprinted in *The Pamphlets of Thomas Robert Malthus.* New York: Kelley, 1970.

———— 1814 (1970). *Observations on the Effects of the Corn Laws, and of a rise or fall in the price of corn on the agriculture and the general wealth of the country.* London: J. Johnson. Reprinted in *The Pamphlets of Thomas Robert Malthus.* New York: Kelley, 1970.

———— 1815a (1970). *The Grounds of an Opinion on the Policy of Restricting the Importation of Foreign Corn, intended as an appendix to "Observations on the Corn Laws."* London: John Murray. Reprinted in *The Pamphlets of Thomas Robert Malthus.* New York: Kelley, 1970.

———— 1815b (1970). *An Inquiry into the Nature and Progress of*

Rent, and the principles by which it is regulated. London: John Murray. Reprinted in *The Pamphlets of Thomas Robert Malthus.* New York: Kelley, 1970.

——— 1817 (1970) . *Statements Respecting the East-India College, with an appeal to facts, in refutation of the charges lately brought against it in the Court of Proprietors.* 2nd ed. London: John Murray. Reprinted in *The Pamphlets of Thomas Robert Malthus.* New York: Kelley, 1970.

[———] 1821 (1963) . "Review of Godwin's *Of Population.*" *Edinburgh Review* 35: 362–377. Reprinted in Semmel, 1963.

[———] 1823 (1963) . "Tooke—On High and Low Prices." *Quarterly Review* 29: 214–239. Reprinted in Semmel, 1963.

——— 1824. "Population." *Supplement to the Fourth, Fifth, and Sixth Editions of the Encyclopaedia Britannica,* VI, 306–333. London: Hurst, Robinson. Printed separately with a few minor changes as *A Summary View of Population.* London: John Murray, 1830. Reprinted with the Pelican edition of the First Essay; see Flew, 1970.

——— 1827. *Definitions in Political Economy, preceded by an inquiry into the rules which ought to guide political economists in the definition and use of their terms; with remarks on the deviation from these rules in their writings.* London: John Murray.

——— 1836 (1974) . *Principles of Political Economy, considered with a view to their practical application.* 2nd ed. London: William Pickering. Reprinted, Clifton, N.J.: Kelley, 1974.

——— 1872. *An Essay on the Principle of Population, or a view of its past and present effects on human happiness, with an inquiry into our prospects respecting the future removal or mitigation of the evils which it occasions.* 7th ed. London: Reeves and Turner.

MAMDANI, MAHMOOD. 1972. *The Myth of Population Control: Family, Caste, and Class in an Indian Village.* New York: Monthly Review Press.

MANN, FRITZ KARL. 1971. "Zu Schumpeters Leben und Werk." *Finanzarchiv* 30: 306–310.

——— 1976. "Adam Smith: The Heir and the Ancestor." *Zeitschrift für die Gesamte Staatswissenschaft* 132: 683–690.

MANNHEIM, KARL. 1953. "Conservative Thought." In *Essays on Sociology and Social Psychology.* New York: Oxford University Press.

MANNING, WILLIAM. 1838. *The Wrongs of Man Exemplified; or An enquiry into the origin, the cause, and the effect of superstition, conquest, and exaction . . .* London: R. Wilks.

MARSHALL, J. D. 1968. *The Old Poor Law, 1795–1834.* London: Macmillan.

MARSHALL, T. H. 1965. "The Population Problem during the Industrial Revolution." In Glass and Eversley, 1965.

MARTINEAU, HARRIET. 1877. *Autobiograhy*. 3 vols. London: Smith, Elder & Co.

MARX, KARL. 1872 (1906). *Capital*. 2 vols. Chicago: Kerr.

———— 1875 (1933). *Critique of the Gotha Programme*. New York: International Publishers.

———— 1919. *Theorien über den Mehrwert*. 3rd ed. Stuttgart: Dietz.

MATHIESON, WILLIAM LAW. 1923. *English Church Reform, 1815–1840*. London: Longmans, Green.

MATTELART, ARMAND. 1969. "Une lecture idéologique de l'*Essai sur le Principe de Population*." *América Latina* 12: 79–114. Reprinted in *Homme et Société,* no. 15 (1970) : 183–219.

MCATEE, W. L. 1936. "The Malthusian Principle in Nature." *Scientific Monthly* 42: 444–456.

MCCAFFREY, LAWRENCE J. 1966. *Daniel O'Connell and the Repeal Year*. Lexington: University of Kentucky Press.

MCCLATCHEY, DIANA. 1960. *Oxfordshire Clergy, 1777–1869: A Study of the Established Church and of the Role of Its Clergy in Local Society*. Oxford: Clarendon.

MCCLEARY, G. F. 1953. *The Malthusian Population Theory*. London: Faber & Faber.

[MCCULLOCH, J. R.]. 1826. "Review of Emigration Report." *Edinburgh Review* 45: 49–74.

MCKEOWN, THOMAS. 1976. *The Modern Rise of Population*. London: Edward Arnold.

———— and R. G. BROWN. 1965. "Medical Evidence Related to English Population Changes in the Eighteenth Century." In Glass and Eversley, 1965.

MCLAREN, ANGUS. 1976. "Sex and Socialism: The Opposition of the French Left to Birth Control in the Nineteenth Century." *Journal of the History of Ideas* 37: 475–492.

MEADOWS, DONELLA H., et al. 1972. *The Limits of Growth: A Report for the Club of Rome's Project on the Predicament of Mankind*. New York: Universe Books.

MEEK, RONALD L., ed. 1953. *Marx and Engels on Malthus: Selections from the Writings of Marx and Engels Dealing with the Theories of Thomas Robert Malthus*. London: Lawrence and Wishart.

———— 1974. "Value in the History of Economic Thought." *History of Political Economy* 6: 246–260.

MESAROVIC, MIHAJLO, and EDUARD PESTEL. 1974. *Mankind at the Turning Point: The Second Report to the Club of Rome*. New York: Signet.

MILLER, GEORGE NOYES. 1891. *The Strike of a Sex: A Novel*. London: W. H. Reynolds.

MINGAY, G. E. 1975. *Arthur Young and His Times*. London: Macmillan.

MOMBERT, PAUL. 1935. "Die Bevölkerungsanschauungen von R. Malthus in seinem Briefwechsel mit Senior und seinen 'Principles of Political Economy.'" *Zeitschrift für Nationalökonomie* 6: 539–547.

MONCK, JOHN B. 1807. *General Reflections on the System of the Poor Laws, with a short view of Mr. Whitbread's bill and a comment on it.* London: R. Bickerstaff.

MORELLET, ANDRÉ. 1822. *Mémoires inédits de l'Abbé Morellet de l'Académie Française* . . . 10th ed., 2 vols. Paris: Ladvocat.

MORISON, SAMUEL ELIOT. 1977. *Sailor Historian: The Best of Samuel Eliot Morison,* ed. Emily Morison Beck. Boston: Houghton Mifflin.

MOSSNER, ERNEST CAMPBELL. 1943. *The Forgotten Hume: Le bon David.* New York: Columbia University Press.

MOUNIER, L. 1873–74. "Le principe de population: Réfutation du malthusianisme." *Revue Catholique des Institutions et du Droit* 3: 162–176 and 299–315; 4: 65–76 and 227–236.

MOWAT, R. B. 1938. *Jean-Jacques Rousseau.* Bristol: Arrowsmith.

MULLER, HERMANN J. 1960. "The Guidance of Human Evolution." In Sol Tax, ed., *Evolution after Darwin.* Chicago: University of Chicago Press.

National Resources Committee. Committee on Population Problems. 1938. *The Problems of a Changing Population.* Washington, D.C.: U.S. Government Printing Office.

NICHOLSON, J. SHIELD. 1902. *Principles of Political Economy.* 2nd ed., 3 vols. London: Black.

NISBET, ROBERT A. 1968. *Tradition and Revolt: Historical and Sociological Essays.* New York: Random House.

O'BRIEN, D. P. 1975. *The Classical Economists.* Oxford: Clarendon.

O'BRIEN, GEORGE. 1918. *The Economic History of Ireland in the Eighteenth Century.* Dublin: Maunsel.

OESTREICH, JOHANNES. 1936. *Die Stellung des Nationalsozialismus zur Bevölkerungslehre von Thomas Robert Malthus und seinen Anhängern: Eine nazionalsozialistische Studie.* Würzburg: Triltsch.

O'LEARY, JAMES J. 1942. "Malthus and Keynes." *Journal of Political Economy* 1: 901–919.

—— 1943. "Malthus's General Theory of Employment and the Post-Napoleonic Depressions." *Journal of Economic History* 3: 185–200.

[OTTER, WILLIAM]. 1836 (1974). "Memoir of Robert Malthus." In Malthus, *Principles of Political Economy.* 2nd ed. London: William Pickering. Reprinted, Clifton, N.J.: Kelley, 1974.

OTTERBEIN, KEITH F. 1977. "Warfare: A Hitherto Unrecognized Critical Variable." *American Behavioral Scientist* 20: 693–710.

Ó TUATHAIGH, GEARÓID. 1972. *Ireland Before the Famine, 1798–1848.* Dublin: Gill and Macmillan.

OWEN, JOHN E. 1974. *L. T. Hobhouse, Sociologist.* London: Nelson.

PAGLIN, MORTON. 1961. *Malthus and Lauderdale: The Anti-Ricardian Tradition.* New York: Kelley.

PAKENHAM, THOMAS. 1970. *The Year of Liberty: The Story of the Great Irish Rebellion of 1798.* Englewood Cliffs, N.J.: Prentice-Hall.

PALEY, WILLIAM. 1786. *The Principles of Moral and Political Philosophy.* London: R. Faulder.

PARKINSON, JAMES. 1807. *Remarks on Mr. Whitbread's Plan for the Education of the Poor; with observations on Sunday schools and on the state of apprenticed poor.* London: H. D. Symonds.

PARREAUX, ANDRÉ. 1969. *Daily Life in England in the Reign of George III.* London: Allen & Unwin.

PARSONS, TALCOTT. 1961. "Introduction" to Herbert Spencer, *The Study of Sociology.* Ann Arbor: University of Michigan Press.

PAUL, C. KEGAN. 1876. *William Godwin: His Friends and Contemporaries.* 2 vols. London: King.

PAYNE, JOHN ORLEBAR. 1890. *Collections for a History of the Family of Malthus.* London: Burns and Oates (privately printed).

PEEL, J. D. Y. 1971. *Herbert Spencer: The Evolution of a Sociologist.* New York: Basic Books.

—— 1972. "Introduction" to *Herbert Spencer on Social Evolution.* Chicago: University of Chicago Press.

PEEL, JOHN, and GRISELDA CARR. 1975. *Contraception and Family Design: A Study of Birth Planning in Contemporary Society.* Edinburgh: Churchill Livingstone.

PENDLETON, BRIAN F. 1978. "An Historical Description and Analysis of Pronatalist Policies in Italy, Germany and Sweden." *Policy Sciences* 9: 45–70.

PERRENOUD, ALFRED. 1974. "Malthusianisme et Protestantisme: Un modèle démographique weberien." *Annales* 29: 975–988.

PERRIN, ROBERT G. 1976. "Herbert Spencer's Four Theories of Social Evolution." *American Journal of Sociology* 81: 1339–1359.

PETERSEN, WILLIAM. 1955a. "John Maynard Keynes's Theories of Population and the Concept of 'Optimum.'" *Population Studies* 8: 228–246.

—— 1955b. *Planned Migration: The Social Determinants of the Dutch-Canadian Movement.* Berkeley: University of California Press.

—— 1957. "Marx versus Malthus: The Men and the Symbols." *Population Review* 1: 21–32.

—— 1960. "The Demographic Transition in the Netherlands." *American Sociological Review* 25: 334–347.

—— 1964. *The Politics of Population.* New York: Doubleday.

—— 1971. "The Malthus-Godwin Debate, Then and Now." *Demography* 8: 13–26.

PETRELLA, FRANK. 1970. "Individual, Group, or Government? Smith, Mill, and Sidgwick." *History of Political Economy* 2: 152–176.

PHILIPS, C. H. 1961. *The East India Company, 1784–1834.* Manchester: Manchester University Press.

PLACE, FRANCIS. 1822 (1930). *Illustrations and Proofs of the Principle of Population, including an examination of the proposed remedies of Mr. Malthus and a reply to the objections of Mr. Godwin and others.* Reprinted with an introduction and critical notes by Norman E. Himes. Boston: Houghton Mifflin.

———— 1972. *The Autobiography of Francis Place (1771–1854)*, ed. Mary Thale. Cambridge, England: University Press.

PLATKY, LEON D. 1977. "Aid to Families with Dependent Children: An Overview, October 1977." *Social Security Bulletin* 40: 17–22.

PLATTER, J. 1877. "Carl Marx und Malthus." *Jahrbücher für Nationalökonomie und Statistik* 29: 321–341.

POLANYI, KARL. 1944. *The Great Transformation.* New York: Rinehart.

PONS, JACQUES. 1919. *L'Éducation en Angleterre entre 1750 et 1800: Aperçu sur l'influence de J.-J. Rousseau en Angleterre.* Paris: Ernest Leroux.

POTTER, GEORGE REUBEN. 1936. "Unpublished Marginalia in Coleridge's Copy of Malthus's *Essay on Population.*" *Proceedings of the Modern Language Association* 51: 1061–1068.

POURSIN, JEAN-MARIE, and GABRIEL DUPUY. 1972. *Malthus.* Paris: Seuil.

POYNTER, J. R. 1969. *Society and Pauperism: English Ideas on Poor Relief, 1795–1834.* London: Routledge & Kegan Paul.

PRICE, RICHARD. 1780. *An Essay on the Population of England, from the revolution to the present time.* 2nd ed. London: T. Cadell.

PROUDHON, P. J. 1886. *The Malthusians.* London: International Publishing Co.

PULOS, C. E. 1952, 1955. "Shelley and Malthus." *Proceedings of the Modern Language Association* 67: 113–124; 70: 555–556.

PUYNODE, GUSTAVE DU. 1849. "Malthus et le socialisme." *Journal des Économistes* 23: 147–155.

QUESSEL, LUDWIG. 1911. "Karl Kautsky als Bevölkerungstheoretiker." *Neue Zeit* 29: 1, no. 16 (January 20) : 559–565.

RAE, JOHN. 1895. *Life of Adam Smith.* London: Macmillan.

RAINWATER, LEE. 1965. *Family Design: Marital Sexuality, Family Size, and Contraception.* Chicago: Aldine.

RASHID, SALIM. 1977. "Malthus' Model of General Gluts." *History of Political Economy* 9: 366–383.

RATZEL, FRIEDRICH. 1897 (1923). *Politische Geographie.* 3rd ed. Munich: Oldenbourg.

RAVENSTONE, PIERCY. 1821. *A Few Doubts as to the Correctness of*

Some Opinions Generally Entertained on the Subjects of Population and Political Economy. London: John Andrews.

RAZZELL, PETER. 1977. *Edward Jenner's Cowpox Vaccine: The History of a Medical Myth.* Firle, England: Caliban Books.

REDDAWAY, W. B. 1939. *The Economics of a Declining Population.* London: Allen & Unwin.

REDFORD, ARTHUR, with W. H. CHALONER. 1976. *Labour Migration in England, 1800–1850.* 3rd ed. Manchester: Manchester University Press.

REED, JAMES. 1978. *From Private Vice to Public Virtue: The Birth Control Movement and American Society Since 1830.* New York: Basic Books.

REISMAN, D. A. 1976. *Adam Smith's Sociological Economics.* London: Croom Helm.

RICARDO, DAVID. 1928. *Notes on Malthus' "Principles of Political Economy,"* ed. Jacob H. Hollander and T. E. Gregory. Baltimore: Johns Hopkins Press.

RICKARDS, GEORGE K. 1854. *Population and Capital; being a course of lectures delivered before the University of Oxford in 1853–54.* London: Longman, Brown, Green, and Longmans.

ROBBINS, LIONEL C. 1927 (1967). "The Optimum Theory of Population." In T. E. Gregory and Hugh Dalton, eds., *London Essays in Economics: in Honour of Edwin Cannan.* Freeport, N.Y.: Books for Libraries Press.

——— 1967. "Malthus as an Economist." *Economic Journal* 77: 256–262.

ROBERTSON, H. M. 1942. "Reflexions on Malthus and His Predecessors." *South African Journal of Economics* 10: 295–306.

ROGERS, JAMES ALLEN. 1972. "Darwinism and Social Darwinism." *Journal of the History of Ideas* 33: 265–280.

ROSE, MICHAEL E. 1971. *The English Poor Law, 1780–1930.* Newton Abbot, England: David & Charles.

——— 1976. "Settlement, Removal and the New Poor Law." In Derek Fraser, ed., *The New Poor Law in the Nineteenth Century.* London: Macmillan.

ROSEN, FREDERICK. 1970. "The Principle of Population as Political Theory: Godwin's *Of Population* and the Malthusian Controversy." *Journal of the History of Ideas* 31: 33–48.

[ROSS, J. C.] John McIniscon, A Fisherman. 1825. *Principles of Political Economy, and of Population: including an examination of Mr. Malthus's Essay on those subjects.* 2 vols. London: Sherwood, Jones.

RUBIN, ERNEST. 1960. "The Quantitative Data and Methods of the Rev. T. R. Malthus." *American Statistician* 14: 28–31.

RUSE, MICHAEL. 1973. "The Nature of Scientific Models: Formal v. Material Analogy." *Philosophy of the Social Sciences* 3: 63–80.

RUSSELL, J. C. 1948. *British Medieval Population*. Albuquerque: University of New Mexico Press.

RUSSELL, W. M. S. 1976. "The Origins of Social Biology." *Biology and Human Affairs* 41: 109–137.

RUSSETT, CYNTHIA EAGLE. 1976. *Darwin in America: The Intellectual Response, 1865–1912*. San Francisco: Freeman.

[RUTHERFORD, ANDREW]. 1816. "Review of Malthus's *Statements respecting the East India Company*." *Edinburgh Review* 27: 511–531.

SAITŌ, KAZUO. 1971. "On the Green Revolution." *Developing Economies* 9: 16–30.

SALLERON, LOUIS. 1972. *Essai sur le principe de population: Malthus*. Paris: Hatier.

——— et al. 1946. *Malthus a-t-il menti? Principes d'action démographique*. Paris: Albin Michel.

SAMUELSON, PAUL A. 1977. "A Modern Theorist's Vindication of Adam Smith." *American Economic Review* 66: 42–49.

SANDERSON, MICHAEL. 1972. "Literacy and Social Mobility in the Industrial Revolution in England." *Past and Present*, no. 56, 75–104.

SAUVY, ALFRED. 1948. "Doctrine soviétique en matière de population." *Rivista Italiana de Demografia e Statistica* 2: 475–484.

——— 1952. *Théorie générale de la population*. 2 vols. Paris: Presses Universitaires de France.

——— 1963. *Malthus et les deux Marx: Le problème de la faim et de la guerre dans le monde*. Paris: Gonthier.

——— 1966. "Les marxistes et le malthusianisme." *Cahiers Internationaux de Sociologie* 41: 1–14.

——— 1968. "Marx et les problèmes contemporains de la population." *Social Science Information* 7: 27–38.

SAVILLE, JOHN. 1957. *Rural Depopulation in England and Wales, 1851–1951*. London: Routledge & Kegan Paul.

SAY, JEAN-BAPTISTE. 1820. *Lettres à M. Malthus sur différens [sic] sujets d'économie politique, notamment sur les causes de la stagnation générale du commerce*. Paris: Bossange.

SCHNEIDER, LOUIS, ed. 1967. *The Scottish Moralists: On Human Nature and Society*. Chicago: University of Chicago Press.

SCHORR, ALVIN L. 1966. *Poor Kids: A Report on Children in Poverty*. New York: Basic Books.

SCHUMPETER, JOSEPH A. 1950. *Capitalism, Socialism, and Democracy*. 3rd ed. New York: Harper.

——— 1954. *History of Economic Analysis*, ed. Elizabeth Boody Schumpeter. New York: Oxford University Press.

SCROPE, G. POULETT. 1832. *Extracts of Letters from Poor Persons Who Emigrated Last Year to Canada and the United States . . .* 2nd ed. London: James Ridgway.

SEMMEL, BERNARD, ed. 1963. *Occasional Papers of T. R. Malthus: On Ireland, Population and Political Economy, from Contemporary Journals, Written Anonymously and Hitherto Uncollected.* New York: Burt Franklin.

——— 1965. "Malthus: 'Physiocracy' and the Commerical System." *Economic History Review* 17: 522–535.

——— 1968. *Imperialism and Social Reform: English Social Imperial Thought, 1895–1914.* New York: Anchor-Doubleday.

SENIOR, NASSAU WILLIAM. 1829 (1966). *Two Lectures on Population, . . . to which is added a correspondence between the author and the Rev. T. R. Malthus.* London: Saunders and Otley. Reprinted, New York: Kelley, 1966.

SEXAUER, BENJAMIN. 1977. "The US Food Stamp Programme." *Food Policy* 2: 331–337.

SHEPARD, LESLIE. 1973. *The History of Street Literature: The Story of Broadside Ballads, Chapbooks, Proclamations, News-Sheets, Election Bills, Tracts, Pamphlets, Cocks, Catchpennies, and Other Ephemera.* Newton Abbot, England: David & Charles.

SHORTER, EDWARD. 1973. "Illegitimacy, Sexual Revolution, and Social Change in Modern Europe." In Theodore K. Rabb and Robert I. Rotberg, eds., *The Family in History: Interdisciplinary Essays.* New York: Harper Torchbook.

——— 1978. "Bastardy in South Germany: A Comment." *Journal of Interdisciplinary History* 8: 459–469.

SIMON, JULIAN L. 1977. *The Economics of Population Growth.* Princeton, N.J.: Princeton University Press.

SKINNER, ANDREW S. 1969. "Of Malthus, Lauderdale and Say's Law." *Scottish Journal of Political Economy* 16: 177–195.

SKLAR, JUNE L. 1974. "The Role of Marriage Behaviour in the Demographic Transition: The Case of Eastern Europe around 1900." *Population Studies* 28: 231–247.

SLAVIN, MORRIS. 1977. "The Terror in Miniature: Section Droits de l'Homme of Paris, 1793–1795." *The Historian* 39: 292–306.

SMITH, ADAM. 1759 (1880). *A Theory of Moral Sentiments.* London: Bell.

——— 1776 (1937). *The Wealth of Nations,* ed. Edwin Cannan. New York: Modern Library.

SMITH, KENNETH. 1951. *The Malthusian Controversy.* London: Routledge & Kegan Paul.

SMITH, ROBERT S. 1954. "Spanish Population Thought before Malthus." In H. Stuart Hughes, ed., *Teachers of History: Essays in Honor of Laurence Bradford Packard.* Ithaca, N.Y.: Cornell University Press.

——— 1969. "The Reception of Malthus' Essay on Population in Spain." *Rivista Internazionale di Scienze Economiche e Commerciali* (Milan) 16: 550–565.

SMITH, V. E. 1956. "Malthus's Theory of Demand and Its Influence on Value Theory." *Scottish Journal of Political Economy* 3: 205–220.

SOETBEER, HEINRICH. 1886. *Die Stellung der Sozialisten zur Malthus'schen Bevölkerungslehre.* Berlin: Puttkammer und Mühlbrecht.

SOUTHEY, ROBERT. 1832. *Essays, Moral and Political.* 2 vols. London: Murray.

SOWELL, THOMAS S. 1963. "The General Glut Controversy Reconsidered." *Oxford Economic Papers* N.S. 15: 193–203.

—— 1967. "Marx's *Capital* after One Hundred Years." *Canadian Journal of Economics and Political Science* 33: 52–74.

—— 1972a. "Sismondi: A Neglected Pioneer." *History of Political Economy* 4: 62–88.

—— 1972b. *Say's Law: An Historical Analysis.* Princeton, N.J.: Princeton University Press.

—— 1974. *Classical Economics Reconsidered.* Princeton, N.J.: Princeton University Press.

SPENCER, HERBERT. 1852. *A Theory of Population, deduced from the general law of animal fertility.* London: John Chapman. Reprinted from *Westminster Review,* April 1852.

—— 1862 (1904). *First Principles.* 6th ed. London: Williams and Norgate.

SPENGLER, JOSEPH J. 1933. "Population Doctrines in the United States: I. Anti-Malthusianism; II. Malthusianism." *Journal of Political Economy* 41: 433–467 and 639–722.

—— 1935a. "Malthusianism in Late Eighteenth Century America." *American Economic Review* 25: 691–707.

—— 1935b. "Malthusianism and the Debate on Slavery." *South Atlantic Quarterly* 34: 170–189.

—— 1936. "Population Theory in the Antebellum South." *Journal of Southern History* 2: 360–389.

—— 1942. *French Predecessors of Malthus: A Study in Eighteenth-Century Wage and Population Theory.* Durham, N.C.: Duke University Press.

—— 1945. "Malthus's Total Population Theory: A Restatement and Reappraisal." *Canadian Journal of Economics and Political Science* 11: 83–110 and 234–264.

—— 1949. "The World's Hunger—Malthus, 1948." *Proceedings of the Academy of Political Science* 23: 149–167.

—— 1965. "Today's Circumstances and Yesterday's Theories: Malthus on 'Services.'" *Kyklos* 18: 601–614.

—— 1966. "Was Malthus Right?" *Southern Economic Journal* 33: 17–34.

—— 1970. "Adam Smith on Population." *Population Studies* 24: 377–388.

———— 1976. "Adam Smith on Population Growth and Economic Development." *Population and Development Review* 2: 167–180.

STANTON, DAVID. 1977. "The Take-up Debate on the UK Family Income Supplement." *Policy and Politics* 5: 27–45.

STAROBIN, LEONARD. 1976. "Our Changing Evolution: Strategies for 1980." *General Systems* 21: 3–46.

STASSART, JOSEPH. 1957. *Malthus et la population*. Liège: Faculté de Droit de Liège.

STEVENSON, J. 1974. "Food Riots in England, 1792–1818." In R. Quinault and J. Stevenson, eds., *Popular Protest and Public Order: Six Studies in British History, 1790–1920*. London: Allen & Unwin.

STIGLER, GEORGE J. 1971. "Smith's Travels on the Ship of State." *History of Political Economy* 3: 265–277.

STOKES, ERIC. 1959. *The English Utilitarians and India*. Oxford: Clarendon.

STONE, LAWRENCE. 1969. "Literacy and Education in England, 1640–1900." *Past and Present*, no. 42, 69–139.

STOPES, MARIE. 1923. *Early Days of Birth Control*. London: Putnam.

SUMNER, JOHN BIRD. 1818. *A Treatise on the Records of Creation, and the Moral Attributes of the Creator; with particular reference to Jewish history and to the consistency of the principle of population with the wisdom and goodness of the Deity*. 2nd ed., 2 vols. London: J. Hatchard.

———— 1824. "Poor-Laws." In *Supplement to the Fourth, Fifth, and Sixth Editions of the Encyclopaedia Britannica*, VI, 293–306. London: Hurst, Robinson.

SWEEZY, PAUL M. 1942. *The Theory of Capitalist Development: Principles of Marxian Political Economy*. New York: Oxford University Press.

TAX, SOL, and LARRY S. KRUCOFF. 1968. "Social Darwinism." *International Encyclopedia of the Social Sciences*, XIV, 402–406. New York: Macmillan.

TAYLOR, ARTHUR J., ed. 1975. *The Standard of Living in Britain in the Industrial Revolution*. London: Methuen.

TAYLOR, GEOFFREY. 1969. *The Problem of Poverty, 1660–1934*. London: Longmans, Green.

TAYLOR, JAMES STEPHEN. 1969. "The Mythology of the Old Poor Law." *Journal of Economic History* 29: 292–297.

TAYLOR, P. A. M. 1976. "Emigration." In P. and G. Ford, eds., *Population and Emigration*. Dublin: Irish University Press.

THORNTON, WILLIAM THOMAS. 1846. *Over-Population and Its Remedy; or, An inquiry into the extent and causes of the distress prevailing among the labouring classes of the British Islands, and into the means of remedying it*. London: Longman, Brown, Green, and Longmans.

TILLY, CHARLES. 1975. "Food Supply and Public Order in Modern Europe." In Charles Tilly, ed., *The Formation of National States in Western Europe*. Princeton, N.J.: Princeton University Press.

TILLY, LOUISE A., JOAN W. SCOTT, and MIRIAM COHEN. 1976. "Women's Work and European Fertility Patterns." *Journal of Interdisciplinary History* 6: 447–476.

TILLYARD, A. I. 1913. *A History of University Reform from 1800 A.D. to the Present Time*. Cambridge, England: Heffer.

TREVELYAN, G. M. 1942. *English Social History: A Survey of Six Centuries, Chaucer to Queen Victoria*. London: Longmans, Green.

TREXLER, RICHARD C. 1974. "Infanticide in Florence: New Sources and First Results." *History of Childhood Quarterly* 1: 98–116.

TU, PIERRE N. V. 1969. "The Classical Economists and Education." *Kyklos* 22: 691–718.

TUAN CHI-HSIEN. 1958. "Reproductive Histories of Chinese Women in Rural Taiwan." *Population Studies* 12: 40–50.

TWISS, TRAVERS. 1845. *On Certain Tests of a Thriving Population*. London: Longman, Brown, Green, and Longmans.

U.S. Council on Environmental Quality *and* Environmental Protection Agency. 1972. *The Economic Impact of Pollution Control: A Summary of Recent Studies*. Washington, D.C.: U.S. Government Printing Office.

UNSHELM, ERICH. 1924. *Geburtenbeschränkung und Sozialismus: Versuch einer Dogmengeschichte der sozialistischen Bevölkerungslehre*. Leipzig: Kabitzsch.

UREÑA, ENRIQUE M. 1977. "Marx and Darwin." *History of Political Economy* 9: 548–559.

VADAKIN, JAMES C. 1968. *Children, Poverty, and Family Allowances*. New York: Basic Books.

VATTER, HAROLD G. 1959. "The Malthusian Model of Income Determination and Its Contemporary Relevance." *Canadian Journal of Economics and Political Science* 25: 60–64.

VAYDA, A. P. 1969. "The Study of the Causes of War with Special Reference to Head-hunting Raids in Borneo." *Ethnohistory* 16: 211–224.

———— 1974. "Warfare in Ecological Perspective." *Annual Review of Ecology and Systematics* 5: 183–193.

VICKERY, ALICE. n.d. *A Programme of Women's Emancipation*. n.p.

———— n.d. *A Women's Malthusian League*. London: Standring. Published also as *Ligue malthusienne des femmes*. Paris: Ligue de la Régéneration Humaine.

VORZIMMER, PETER. 1969. "Darwin, Malthus, and the Theory of Natural Selection." *Journal of the History of Ideas* 30: 527–542.

WALLACE, ALFRED RUSSEL. 1870. *Contributions to the Theory of Natural Selection: A Series of Essays*. London: Macmillan.

———— 1905. *My Life: A Record of Events and Opinions.* 2 vols. London: Chapman & Hall.

———— 1908. "Note on the Passages of Malthus's 'Principle of Population' Which Suggested the Idea of Natural Selection to Darwin and Myself." In Linnaean Society of London, *The Wallace-Darwin Celebration held on Thursday, 1st July, 1908.* London.

WALLACE, ROBERT. 1761, 1809. *A Dissertation on the Numbers of Mankind, in Ancient and Modern Times.* 1st and 2nd eds. Edinburgh: Constable.

WEBB, SIDNEY. 1913. *The Decline in the Birth-Rate.* London: Fabian Society.

———— and BEATRICE WEBB. 1919. *Industrial Democracy.* London: Longmans, Green.

WELLS, ROBERT V. 1975. *The Population of the British Colonies before 1776: A Survey of Census Data.* Princeton, N.J.: Princeton University Press.

———— 1978. "Fertility Control in Nineteenth-Century America: A Study of Diffusion, Technique, and Motive." In American Academy of Arts and Sciences, "Historical Perspectives on the Scientific Study of Fertility in the United States." Mimeographed. Boston.

WEYLAND, JOHN. 1807. *Observations on Mr. Whitbread's Poor Bill, and on the population of England* . . . London: J. Hatchard.

———— 1816. *The Principles of Population and Production, as they are affected by the progress of society; with a view to moral and political consequences.* London: Baldwin, Cradock, and Joy.

WHATELY, RICHARD. 1855. *Introductory Lectures on Political Economy* . . . 4th ed. London: Parker.

WHEWELL, WILLIAM, ed. 1859. *Literary Remains, consisting of lectures and tracts on political economy of the late Rev. Richard Jones.* London: Murray.

WHITBREAD [SAMUEL]. 1807. *Substance of a Speech on the Poor Laws: Delivered in the House of Commons on Thursday, February 19, 1807.* London: J. Ridgway.

———— 1971. *Notebooks, 1810–11, 1813–14,* ed. Alan F. Cirket. Bedfordshire Historical Record Society, *Publications,* vol. 50.

WHITNEY, VINCENT H. 1968. "Fertility Trends and Children's Allowance Programs." In Eveline M. Burns, ed., *Children's Allowances and the Economic Welfare of Children.* New York: Citizens' Committee for Children of New York.

WIKMAN, K. R. V. 1937. *Eine vergleichende ethno-soziologische Untersuchung über die Vorstufe der Ehe in den Sitten des schwedischen Volkstums.* Abo: Abo Akademi.

WILLIAMS, BERNARD. 1973. "A Critique of Utilitarianism." In J. J. C. Smart and Bernard Williams, *Utilitarianism, For and Against.* Cambridge, England: University Press.

WILLIAMS, DALE EDWARD. 1976. "Were 'Hunger' Rioters Really Hungry? Some Demographic Evidence." *Past and Present,* no. 71, 70–75.

WILSON, EDWARD O. 1975. *Sociobiology: The New Synthesis.* Cambridge, Mass.: Harvard University Press.

WINSTANLEY, D. A. 1935. *Unreformed Cambridge: A Study of Certain Aspects of the University in the Eighteenth Century.* Cambridge, England: University Press.

WOODROOFE, KATHLEEN. 1977. "The Royal Commission on the Poor Laws, 1905–09." *International Review of Social History* 22: 137–164.

WOODRUFF, PHILIP. 1953. *The Men Who Ruled India: The Founders.* London: Cape.

WRIGHT, HAROLD. 1923. *Population.* New York: Harcourt, Brace.

WÜRGLER, HANS. 1957. *Malthus als Kritiker der Klassik: Ein Beitrag zur Geschichte der klassischen Wirtschaftstheorie.* Winterthur: P. G. Keller.

WYNNE-EDWARDS, V. C. 1967. *Animal Dispersion in Relation to Social Behaviour.* Edinburgh: Oliver and Boyd.

YOUNG, ARTHUR. 1774 (1967). *Political Arithmetic, containing observations on the present state of Great Britain and the principles of her policy in the encouragement of agriculture.* London: Nicoll. Reprinted, New York: Kelley, 1967.

——— 1898. *The Autobiography of Arthur Young, with Selections from His Correspondence,* ed. M. Betham-Edwards. London: Smith, Elder.

[YOUNG, GAVIN] Author of "Reflections on the Present State of British India." 1832. *Observations on the Law of Population; being an attempt to trace its effects from the conflicting theories of Malthus and Sadler.* London: B. Fellowes.

YOUNG, ROBERT M. 1969. "Malthus and the Evolutionists: The Common Context of Biological and Social Theory." *Past and Present,* no. 43, 109–145.

ZINKE, GEORGE W., ed. 1942. "Six Letters from Malthus to Pierre Prévost." *Journal of Economic History* 2: 174–189.

——— 1967. *The Problem of Malthus: Must Progress End in Overpopulation?* Boulder: University of Colorado Press.

ZIRKLE, CONWAY. 1957. "Benjamin Franklin, Thomas Malthus and the United States Census." *Isis* 48: 58–62.

Index

Index

T